More praise for *A Chainless Soul*

"A graceful, sympathetic, agreeably succinct account of these fragile yet productive and often heroic sisters."

USA Today

"*Wuthering Heights* may be the most passionate, emotionally intense novel in the English language, yet Emily Brontë lived one of the most passionless lives imaginable, at least on the surface. . . . It is to biographer Katherine Frank's great credit that she manages to capture so vividly the turbulence of this anorexic, agoraphobic spinster's inner life. Drawing heavily on the poems, Frank shows how Brontë used both writing and fasting to declare her independence from the outer world, even from her own body. . . . We'll never know exactly what Emily felt out on the moors in the dark of night, but Frank makes us wish we did."

Booklist

"In an extraordinary, remarkably intimate biography that is as emotionally charged as a Brontë novel, Frank dismantles the conventional, rhapsodic family story of the storm-tossed Brontës."

Publishers Weekly

BOOKS BY KATHERINE FRANK

A Voyager Out:
The Life of Mary Kingsley

KATHERINE FRANK

A Chainless Soul

A Life of Emily Brontë

Fawcett Columbine
New York

A Fawcett Columbine Book
Published by Ballantine Books

First published by Houghton Mifflin Company.

This edition published by arrangement with Houghton Mifflin Company.

All photographs are reproduced by kind permission of the Brontë Society, with the exception of the photograph of Law Hill School (Halifax Public Library), the first page of the Gondal Poems (British Library), the drawings of Branwell Brontë (Brotherton Collection, Leeds University Library) and the 'pillar portrait', the 'profile portrait' and the photograph of Charlotte Brontë in 1854 (National Portrait Gallery)

Library of Congress Catalog Card Number: 91-72894

ISBN: 0-449-90661-2

Cover design by William Geller
Cover art courtesy of the National Portrait Gallery, London

Manufactured in the United States of America

First Ballantine Books Edition: February 1992

10 9 8 7 6 5 4 3 2 1

For Rosemary Grave and Laura Kalpakian

Riches I hold in light esteem
And Love I laugh to scorn
And lust of Fame was but a dream
That vanished with the morn –

And if I pray, the only prayer
That moves my lips for me
Is – 'Leave the heart that now I bear
And give me liberty.'

Yes, as my swift days near their goal
'Tis all that I implore –
Through life and death, a chainless soul
With courage to endure!

Emily Brontë

Contents

A Chainless Soul

Preface

A new Brontë biography inevitably requires some explanation: there are so many books on the Brontës already, and can it be that any more materials have come to light? As it happens, though Emily Brontë has been the object of a great deal of literary criticism of late, there hasn't been a full-length biography of her in nearly twenty years.[1] And while no dramatic revelations about the facts of her life have been made, our understanding of her personality, experience and writing has changed in fundamental ways in the last two decades. In part this has been due to the new emphases and points of view, as well as knowledge, yielded by recent scholarship on the social and literary history of women in the nineteenth century. A demythologizing process has taken effect, and among the Victorian idols it has dismantled is the mystical, oracular Emily Brontë – 'the sphinx of English literature' canonized by Elizabeth Gaskell in her pioneering life of Charlotte Brontë published in 1857, and cherished and perpetuated by nearly every Brontë biographer since.

My vision of Emily Brontë's life is quite different from that held dear by what has been called 'the purple heather school of Brontë biography': the rhapsodic, storm-tossed, fundamentally sentimental version of the family's story. I see Emily Brontë's life as far more troubled, solitary and austere. And yet it will not do to reduce her to another victim of nineteenth-century patriarchy. For all the eventlessness of her life, she was not passive. She made her own choices boldly and stuck by them. She cared nothing for the opinions and values of others. Her will was inflexible and her courage immense. There was much that was dismaying, even forbidding, in her personality, and the story of her life is riddled with misfortune, loss and failure. She died at the age of thirty with her one novel misunderstood and condemned, in silence and, despite the presence of her sisters, essentially alone. And yet there was an undercurrent of triumph in this life and death. Not the triumph of a mystical spirit, but of a woman who lived bravely, consistently and purely, with unassailable integrity. Her life was unmarred by the compromises and faintheartedness, the needs and desires and insecurities, the petty acts of selfishness, the doubts and deceptions and self-deceptions which disfigure most of our lives, and yet also, perhaps, enable us to survive in a world that Emily Brontë scorned and repudiated. It was a life, too, of rare and awesome autonomy. The rest of us are linked and yoked to the fates of others: we are obligated, committed, beholden and not free. Emily Brontë was, as she herself affirmed, a 'chainless soul'.

It is partly this very 'chainlessness' which makes her seem so inaccessible. She is not 'one of us', and we are accustomed to glimpsing the plots of our own lives when we read the biographies of others. But Emily Brontë's remoteness is also due to the fact that, as Charlotte Brontë said, 'an interpreter ought always to have stood between her and the world.' It is not so much that an interpreter *ought* to have mediated between Emily and the world as that one – very often Charlotte herself – almost invariably did. We perceive Emily Brontë nearly always at second hand: in Charlotte's letters, in the reminiscences of family friends, acquaintances and servants, and in Elizabeth Gaskell's life of Charlotte. Mrs Gaskell didn't know Emily herself – she befriended Charlotte in the years after Emily's death – but Charlotte spoke freely and at length of her sister to the sympathetic and warm-hearted Mrs Gaskell, who was a successful novelist in her own right. Very few of Emily's own letters survive. She wrote regularly to Charlotte during the periods when Charlotte was away from home working as a governess or studying alone in Brussels. Charlotte herself may have destroyed Emily's letters, or perhaps Charlotte's husband, Arthur Bell Nicholls, did after Charlotte's death. In any event, the scant correspondence by Emily which has come down to us consists of a handful of perfunctory notes to acquaintances beyond the family circle, such as Charlotte's friend Ellen Nussey.

Even when Emily speaks to us in her own voice, in her poetry and her novel, she does so indirectly – in the language and accents of her imaginary kingdom, Gondal, the setting and domain of so much of her poetry, and from behind the 'veil' of the pseudonym Ellis Bell. Only in her four laconic 'diary papers', written at four-year intervals in collaboration with her younger sister Anne, does Emily speak to us directly. But charming as these bulletins of daily life in the parsonage are, they remain curiously uninformative, fugitive pieces.

Most of what we know of Emily Brontë is perceived through the refracting and sometimes distorting lens of Charlotte Brontë's vision. Thus I have attempted to illuminate Emily's dark silhouette by the light of Charlotte's much more fully documented life. More fully documented because Charlotte's friends, especially Ellen Nussey, preserved hundreds of her letters, and also because Mrs Gaskell collected so much information about Charlotte from Charlotte herself, from her father and husband, friends and acquaintances and from Charlotte's editor and publisher. Inevitably, then, Charlotte and, to a lesser degree, Emily's older brother, Branwell, and younger sister, Anne, and their father, Patrick Brontë, all play a large role in my story. Indeed, it is not possible to write a biography of one Brontë without writing a book on them all. Emily's Belgian schoolmaster, Constantin Heger, said she would have made a great navigator. Negotiating the troubled waters of her life, I have sometimes felt as if I were following the charts of celestial navigators, where continents and islands are blank, featureless deserts in contrast to oceans inscribed and crossed and carved out by currents, reefs, shallows, and the precipitous descents of continental shelves. The rest of the Brontës stand on the shore while Emily's life is a tale of sea changes.

It is also a tale of hunger and starvation, and this is where I depart most radically from previous biographers. If Emily Brontë were alive today and could be prevailed upon to submit to psychiatric treatment (a most unlikely prospect), she would almost certainly be diagnosed as suffering from anorexia nervosa. Not merely her refusal to eat and her extreme slenderness and preoccupation with food and cooking, but also her obsessive need for control, her retreat into an ongoing, interior fantasy world, and her social isolation are all characteristic of the 'anorectic personality' described by psychiatrists such as Hilde Bruch, Peter Dally and R. L. Palmer, and also by feminist writers on anorexia such as Susie Orbach, Kim Chernin and Sheila MacLeod. Joan Jacobs Brumberg's historical exploration of anorexia nervosa as a social and cultural malady with roots in the nineteenth century also illuminates Emily Brontë's particular case, as does Brumberg's discussion of the connection between religious asceticism and anorexic fasting.

It is my contention, then, that Emily Brontë's oft celebrated mystical temperament has been mistaken for what, in reality, was her anorexia nervosa. Of course, the two conditions can be easily confused: voluntary fasting has long been a route to transcendence for religious mystics, and anorexic women often experience alterations in consciousness and distorted sense perceptions akin to those described in accounts of mystical trances. But the mystic is not overwhelmingly hungry, preoccupied with food, obsessed with power and control, and terrified of disorder. The anorexic woman is all these things, and I hope to show that Emily Brontë, for all her 'chainlessness', was not free from these obsessions.

I am less interested in retroactive medical diagnosis, however, than in what must have been the experience of her 'illness' for Emily. How did it feel to be perpetually hungry and to deny that hunger? Even more importantly, how was this physical hunger related to a more pervasive hunger in her life – hunger for power and experience, for love and happiness, fame and fortune and fulfilment? In the same poem from which I take my title, Emily proclaimed:

> Riches I hold in light esteem
> And Love I laugh to scorn
> And lust of Fame was but a dream
> That vanished with the morn – [2]

This arresting stanza articulates a kind of metaphysical fasting: she spurns everything which is ordinarily considered to make human life valuable, just as she habitually refused the nourishment of food for her body.

When we move from the physical, bodily desire for food and

perceive that hunger is a metaphor of sorts in the anorectic's life, it becomes clear that anorexia nervosa is not merely an 'eating disorder' but a psychiatric state characterized by an over-whelming fear of chaos and an obsession with order and control. As a Victorian woman, as the unendowered daughter of an obscure clergyman, Emily Brontë possessed scant power or control over the world she inhabited or over the course of her own life. She responded to her helplessness in two ways, both of which granted the illusion of power: through anorexic behaviour and writing. By refusing to eat she seized control of the only thing which was malleable: her own body. This was an essentially destructive reaction to the chaos she felt impinging on her. Her creative response was to reorder and rewrite the world in which she felt herself entrapped, bestowing on it, in the process, order, harmony, meaning and beauty. What is important in the end, then, is not Emily Brontë's anorexia in itself, but the way in which it shaped her life and writing as well as her body.

Anyone working on the Brontës owes a great debt to those biographers, scholars and critics who have gone before. A complete list of the works I have consulted may be found in the Bibliography. But here I would like to make special mention of the biographies of Anne, Branwell, Charlotte and Emily Brontë writtten by Winifred Gérin between 1959 and 1971, and also Margot Peters' and Rebecca Fraser's more recent lives of Charlotte Brontë. Christine Alexander's study of the Brontë juvenilia has been very helpful. John Lock and W. T. Dixon's biography of Patrick Brontë and John Cannon's and Edward Chitham's books on the Brontës' Irish background have all proved valuable. I must also thank Dr Juliet R. V. Barker, former Curator and Librarian at the Brontë Parsonage Museum, for generous assistance and expertise. Helena Whitbread, the editor of Anne Lister's diaries, was a boon companion in Yorkshire.

The writing of the book was far from a solitary labour. From the beginning I had encouragement and wise counsel from my agent, Jennifer Kavanagh. I'm also grateful, once again, for the creative editing of Signe Warner Watson of Houghton Mifflin. At Hamish Hamilton, Andrew Franklin and Sophie Ovenden gave valuable editorial guidance while tempests raged outdoors.

Dr Peter Dally discussed anorexia nervosa in the nineteenth century and Emily Brontë with me. Laura Kalpakian, my old and valued collaborator in life and books, told me which biography to retrieve from an unwieldy manuscript and how to do it. Michael David Anthony read every word with scrupulous care, intelligence and sympathy. At the end, Naseem Nathoo provided excellent technical and unflagging moral support. Belated thanks, too, to Robert Kelley and Florence Boos for encouraging me years ago to write a biography of Emily Brontë.

For acts of love, friendship and support which sustained me, I am deeply grateful to Isabel and Arthur Voss, Margaret Voss-Pierce, Art Voss, Justin Frank, Anthony Mann, William Kupersmith, Stephen Riley, Abubakar Rasheed, Antonia Shooter, and, above all, Rosemary Grave. My greatest debt, though, is to my late husband, Saeed-ul-Islam, who died shortly before the book was finished, in the middle of our journey.

Prologue

October 1845. It was a long way from London to Haworth in the autumn of 1845: you travelled far in terms of space and time, boarding the train at Euston Station in the early hours of the morning and then steaming like a tornado of noise and dust and soot north through Leicester, Nottingham and Sheffield to Leeds, where it was necessary to change to the smaller branch line that ran along the deep valley of the Aire to Bradford and Keighley. By the time you reached Keighley, dusk was falling, and, more likely than not, it had begun to rain too, not a proper storm, but a monotonous, chill drizzle that saps the spirit as well as penetrates cloaks and gloves and bonnets. It is four more miles from Keighley to Haworth and for this last leg of the journey, you had to hire a gig. Or, you could send a cart ahead with your luggage and then walk across the fields and 'bottoms', crossing stiles and icy cold becks littered with round smooth rocks – slippery stepping stones across the streams. Not that the way was very picturesque, for all you passed were 'grey, dull-coloured rows of stone cottages', stone factories, 'poor, hungry-looking fields; – stone fences everywhere, and trees nowhere.'[1] Approaching Haworth, the landscape becomes even more leaden and inanimate. The soil and vegetation get poorer; trees give way to stunted shrubs and bushes; 'what crops there are, on the patches of arable land consist of pale, hungry-looking grey green oats.'[2]

Haworth itself is the most meagre of villages, clinging to a hillside so steep that the cobblestones on Main Street had to be laid end-ways to give horses (and humans) a grip on the road, and to prevent them from sliding all the way back down to the Baptist chapel and sixteenth-century Emmott Hall at the junction of Bridgehouse Lane and the precipitous Main Street. More than 1200 handlooms were operating in the village in the 1840s, and many of the parish's 6000-odd inhabitants were connected in one way or another with the textile industry.

A rough, provincial people were the citizens of Haworth – hostile to strangers and taciturn and 'close' to a fault. When they did divulge a few crusty words – a warning more likely than a greeting – their thick Yorkshire accent rendered them nearly incomprehensible to visitors. On Sundays they wore sturdy wooden clogs to church and when the Reverend Brontë's predecessor, one Mr Redhead, displeased them, his congregation clattered and clumped out in the middle of the sermon. When this failed to drive Redhead away, on the following Sunday one member of the congregation rode into the church on an ass, the rider's head – adorned with a pile of old hats – facing the animal's rear. Of the Reverend Brontë they were more appreciative because, as one of them put it, 'he minds his own business, and ne'er troubles himself with ours.'[3]

Towards the top of Main Street were to be found a chemist's shop, post office and a public stocks, which had probably fallen into disuse by the Brontës' day. Haworth also boasted four inns: the Kings Arms, the White Lion, the White Cross and the Black Bull, all within a stone's throw of each other at the top of Main Street. And here the village proper as a weaving centre and sandstone-quarrying area ended.

Just beyond the Black Bull lay the Parish Church of St Michael and All Angels, and across the small lane, the Sunday school and sexton's house. Imagine the church and Sunday school forming two sides of a rectangle meeting at right angles. Filling in the space between the two is a sea of gravestones – more than a thousand of them – upright and horizontal and every conceivable angle in between, the oldest crumbling and leaning, their inscriptions effaced by seasons of rain, snow and wind. Across from the Sunday school, the graveyard dissolves imperceptibly into the surrounding, heather-covered moors. And across from the church was the Brontës' home, the parsonage of the incumbent of Haworth, in 1845 the very last house or structure of any kind in the village. There it is perched still, on the edge of the village, belonging neither to the human community it culminates nor to the boundless natural world which rises up behind it. Instead, the house is precariously balanced between the two, a boundary, an indeterminate zone, between two well-defined realms: hemmed in by the Death all those gravestones speak of, and also yielding a liberating access to a natural world beyond human needs, cares or dreams.

In the autumn of 1845 the parsonage was, however, a beleaguered house: a house of failure, of blasted hopes, of paralysing depression, of blindness. Even more, it was a house of hunger – a gnawing, wasting hunger of the heart and intellect and spirit, a mental and emotional starvation. Emily Brontë's poems were to be the crumbs to feed that heart hunger. She was born on 30 July 1818, but it was on the otherwise wholly unremarkable October afternoon in 1845, when her older sister Charlotte 'accidentally lighted' upon Emily's poetry manuscript book, that Emily was ineluctably destined to live for us. Every writer possesses this double sort of birth certificate: the day when she came into the world a red-faced, protesting scrap of humanity, and the far more important date when she was discovered as the writer of books which ensured that she would never be entirely lost to it.

The day began, as every day did, shortly after dawn with an ear-piercing pistol shot and a bullet sailing across the crowded field of crumbling, leaning graves to the squat church tower which lay directly in line with the Reverend Patrick Brontë's first-floor bedroom window. Not that there were thieves or any other offensive beings, human or animal, clinging to or perched on the church tower just below the blue and gilt face of its clock. The sleepers in the quiet earth of the graveyard (whatever some of the old superstitious villagers might hint about their goings-on in the dead of night) were as safe from the bullets that whistled by them each morning as they were oblivious to the cawing rooks winging overhead. And invulnerable, too, were 'Maria, wife of the Reverend P. Brontë', and 'Also Maria, their daughter', and 'Also Elizabeth their daughter', all dead these twenty years and more, and buried in a vault inside the church, under the stone-flagged floor. John Brown, the sexton who lived across the way from the churchyard, heard the pistol shot and knew it was time to face another day. No doubt William Wood, the village carpenter, and John Greenwood, the stationer, and Abraham Wilkinson, the proprietor of the Black Bull, and the chemist and postmaster at the top of Main Street were all similarly roused. The incumbent of Haworth was signalling the start of a new day – a frosty, grey one, for the golden late summer of September had given way to the withering of autumn and there was scarcely a sprig of purple heather left on the distant hills.

The Reverend Patrick Brontë was discharging the bullet which had lain in his cocked pistol next to his gold pocket watch at his bedside all night, the bullet he had not been called upon to use in the course of that night – or any other night for that matter – against housebreakers, thieves or murderers. But he was discharging, too, in his own peculiar way, his dashed dreams, gnawing regret and abiding loss. The church tower had become pock-marked by his bullets over the years, but there was no real target for Patrick Brontë's morning pistol shooting or for his bitterness. Yet this did not diminish by a fraction of a degree the animus with which he pulled the trigger.

The shot rang out far more forcefully within the house than without: it must have penetrated even the heavy opium- and gin-induced slumber of the minister's only son, Branwell; it momentarily interrupted, perhaps, the morning prayers of his youngest daughter, Anne. Emily and Charlotte Brontë may have paused as they pulled up the white counterpanes which covered their beds. As Patrick Brontë reloaded his smoking pistol and attached his watch guard to his waistcoat, his daughters dressed and hastened down to the kitchen to help old Tabby, the servant, to prepare breakfast: porridge, oatcakes and tea. Meagre, plain Yorkshire fare for a family plagued by stomach and eating ailments: dyspepsia, loss of appetite, nausea. With the simplest and smallest portions and a few sips of weak, milky tea they were satisfied. And it was only this skimpy, bland morning meal that they ate together with their father. Dinner and evening tea he insisted upon eating alone in silence in his study, and he remained immured in his room a good hour or more after completing the meal lest conversation or any other sort of stimulation might trigger an attack of 'bilious' indigestion.

After breakfast and washing up, after the carpet had been

swept in the parlour and Mr Brontë's study, after the grocer's boy had delivered the meat and potatoes for dinner and the bread had risen and been baked and the apple pudding was prepared; after the postman's bell had brought no letters from Brussels or even from Birstall, after the mending of shirts, and pelisses and stockings, after the mid-day dinner had been consumed by the sisters in the dining room where they picked over the food, and by their father in his dyspeptic isolation in his study, after all this, Emily and Anne may have braved the chill wind and impending darkness and gone out for a ramble on the rusty brown moors rising upwards behind the house. Emily knew the landscape the way others know every mood and expression and tone of voice of a lover – intimately, deeply, in every season and in all weathers. Or perhaps she and Anne merely stepped across the hall to their father's study and, because the old man's cataracts had by this time rendered him nearly blind, read to him the latest issues of the *Leeds Intelligencer* or the *Halifax Guardian* or the great family favourite, *Blackwood's Magazine*. Or if he felt particularly melancholy, Patrick Brontë might ask Emily to play a bit of Handel or Bach on the small upright piano in the study. Branwell would still be in bed, for he rarely got up before early evening these days, and then he went out to the Black Bull or the Old White Lion as soon as he was dressed and had run his hands through his carrot-coloured hair.

Charlotte was now left alone in the small parlour with her familiar companions: a dull, throbbing headache that made reading or needlework impossible and hence left her vulnerable to haunting memories of every pain and misery in her past and the hopeless blank prospect of the future – a future that resembled one of the worn-down, indecipherable stone slabs of the graves she could see through the uncurtained parlour windows. There were still three hours before tea time and then another two before evening prayers, and then God knows how many more to be endured before sleep granted its brief reprieve and dawn broke, and the pistol shot began the whole cycle over again.

At some point during that long afternoon alone in the parlour, Charlotte noticed Emily's rosewood lap desk lying open on the table where Emily had carelessly left it before going out on the moors or across the hallway to her father's study. Knowing full well that she would be committing a violation, Charlotte nevertheless was drawn to the desk the way a starving prisoner grabs at a crust of bread or a drowning man a lifeline. Charlotte was nearly thirty years old – two years older than Emily – with nothing but the wreckage of earlier plans and hidden heartbreak to show for her years. The parsonage to Charlotte seemed an extension of the graveyard: a tomb in which she and Emily and Anne were 'buried alive'. Emily's desk might harbour the means to work their resurrection.

At first glance, though, it merely contained a cluttered jumble of things: coloured sealing wax, bottles of ink and steel pen nibs, a silver pen holder with the initials T.B. which had once belonged to their maternal grandfather, Thomas Branwell, stray buttons, an ivory-handled brass seal, several French coins, and a packet of 'Clark's Enigmatic and Puzzle Wafers' – small circular seals with mottos such as 'UCIXL', 'UR Cautious', 'ICUR Temptations'.

All of these things were stuffed into one compartment of the desk; in the other were two small manuscript notebooks bound in soft, dark crimson leather, with lined leaves of paper inside: the sort of booklet one could keep accounts in, or a diary. But these, to Charlotte's mounting excitement, contained neatly copied out and carefully dated poems. The first page of one of the booklets was headed 'E.J.B. Transcribed February 1844', and the other began with 'Emily Jane Bronte. Transcribed February 1844. GONDAL POEMS'. Charlotte saw, however, as she furtively leafed through them, that the poems bore dates as far back as 1836 and came right up to the present; one, indeed, was dated 9 October 1845.

Formerly they had shared their writing with each other, reading it aloud far into the night, when their father and aunt were in bed and Branwell had gone out to drink and carouse. But for some time now they had ceased this communal creative activity. Most likely this was Emily's doing; since she had returned from school in Brussels three years earlier, her natural secretiveness had become more and more zealous. As Charlotte put it later, the 'habit of communication and consultation had been discontinued; hence it ensued that we were mutually ignorant of the progress we might respectively have made.'[4] Even

Anne, Emily's collaborator in their imaginary kingdom of Gondal – the world of so much of Emily's writing – had not been allowed to read Emily's most recent poems. In her journal in July Anne had noted that Emily 'is writing some poetry ... I wonder what it is about.'[5]

Added to Charlotte's guilt – for reading Emily's poems was tantamount to, perhaps even worse than, opening another person's mail or prying into their diary – was the extreme difficulty she had in deciphering them. For, unlike Charlotte and Anne, Emily had continued to write in the diminutive print-like hand they had all used in their childhood writing when they wished their stories to appear like miniature books. As Charlotte held up the pages close to her eyes and squinted through her spectacles, in her own words, 'something more than surprise seized me, – a deep conviction that these were not common effusions, ... I thought them condensed and terse, vigorous and genuine. To my ear, they had also a peculiar music – wild, melancholy, and elevating.'[6] To a friend she later wrote how the 'startling excellence' of Emily's poems 'stirred my heart like a trumpet when I read them alone and in secret.'[7]

One of the most arresting poems in the notebook was addressed 'To Imagination' and dated 3 September 1844. The second stanza held the seeds of the struggle soon to ensue between Charlotte and Emily over the poems, and also the map of their lives, past, present and to come:

> So hopeless is the world without
> The world within I doubly prize
> The world where guile, and hate, and doubt,
> And cold suspicion never rise;
> Where thou and I and Liberty
> Have undisputed Sovereignty.[8]

By reading Emily's poems Charlotte had intruded into Emily's 'world within', the fantasy world of Gondal and imagination and secret writing, a safe, interior realm that protected Emily from all the lures and disappointments and broken dreams of the 'world without'. But Charlotte herself still dwelt there, outside in the unresponsive, corrupt, unjust 'world without'. Year in and year out she had toiled to carve out some sort of niche in it for herself and her sisters, however small and insignificant that might be. But governessing positions, foreign study, a plan for the 'Misses Brontë's Establishment' for the education of young ladies, had all come to naught. So, too, had their 'very early cherished dream', as Charlotte put it, 'of one day becoming authors.' Ten years before, Charlotte had sent some of her poems to the Poet Laureate, Robert Southey, and he had replied with a 'cooling dose' of advice that she should keep to her sewing. Branwell's importunate submissions to *Blackwood's Magazine* had been ignored. And so they had gone underground with their writing, scribbling their poetry into private notebooks, unbeknownst not only to the 'world without' but also to each other.

Now, on that grey afternoon in October 1845, Emily's poems seemed to promise a way forward; they acted upon Charlotte like a sorely needed, invigorating draught of courage. Why not display the treasures of the 'world within' – their writing – to the 'world without'? Why not publish a volume of their poetry, embark on a career as poets, pursue their long-cherished, stifled, but never relinquished, hoped-for destiny as writers?

Such was the vision and exorbitant hope that welled up within Charlotte as she read through her sister's work with a pounding heart. Beneath one poem she hastily scribbled: 'Never was better stuff penned', a message for Emily to find when she read through her poems again. But Charlotte couldn't wait to divulge her discovery. Just when and how the confrontation – Charlotte's revelation of what she had done and Emily's enraged response – took place is not recorded. No doubt that very afternoon, when Charlotte's 'deep excitement' was still coursing through her like a drug in her veins. Of this momentous scene she later wrote only that 'my sister Emily was not a person of demonstrative character, nor one, on the recesses of whose mind and feelings, even those nearest and dearest to her could, with impunity, intrude unlicensed; it took hours to reconcile her to the discovery I had made, and days to persuade her that such poems merited publication.'[9] But 'by dint of entreaty and reason' Charlotte 'at last wrung out a reluctant consent to have the "rhymes" as they were contemptuously termed [by Emily] published.'[10]

Left to her own resources, Emily would have protected and kept hidden her 'world within' and never have exhibited a word or line of it to the alien eyes of her older sister, much less to those of an anonymous public in the 'world without'. Charlotte had to engage in an exceedingly hard struggle to win over Emily. Anne, meanwhile, proved an ally when she 'quietly produced some of her own compositions, intimating that since Emily's had given [her] pleasure, [Charlotte] might like to look' at Anne's too.[11] Charlotte was moved by their 'sweet sincere pathos', but she knew that her own and Anne's verse were as base metal, mere alloys, compared to the pure gold of Emily's. Only under the protection of Emily's precious wares could they hope to gain an audience.

Of one thing Charlotte could, however, reassure her sister. If Emily would give in to the publishing plan, her identity would still be concealed. No one need ever know who were the real authors of their work. For side by side with Charlotte's abiding dream, and now positive resolve, to become a writer was a horror of being classified as a mere authoress – a 'silly lady scribbler', as they were scornfully dismissed in the press of the day. Emily's poems, Charlotte insisted again and again, transcended the accident of her sexual identity: 'I know no woman that ever lived ever wrote such poetry,' she confided to a friend.[12] And to the public much later she asserted that Emily's were not 'at all like the poetry women generally write.'[13] If Emily sought concealment of her identity, Charlotte wished to disguise their sex. Hence, she explained, they 'veiled' their own names under those of Currer, Ellis and Acton Bell. She might more accurately have said 'cloaked', for the names, though not blatantly masculine, certainly wouldn't be taken as women's. Currer, Ellis and Acton were all unusual, slightly ambiguous Christian names. 'Bell' was more straightforward: a sort of private joke, in fact, for it was the middle name of the newly hired curate, Arthur Bell Nicholls, the most recent in the 'highly uninteresting' (as Charlotte described them) series of assistant clergymen that Patrick Brontë, in his growing blindness, had increasingly to rely upon.

Now, after evening prayers at eight o'clock, after Patrick Brontë had ascended the stairs to his bedroom, pausing on the landing to wind the tall grandfather clock whose ticking pendulum could be heard all over the house, after Branwell had sallied out to his usual haunts, Emily and Charlotte and Anne sat together at the square dining room table writing in a sea of paper, passing manuscript pages back and forth, reading them out aloud, discussing the merits of this or that metaphor, the rigidity of metre in one stanza or slackness in another, devising titles for all the poems they had merely labelled 'Stanzas' or 'Song', or, particularly in Emily's case, had composed with no heading whatsoever. Furthermore, self-sufficient poems had to be plucked out of longer Gondal or Angrian (Charlotte's imaginary domain) productions – names expunged, locations generalized, dates eradicated. Demanding work often, but also, as they progressed and became more and more committed to the project, increasingly exhilarating. And intensifying their excitement was the fact that the whole enterprise was clandestine – a closely guarded secret, kept even from their father and brother. Hence the night-time flurry of activity when the first was abed and the second abroad. During the day they continued their 'buried alive' routine: sewing and ironing and brushing the carpet and baking, their minds all the while teeming with images and phrases and lines they had to wait until evening to transcribe.

Slowly the volume began to take shape during the cold, dark evenings of November and December. Individual poems were revised, polished and given appropriate titles. Then they painstakingly arranged them into a coherent collection, alternating poems by 'Currer', 'Ellis' and 'Acton', and also alternating lyrics with narrative poems, philosophical meditations with songs, elegies with celebrations. When, at last, the volume was completed and ready, even to Emily's grudging satisfaction, the next quandary they faced was how to get it published.

'The bringing out of our little book was hard work,' Charlotte later wrote: 'neither we nor our poems were at all wanted ... The great puzzle lay in the difficulty of getting answers of any kind from the publishers to whom we applied.'[14] Very likely Charlotte began by writing to the publishers of their favourite poets, especially the famous Edward Moxon, who numbered Wordsworth, Shelley, Coleridge, Keats and Tennyson among his authors. But Charlotte's queries to Moxon and whomever else she approached probably ended up where so many hopeful appeals from would-be authors land: in the dustbin. Moxon and company had no time to waste replying to, much less reading, the manuscript of the three Bell brothers up in Yorkshire. Any and everyone who had read the Romantics and taken a turn at versifying fancied himself a poet, and publishers routinely found themselves deluged with unpublishable odes and sonnets and epics containing a dozen or more cantos. It is no wonder that not one of Charlotte's letters to established publishers elicited a response. The wonder, rather, is that she had the heart to persist in their quest.

Finally Charlotte wrote to Messrs Chambers, Edinburgh publishers of some repute, not to offer the spurned volume of poems, but rather for advice on how she might go about getting them published. Chambers, to their everlasting credit, did not throw her letter into the waste basket; they responded with 'a brief and business-like, but civil and sensible reply' on which Charlotte swiftly acted.[15] The gist of their advice was that the Bells needed a printer, not a publisher, for their poems, what would later be called a 'vanity press', and apparently Chambers even referred them to the firm of Aylott and Jones of 8 Paternoster Row, London.

Aylott and Jones were actually booksellers and stationers, but they sometimes published religious poetry and theological works at the authors' own expense. Charlotte first wrote to them on 28 January 1846:

> Gentlemen, –
> May I request to be informed whether you would undertake the publication of a collection of short poems in 1 vol. oct.
> If you object to publishing the work at your own risk – would you undertake it on the Author's account?
> I am, gentlemen, your obdt. hmble. servt.
>
> C. Brontë[16]

Aylott and Jones immediately 'accepted' the volume of poems, sight unseen, and three days after her initial query had received a positive response, Charlotte wrote to her 'publishers' that she would like the poems to be published 'in 1 octavo volume of the same quality of paper and size of type as Moxon's last edition of Wordsworth.'[17] She also asked in this letter for an estimate of the cost of publication, and it was only at this juncture, when she required a calculation of the expense they were about to incur, that Aylott and Jones asked to see the manuscript.

It was dispatched to them on 6 February. Then there was a break in communication so that on the 15th Charlotte anxiously enquired if the manuscript (of which they had kept no copy in Haworth) had safely reached London. Reassured that it had, on 3 March she then sent a draft for £31 10s. for initial publishing expenses, a sizeable portion of the legacy their aunt had left them. This set the wheels of the enterprise in motion: Aylott and Jones began setting the manuscript in type, and the first proof sheets reached Haworth by the middle of March.

The proofs caused no small degree of consternation and anxiety at times: Charlotte complained that 'such a mistake for instance as *tumbling* stars instead of *trembling* would suffice to throw an air of absurdity over the whole poem.'[18] She requested that they be allowed to check all the proofs themselves and also explained that though all their previous correspondence had been safely delivered to 'C. Brontë, Esq.', 'a little mistake having occurred yesterday' made it advisable that future letters be addressed to 'Miss Brontë', care of Reverend Brontë of the same address.[19] Apparently the postman had tried to give the proofs to Patrick or Branwell, or enquired if a male relation was staying at the parsonage.

Early in May the book was printed and ready to be bound. On the 7th three presentation copies arrived at the parsonage, stamped in gilt lettering on the cover: *Poems by Currer, Ellis and Acton Bell*. But the physical, material existence of the book was not sufficient to allay Charlotte's hunger for their recognition as writers. On the same day that the three copies of the *Poems* were delivered, she wrote back to Aylott and Jones, requesting them to send review copies to a long list of magazines, including *Bentley's Miscellany*, *Blackwood's Magazine*, the *Edinburgh Review*, and to the *Daily News*, and *Britannia Newspaper* as well. And she remitted some additional money for advertising.

Poems by Currer, Ellis and Acton Bell was officially published in late May. One thousand copies were printed at a total cost of £37 (covering printing, paper and advertising), incalculable hours of labour, interminable discussion and inestimable anxiety and hope to its three authors. A meagre little book it was, with a dull, dark green cloth binding, poor-quality paper and a standard, undistinguished typeface. It contained twenty-one poems each by Emily and Anne and nineteen by Charlotte; sixty-one poems altogether covering 165 pages, including the Table of Contents and a page of Errata.

As far as one of the contributors was concerned, the whole production might well have been entitled *Errata*. Out of sympathy and pity for Charlotte, Emily had consented to have her 'rhymes' published. Never was there a more reluctant author. And the reading public seemed to confirm Emily's conviction of the folly of their enterprise. Despite the fact that the book sold for only 4s. (Charlotte had suggested 5s.) and despite two favourable reviews in the *Athenaeum* and the *Critic*, the book almost immediately sank without leaving a trace. None of the magazines on the long list Charlotte had sent to Aylott and Jones deigned to notice it; the few advertisements that appeared were ignored. The Bells' little book fared no better than any of the other schemes for their advancement they had energetically 'hatched' in the past. Exactly two copies were sold (we shall never know to whom) before Charlotte apologetically sent off gift copies more than a year later to Wordsworth, Tennyson, De Quincey and several other leading writers of the day, copies rescued from what she assumed was the ultimate fate of their creative effort: the trunk makers and fish-and-chip sellers.

A copy of *Poems by Currer, Ellis and Acton Bell* now joined the pen nibs and scraps of paper and notebooks and enigmatic wafers in Emily Brontë's desk. Henceforward her life would no longer be her own possession. Charlotte had coaxed and cajoled and finally piloted Emily from the 'world within' to the 'world without'. Though the latter seemed for the present largely indifferent to Emily's poetic gifts, in a year's time it would be scandalized by her powerful, unprecedented novel, *Wuthering Heights*. Never would life be the same for Emily Brontë, for all the inhabitants of the unprotected stone house, perched at the top of an inhospitable village, hemmed in by graves, opening out behind to a limitless expanse of moors.

· I ·

Seed Time

We are so accustomed to thinking of the Brontë story as a Yorkshire saga, one permeated by the 'Spirit of the Moors', that we tend to forget that it actually began somewhere else: in County Down, Northern Ireland, in a two-room, thatched-roof cottage in the hamlet of Imdel, some thirty miles south of Belfast and seventy miles north of Dublin. Here Patrick Brontë, the first son and eldest child of Hugh and Alice (or, according to some records, Ellis) Brunty was born on 17 March, St Patrick's Day, 1777. Forty-three years later, when Patrick Brontë moved to Haworth with his wife Maria and their six young children, they were considered interlopers, 'strangers in a strange land', as Patrick himself put it, though he did his best to cover his own traces.

For a class-bound society such as Britain's still was in the eighteenth and nineteenth centuries, despite the spectre of revolution across the English Channel and Atlantic Ocean, and the agitation for reform bills and other radical innovations at home, Patrick Brontë's lowly origins did not bear much looking into. The very name *Brontë* was strange, singular, and completely absent from all the county records and parish registers of County Down. It was almost equally unknown in England. In 1799, however, Lord Nelson had bestowed upon him by the King of Naples the title of Duke of Brontë. Far away in Northern Ireland young Patrick Brunty – whose forebears had called themselves O'Prunty – was struck by the celebrated Nelson's exotic new title and its closeness to his own surname, and in time he appropriated 'Brontë' for himself.

By the age of twenty-two Patrick had worked for a time as an

20

agricultural labourer and then pulled himself up from his humble origins during apprenticeships as a blacksmith and weaver, and finally secured employment as a schoolteacher under the auspices of a wealthy, university-educated clergyman, the Reverend Thomas Tighe, rector of the parish of Drumballyroney. Tighe was a clergyman in the evangelical mould of John Wesley. Patrick, the son of a Protestant father and Catholic mother, had been raised in no particular religion at all. His parents, Hugh and Alice, had had enough to do eking out a living for themselves and their five sons and five daughters by means of their corn-drying kiln and by spinning and weaving wool. They were simple, probably illiterate folk, though the house contained two books which Patrick read and reread until he knew them by heart: the Bible and *Pilgrim's Progress*. These nourished his imagination as surely as the Bruntys' frugal diet of potatoes, oats and milk sustained his body.

Patrick's lifelong addiction to the Bible and *Pilgrim's Progress*, however, was more literary than religious. Tighe convinced Patrick that his true calling was that of a servant of God, and Patrick started to attend church regularly under Tighe's patronage and influence. But he also began at about this same time to write poetry. He scraped together enough of his meagre wages to buy Milton's *Paradise Lost*, more food for his imagination, and he memorized all of it as he had the Bible and *Pilgrim's Progress*. The boundary between the theological and literary realms was rather tenuous and indefinite. Patrick could indulge his literary hunger while he followed Tighe's benevolent plan for him to attain, via higher, university education, the genteel position of an Anglican clergyman.

Years later, when Patrick Brontë was dead and fossilized as the tyrannical patriarch of the Brontë myth, it was said that his heart really lay in the direction of the military, that he should have been a soldier and fired his pistols at something more dangerous than his own church tower. Yet this passionate, often volatile young man wanted above all else to become an author, a poet. What he lacked in the way of poetic gifts he made up for by his absorption in and commitment to his literary efforts. His father, Hugh Brunty, had been a great story-teller, spinning out grim, gripping, supernatural tales to an audience of Irish peasants and his own children gathered round the glowing fire of the corn kiln, while his wife Alice spun out wool to be woven and fashioned into their clothing.

We might say that Patrick Brontë had the tale-telling gift and the identity of an author in his blood and hence that his children inherited it too. Certainly he experienced the keen, pleasurable transports of all-consuming composition, when, as his daughter Emily said much later, 'the world was lost to me'. Referring to himself in the third person in a Preface to his first book, *Cottage Poems*, Patrick described how he wrote from morning to noon and from noon to dusk 'full of indescribable pleasure such as he would wish to taste as long as life lasts. His hours glided pleasantly and almost imperceptibly by,' and when it came time to go to bed, he could scarcely sleep for thinking of the day's writing. *Cottage Poems*, like *Poems by Currer, Ellis and Acton Bell*, was published, as were all four of Patrick's books, at the author's own expense. It contained wooden, hackneyed verse unrelieved by any kind of stylistic or imaginative merits. 'Vision of Hell', for example, began:

> At midnight, alone, in the lonely dell
> Through a rent I beheld the court of hell;
> I stood struck dumb by the horrid spell
> Of the tide of wailing that rose and fell.

'Vision of Hell', like almost everything Patrick wrote, was highly religious and didactic. Art must serve God, the origin of all human gifts and talents. Patrick had not been endowed with literary gifts commensurate to his sense of poetic calling, and in the end his creative talents found their best outlet in his inspired, extempore preaching. But he did possess the true writer's passion, exhilaration, and commitment. For us he is the 'Father of the Brontës', and at the end of his long life he himself embraced this identity gladly. Through his daughters he finally realized vicariously the dreams of his youth. But at the turn of the century, as the Reverend Tighe's schoolmaster and protégé, Patrick wasn't the father of anybody nor likely soon to be. He was an eager, high-spirited schoolteacher who had already got into one scrape on account of a fetching fifteen-year-old girl pupil. Tighe decided that Patrick should go to Cambridge, to Tighe's own college, St John's, get a degree, and become an ordained minister of the Anglican Church.

Given the times, this was an extraordinary fate for the son of Irish peasants. Perhaps it still is. In 1802, when Patrick first enrolled at Cambridge, no one from Imdel or the neighbouring town of Ballynaskeagh, where his family had moved, had ever gone to Cambridge, and to the present day no one has ever gone again.[1] Patrick left Ireland with seven pounds in his pocket, and upon arriving at the university must have seemed a queer character in his homespun clothes, heavy boots and with his shock of red hair. He entered St John's under the name of Patrick Branty (the internal vowel change apparently reflecting his rise in the world) as a 'Sizer' or poor student whose fees were paid in return for personal services rendered to the two other classes of fee-paying students: 'Pensioners' and 'Fellows'. 'Branty' was an evolutionary name midway between O'Prunty, Brunty and the subtle distinctions (hinging on the final vowel *e*) of Bronte, Bronté and the final, definitive Brontë. Patrick Branty enrolled at St John's in 1802, but Patrick Brontë took the degree of Bachelor of Arts or A.B. in 1806 and was ordained in the same year by the Bishop of London at the Bishop's Palace, and duly licensed as a Curate of the Church of England. The following year he was ordained as an Anglican Priest by the Bishop of Salisbury. It was also Patrick Brontë who never in the course of his long life returned to Ireland, and who deliberately concealed his Irish background.

By 1807, then, the metamorphosis was complete. Patrick Brontë, Anglican priest and aspiring poet, had supplanted Patrick Brunty, humble blacksmith, weaver and village schoolmaster. The Brontës' 'Irish connection' was thus lost in the mists of time and was only recovered long after they were all dead and past caring about their humble roots. But Patrick Brontë's rags-to-riches saga (in terms of station more than wealth, for he never earned more than £200 per annum) was probably divulged to his children and absorbed in particular by Emily. In *Wuthering Heights* Emily's romantic hero Heathcliff has a lowly beginning. And Emily very likely also heard her father tell stories of Hugh Brunty, their grandfather, who had been orphaned, like Heathcliff, and adopted by his wicked uncle, Welsh Brunty. Welsh, himself, possessed strange origins: he, too, was an orphan and had been found as a starving stowaway on a trading ship bound from Liverpool to Ireland. In the lives of her father's family Emily found the broad outlines of her hero's mysterious past.

Before coming to Haworth, Patrick Brontë held a series of curacies, the first of which was in Essex at Wethersfield, and the only reason why this is of any note is that here he fell in love with his landlady's niece, a pretty eighteen-year-old girl named Mary Burder, who lived with her wealthy, widowed mother at a large house called Finchingfield Park. Many were Patrick Brontë's calls at Finchingfield Park despite Mrs Burder's increasingly frosty reception of him and the disapproval, too, of Mary's elder brother and her uncle, who was also her legal guardian. No one in the Burder family could countenance this romance between Mary and the new upstart Irish curate. Undaunted, however, Patrick pressed his suit, proposed and was accepted. And then, quite unaccountably, the courtship was broken off, the engagement cancelled. Patrick abruptly retracted his proposal and just as precipitately retreated from Wethersfield to another temporary post at Wellington, Shropshire. He then quickly moved on to a better and more distant curacy at Dewsbury, Yorkshire.

Here Patrick found a true friend in his vicar, the Reverend John Buckworth, with whom Patrick lodged, though even at this early date he insisted upon dining alone in his room to promote his digestion, and perhaps, too, to avoid the Buckworths' teasing him about his spartan eating habits, especially his fondness for bland, watery porridge. Besides his eccentric diet and solitary meals, another striking characteristic of Patrick's was his voluminous cravat – yards and yards of fine white silk wrapped round and round his neck, creeping ever higher and quite muffling up his chin. Patrick had, or believed he had, delicate lungs. The distinctive cravat, visible even in an early oil painting of him as a young man, was intended to ward off chills and the colds, bronchitis and even pneumonia that could descend in their wake.

Buckworth recognized the intelligence and independence of his curate, now nearing the age of thirty-four, and in 1811 appointed Patrick minister at the nearby church at Hartshead.

Here Patrick would be his own master, not the assistant to a senior clergyman. As befitted his new self-sufficiency, he soon took two decisive steps: he had his first collection of verse, *Cottage Poems*, published the same year he moved to Hartshead, and the following year he got married.

Despite his long journey – in every sense – from the two-room Brunty cottage in Imdel to his own incumbency as a university-trained Anglican priest at Hartshead, emotionally, at least, Patrick did not renounce the simple, humble world from whence he had sprung. *Cottage Poems* was addressed to 'the lower classes of society'. Not that Patrick romanticized rural life as his contemporary Wordsworth did. Wordsworth's pastoral poems were *about* simple rustics, not written *for* them. Patrick, in contrast, spoke directly to:

> All you who turn the study [*sic*] soil
> Or ply the loom with daily toil
> And lowly on, through life['s] turmoil
> For scanty fare;
> Attend: and gather richest spoil
> To sooth your care.

Some 500 miles south-west of Hartshead, in the pleasant seaside resort town of Penzance in Cornwall, a woman past her first bloom and fast approaching thirty was also at about this same time plying her pen to solace the poor. But Maria Branwell was writing in prose, not verse, and her essay, 'The Advantages of Poverty in Religious Concerns', was never published, not even privately, at her own expense. Like Patrick, Maria could see nothing but good arising out of the life of impoverished labourers. Maria, fortunately, was not writing out of first-hand experience; she could be complacent about poverty given the fact that her late father – a well-off Penzance wine merchant – had left her with a useful legacy of £50 a year.

If we had only their literary efforts to go by, we should judge Patrick Brontë and Maria Branwell a most tedious, spiritually smug and self-satisfied pair. Patrick, in any event, soon changed his mind about the edifying benefits of poverty as clearly indicated by the title of his first novel, *The Cottage in the Wood or the Art of Becoming Rich and Happy*, published (privately again) in

1815. But, fortunately, we have some private letters of Patrick and Maria as an invigorating antidote to their stilted pronouncements on the lot of the poor.

The outward facts and events of their meeting were prosaic enough, and in no way prepared for the extraordinary outcome of their union. During his brief sojourn at Wellington Patrick had become fast friends with another curate, William Morgan, whom he saw a great deal of when Morgan took up a post at Bierly not far from Hartshead. Shortly after coming to Bierly, Morgan became engaged to a young woman named Jane Fennell, the only daughter of a Wesleyan preacher, John Fennell, who was the headmaster of a Wesleyan school at Woodhouse Grove, near Bierly and some ten miles away from Hartshead. In the spring of 1812 Jane Fennell wrote to her cousin, Maria Branwell, in Penzance and invited her to come to stay for an indefinite period at Woodhouse Grove. Maria eagerly accepted and left her three sisters and brother in Penzance, never, as it turned out, to return.

She arrived in Yorkshire in the summer, 'extremely small in person; not pretty but very elegant ... and always dressed with a quiet simplicity of taste,' according to Charlotte Brontë's friend and first biographer, the novelist Elizabeth Gaskell.[2] William Morgan must have taken Patrick over to the Fennells' home at Woodhouse Grove in order to introduce his betrothed and her family soon after Maria's arrival. Patrick and Maria fell in love at this first meeting, and by the end of August they were exchanging letters full of declarations and the pain of separation despite the fact that they were only ten miles apart and Patrick was a very regular and frequent visitor to Woodhouse Grove: Their all-consuming attraction made everything unconnected with their intimacy shrink to a pale unreality. Maria could scarcely bear strolling out with her cousin over the same paths that she and Patrick had walked, so urgent was her desire to be with him again. All this she freely confessed to Patrick because, as she put it, 'I wish to write the truth and give you satisfaction, yet fear to go too far, and exceed the bounds of propriety.' And so she advanced and retreated in her letters: 'I rely on your goodness', she wrote, 'to pardon everything in this which may appear either too free or too stiff.'[3] Maria could not play the conventional role of reluctant maiden; she was passionately in love and, throwing caution to the winds, she openly, if sometimes guiltily, declared herself to be.

By early September, scarcely a month after they first met, Maria and Patrick were engaged, and Maria's letters to her 'dearest friend' became even more frank and open. When he promised to write on a certain day and no letter arrived, she was consumed with disappointment and anxiety, and begged him never to lead her to 'expect a letter without receiving it ... what many would deem a trifling incident, has so much disturbed my mind'... But what nonsense I am writing', she confessed, and then drew the moral of the 'trifling' episode: 'Surely after this you can have no doubt that you possess all my heart. Two months ago I could not possibly have believed that you would ever engross so much of my thoughts and affections and far less could I have thought that I should be so forward as to tell you so.'[4]

Another letter begins: 'With the sincerest pleasure do I retire from company to converse with him whom I love beyond all others.' Everyone, everything else, diminished in value as Maria's love for Patrick grew and deepened. It was a love worthy of any sacrifice: 'Unless my love for you were very great how could I so contentedly give up my home and all my friends – a home I loved so much that I have often thought nothing could bribe me to renounce it for any great length of time ... and friends with whom I have been so long accustomed to share all the vicissitudes of joy and sorrow. Yet these have lost their weight ... the anticipation of sharing with you all the pleasures and pains, the cares and anxieties of life, of contributing to your comfort and becoming the companion of your pilgrimage, is more delightful to me than any other prospect which the world can possibly present.'[5] 'I freely declare I love you above all the world,' she wrote to Patrick in November, and again in early December, 'I am certain no one ever loved you with an affection more pure, constant, tender, and ardent than that which I feel.'[6] What Patrick's side of the correspondence was like we do not know, but even if he matched Maria's fervour of devotion and love, her letters remain extraordinary.

And yet Maria, despite the strength and conviction of her love for Patrick, had her doubts. The other great theme of her letters besides love is religion. She exhorts her fiancé to look to God and pray for them both, a strange command given the fact that her future husband was an ordained clergyman who had never been negligent in performing his religious duties. It does not seem to have mattered that Maria was a Methodist and Patrick an Anglican; both were evangelical in their religious practices. But Maria harboured misgivings that perhaps her love for Patrick exceeded human bounds and encroached upon, or at least distracted her from, her love of God. In a note dated 'Sunday morning', when presumably she should have been devoting all her attention to spiritual matters, she guiltily wrote to Patrick that 'I feel that my heart is more ready to attach itself to earth than heaven. I sometimes think there never was a mind so dull and inactive as mine is with regard to spiritual things.'[7]

No doubt Patrick basked in, rather than tried to dampen, Maria's idolatry at the same time as he quelled her doubts. They prayed together and for each other. For Maria, especially, wanted theirs to be a spiritual as well as earthly 'pilgrimage', her favourite image for their love and future life together. Soon she was writing with a light heart again to her 'dear saucy Pat', and yet the undercurrent of doubt and fear remained, though it did not always manifest itself in religious terms. Sometimes, indeed, she doubted Patrick himself, for hers was the peculiar anxious vulnerability born of great and as yet unconsummated love. Scarcely three weeks before their wedding she wrote in response to his latest letter, 'I fancied there was a coolness in it which none of your former letters had contained ... Real love is ever apt to suspect that it meets not with an equal return; you must not wonder that my fears are sometimes excited.'[8]

But such doubts over Patrick's constancy were baseless; in his own less articulate way he must have loved Maria as passionately as he was loved by her. Theirs was the mature, adult love of people past the period of infatuation. He was thirty-five and she nearly thirty; they had spent long years waiting for love, and when it finally came it came, not with the diluted affection of many middle-aged marriages, but with a depth and intensity that only those who have endured long years of emotional isolation can know.

On 29 December 1812 Maria and Patrick were married in a

double ceremony along with Jane Fennell and William Morgan at Guiseley Church, near Bradford. Jane's father gave away both brides, while Morgan first joined Maria and Patrick and then Patrick performed the same task for Jane Fennell and Morgan.

After their wedding, in the dead of winter but on the brink of a new year, Maria begins to fade from the foreground of our story, and babies and illness and ceaseless domestic chores and too little money – all the realities of nineteenth-century married life – obscure our vision and perhaps obscured too the love with which Maria and Patrick had embarked on their 'pilgrimage'. The marriage was only to last nine years, and what those years were for them both we can only guess. Certainly Maria's continuous pregnancies show that the passion of their union did not wane, at least not on Patrick's side. Certainly, too, in the beginning, at Hartshead, they must have been extremely happy. Here their first two children, Maria and Elizabeth, were born, in late 1813 (less than a year after the marriage) and in February of 1815.

After two years of family life at Hartshead, they moved to Thornton, close to Bradford, where Patrick Brontë preached in 'a building of unredeemed ugliness' called the Old Bell Chapel.[9] They inhabited a cramped parsonage on Market Street, a dwelling not much more than a cottage, which could scarcely accommodate the ever-increasing family: Charlotte was born in April 1816, Patrick Branwell in June 1817, Emily Jane in July 1818, and, finally, Anne in January 1820. Elizabeth Branwell came from Penzance to help her younger sister cope with the babies shortly before Charlotte was born, and stayed on some months. Patrick Brontë, who could so easily produce offspring, was dismayed at the noise and disorder they wrought, and retreated as much as possible to his study and parish rounds. Maria was often unwell and always exhausted; there was neither privacy nor time nor energy to nourish the precious intimacy they had known in the early days of their marriage. If Maria wasn't recovering from childbirth, she was suffering early-pregnancy morning sickness or mid- and late-pregnancy fatigue and lethargy. The children, too, were often ill with colds and whooping cough and influenza and needed special nursing. Someone was always hungry or waking from a nap or crawling into the sitting room grate. They hired a twelve-year-old servant girl named Nancy Garrs as a nursemaid, and, shortly after, her sister Sarah joined the household as well.

And yet despite the noise of crying children, their colds and coughs and the mounds of laundry to be washed, the lack of privacy and the rigours of the North Yorkshire climate, life at Thornton was not a grim or lonely existence for Maria and Patrick and their children. A young lady named Elizabeth Firth, who lived with her widowed father at Kipping House in Thornton, kept a diary of all the outings, comings and goings of the small village's more prominent inhabitants, including of course the minister and his growing family, and we learn from Miss Firth that Maria, when she was able to go out, and her husband, sister and children all enjoyed a continual round of visits, teas, and walks in the surrounding countryside.

Elizabeth Firth, along with Elizabeth Branwell, was godmother to the second Brontë daughter, their namesake, and we find also in her diary not only a steady catalogue of the Brontës' social activities, but also a record of the arrival of each new baby, Maria's health, christenings, and Elizabeth Branwell's departure from Thornton in July 1816. On 14 November of this same year, Elizabeth Firth took tea at the Brontës' and recorded in her diary that 'we observed a beautiful eclipse of the sun; the sky was very clear till it arrived at its greatest obscurity; it was afterwards enveloped in clouds – a great gloom.'[10] When Branwell was born the following year, Elizabeth visited Maria at home on the day of her little son's birth – a great event coming as it did after three daughters. In early January 1819, Elizabeth had a special tea party for the three eldest little girls, Maria, Elizabeth and Charlotte. At six months, Emily was the baby of the family and too young to be included. But when Anne was born on a frozen January morning in 1820, one-and-a-half-year-old Emily and all the others went to Kipping House to spend the day. During the five years the Brontës lived in Thornton, they got together with the Firths and other village neighbours at least weekly or more often.

All this changed – the visits and calls and tea parties – when the Brontës moved to Haworth in April of 1820. For a salary of just £180 per annum, plus surplice fees of £14 (hence Patrick

Brontë's repeated, slightiy inflated quotation of his salary as
£200), he assumed the spiritual leadership of the parish where
the famous eighteenth-century clergyman William Grimshaw
had been incumbent and where the even more famous John
Wesley had often preached. There was very little else to recommend this new position other than the illustrious evangelical
predecessors who had held it in the past.

The villagers watched the Brontës' advent suspiciously and
warily: on the grey, chill morning of 20 April the family lumbered
up Main Street in a covered wagon, followed by seven carts
containing all their worldly possessions. When they arrived at
the brow of the hill they saw their new home, a square, sandstone
parsonage, surrounded by graves and unsheltered by trees to
protect it from the blasts and storms that the rigours of the
climate inflicted on the hillside village.

But it wasn't merely inclement weather that would make their
new life in Haworth a trial. The village was decidedly unhealthy.
There was no proper sewage system, and the open drains along
Main Street and the back lanes and the cesspools were an ideal
breeding ground for all sorts of diseases. Privies were shared by
up to a dozen families, and the water supply was limited and
impure, especially in the summer. In addition, the church graveyard was dangerously overfilled, and hence an additional source
of pollution to the erratic water supply. As a consequence of
all these hygienic nightmares, the Haworth mortality rate was
fearsomely high: nearly half of the children born in the village
died before they were six. The average age of death was only
about thirty.

The Brontës literally turned their back on the village and its
piles of refuse and clogged drains and open cesspools. But not
merely because of the threats to their health. There were no Miss
Firths in this grim, isolated place, no congenial neighbours to
drink tea with or receive calls from. The people of Haworth were
humble weavers and labourers. As Mrs Gaskell described them,
'there is little display of any of the amenities of life among this
wild, rough population. Their accost is curt, their accent and tone
of speech blunt and harsh.'[11] They did not take to newcomers,
especially those of a higher class and from alien places beyond
Yorkshire, as both Patrick and Maria were. In the coming years

the Brontë children walked the hills and moors rising up behind the parsonage in all weathers, at all times of year, but only rarely did they venture in the opposite direction down Main Street or hold any commerce with their neighbours.

The villagers had already ousted Mr Redhead, Patrick Brontë's immediate predecessor, because he pried too much into their ways and doings. Patrick wisely left his parishioners alone, as far as responsibility and duty to them allowed. He took them to task only over irreverent practices such as drying their laundry on the tombstones in the church graveyard. Otherwise he left them undisturbed, with the result that he and his family lived in almost total isolation at the summit of the village in the bare, exposed house on the hill.

Haworth Parsonage, a Georgian structure built in 1799, was larger than the one they had nearly burst at the seams in Thornton. On the ground floor, on either side of the stone-flagged hallway, were four rooms: the 'dining room', which also served as the parlour, on the left at the front, and across from it, Patrick Brontë's study. Behind these two rooms were the kitchen and a storage room. Directly above the four ground-floor rooms were four identically sized ones on the first floor. Patrick and Maria Brontë and the two youngest children, Emily, who was fast approaching two, and Anne, who was still a baby at four months, slept in a large bedroom overlooking the churchyard. But the four older children were crammed into a small box-shaped room, without a fireplace, above the ground-floor entrance way, a tiny place, measuring just 9 feet by 5 feet $7\frac{1}{2}$ inches, which was called the 'children's study' rather than the nursery. Water was supplied by a well that had not been cleaned in years and was situated perilously close to the over-crowded graveyard. Behind the house there was an outdoor privy with two seats, one for adults and the other for children. At night the parsonage was dimly lit with candles and oil lamps. To add to its general discomfort were the cold and often damp bare stone floors and curtainless windows. Patrick Brontë had a morbid fear of fires and as a precaution against them banned curtains from the house and also insisted that all its inmates be dressed in either silk or wool – never cotton, which he deemed highly inflammable.

Within months of their arrival in Haworth Maria Brontë was

taken seriously ill. At first she and her husband no doubt suspected yet another pregnancy, a most unwelcome prospect to them both. Maria was exhausted after all her confinements and the demands of six little children under the age of seven. Patrick Brontë, like so many other Victorian patriarchs, 'was not naturally fond of children and felt their frequent appearance on the scene as a drag both on his wife's strength and as an interruption to the comfort of the household.'[12]

Soon, however, it became clear that there would be no addition to the family. On the contrary, a terrible loss loomed ahead. By January of 1821, it was obvious that Maria was dying, perhaps of stomach cancer or of a chronic infection resulting from all her pregnancies and childbirths.[13] Patrick moved into the bedroom across the hall and Emily was exiled from her mother to the tiny, unheated 'children's study'. Maria remained in her bed in the room above the dining room, and down below her children's happy prattle ceased. Emily was only three, but along with the others she must have felt the dull terror gathering upstairs. To the servants and the special nurse brought in to care for Maria, the little ones seemed 'spiritless': 'they were grave and silent beyond their years; subdued ... by the presence of serious illness ... you would not have known there was a child in the house, they were such still, noiseless ... creatures.'[14] Maria did not often ask to see them; she had sunk into a listless kind of despair, and the pain of her illness enveloped her like a shroud. On her better days she would ask her nurse to raise her in bed so that she could watch the grate being cleaned as it was done in Cornwall. Her mind wandered back to Penzance and whatever soothing reveries she could summon from the memories of her youth. To think about her husband, behaving ever more eccentrically as she worsened, or of her children was unbearable.

Patrick, for his part, fired his pistol out of the kitchen door. And one day, when the children had all gone out for a walk on the moors rising up behind the village, in what frame of mind can only be imagined, Patrick burned the little pairs of coloured boots the nurse had set out for their return when their feet would be wet and cold from wandering the pathless, muddy hills. But Patrick Brontë could not discharge his overwhelming anxiety and fear out of the kitchen door or watch them go up in flames in the dining room fireplace. Some days were insupportable. Patrick wrote to his old Dewsbury friend, John Buckworth, of these wretched days and how on one, 'a gloomy day of clouds and darkness, three of my little children were taken ill of ... scarlet fever, and the day after, the remaining three were in the same condition.' Maria was ever more remote and unresponsive: 'she was cold and silent and seemed hardly to notice what was passing around her.'[15]

Elizabeth Branwell was once again summoned from Penzance to nurse her dying sister and help care for the children, who, however, had already found a second mother in their oldest sister, the precocious seven-year-old Maria. Maria shepherded them about on their rambles on the hills, and read to them sotto voce in the 'children's study' so as not to disturb their parents. She read to them from the newspapers (not children's books, which they did not possess), and she reported and explained to her audience the minutest details of all the parliamentary debates and other political developments.

As the natural world came to life in the spring and summer of 1821, with its daffodils and bilberries and ling and blackcurrants in the kitchen garden, Maria Brontë's existence ebbed away in the dark, stuffy bedroom overlooking the graveyard. But not peacefully or tranquilly, not without conflict and doubt and despair. While the doctors and the nurse Patrick Brontë called in struggled to preserve Maria's life, he wrestled for her soul. The religious doubts Maria had written about in her letters before her marriage returned to her now on her deathbed. Patrick wrote to Buckworth how 'Death pursued her unrelentingly. Her constitution was enfeebled and her frame wasted daily.' For seven months she endured 'more agonising pain than I ever saw.' And all this pain, the approaching severance from her husband and children, and their bleak future – all this undermined Maria's faith. 'During many years she had walked with God,' Patrick explained, 'but the great enemy, envying her life of holiness, often disturbed her mind in the last conflict.' The World, God, heaven and hell all seem to have become 'mighty strangers' to Maria as she lay dying.

In September, just when the moors cast off their habitual dress of dark greenish-brown heath and the heather bloomed a vibrant purple, Maria Brontë died, 'not triumphantly', her husband confessed, but, he still hoped, 'with a holy yet humble confidence that Christ was her Saviour and heaven her eternal home.'[16] And yet Maria's cry 'Oh God, my poor children – oh God, my poor children' slashed like a dagger through Patrick Brontë's pious account of his wife's end. Downstairs, alone, 'reading or whispering low', Emily and the other children must have heard their mother's anguished cry, though in later years it was only Charlotte who had any memory of her – a soothing one, not of suffering and pain or disembodied cries, but of her mother playing with Branwell at twilight in the dining room. In later years, Emily could summon no recollection or even half-dreamt-up impression of her at all.

· 2 ·

A Small but Sweet Little Family

It is a truth universally acknowledged that a middle-aged widower with six small children under the age of eight and an income of scarcely £200 per annum must be in want of a wife. Or if not universally acknowledged, the veracity of this statement must have been borne home more and more urgently to Patrick Brontë in the cold winter months of 1821 following his wife's death. And so, after the acute grief of his bereavement began to subside, he cast about himself, as John Bunyan would say, for another companion and helpmeet to share his life's pilgrimage. Elizabeth Branwell, who had returned to Yorkshire from Penzance to nurse her dying sister, agreed to stay on for the duration, and little Maria, already so precocious in every way, showered the caresses, reassuring words of comfort, diverting tales and other maternal gifts that Aunt Branwell lacked on her younger sisters and brother. But another mother, a loving stepmother, was what was needed to nurture and care for Patrick Brontë's little brood.

The youngest of them, Anne, was still in her wooden cradle when Patrick Brontë proposed to the most likely and suitable candidate for a wife for himself and new mother for his children: Elizabeth Firth, their old family friend from Thornton. Since their move to Haworth the Brontës' relations with the Firths of Kipping House had remained cordial and warm. Elizabeth Firth had visited the family in February, shortly after Maria fell ill, and for almost the whole of June – by which time it had become clear that Maria was unlikely to recover – the two eldest children, Maria and Elizabeth, had stayed with the Firths in Thornton to lessen the burden of childcare and nursing at Haworth Parsonage.

In early December, just two months after his wife's death, Patrick Brontë made a solo visit of his own to Kipping House, but after only two days he returned alone and – however kindly and delicately – rejected. There are limits to feminine compassion and altruism even with the Elizabeth Firths of this world. Elizabeth was still an attractive, young woman, twenty years or so younger than her rather desperate if over-confident suitor. Perhaps Maria Brontë had confided now and then some of her husband's eccentricities to her younger friend – his phobia about fires, for example, or his strange eating habits and purposeless pistol shooting. And then there were practical considerations: a yearly salary of less than £200 in that remote, isolated village after Elizabeth's comfortable, sociable existence with her father and his new wife at Thornton.

Elizabeth's new stepmother, indeed, may have also influenced her decision. It was not an easy role to be cast into, even with one grown daughter such as herself. To have instant motherhood thrust upon her, despite her deep and abiding affection for the little Brontës, when she had been an indulged and carefree only child all her life, was a prospect Elizabeth was reluctant to contemplate. She had seen at first hand, over a period of years in Thornton, how harassed and overworked Maria had often been with all her babies. And it was unlikely that Patrick Brontë would welcome the addition of any more of Elizabeth's own. In the space of his brief visit to Kipping House Elizabeth Firth searched her soul, prayed, listened perhaps to a persistent voice of self-preservation within, and then refused Patrick Brontë's offer – hesitantly, no doubt, and with more than a modicum of guilt – but still she said no. (Three years later she married the Reverend James Franks of Huddersfield; on their honeymoon, in September 1824, they visited the three eldest Brontë daughters, Maria, Elizabeth and Charlotte, at Cowan Bridge School, and gave each of them a half-crown.)

Elizabeth's rejection was a stunning blow to Patrick Brontë. For nearly a year he brooded on his failure while Aunt Branwell continued to run the household (and contributed to it by paying for her own room and board), and Maria saw, as best she could, to the emotional needs of her little sisters and brother. At some point during 1822, however, Patrick Brontë pulled himself together again and proposed to one Isabella Drury in nearby Keighley, about whom we know nothing other than the fact that she bluntly told her suitor that she was 'not so stupid' as to accept his offer. With those three decisive words Isabella Drury sinks back into the irrecoverable past, to what fate we shall never know.

But Patrick Brontë's quest for a 'fool' or martyr to marry, though again halted for a period by this second refusal, was not yet abandoned. Where Elizabeth Firth's charity and Isabella Drury's lack of stupidity fell short of the mark, perhaps love – or the protestation of it – might succeed. Patrick Brontë, forty-six years old, with a cramped house full of little children and not very much money, cast himself into the unlikely role of a romantic hero in search of a heroine. And scanning the past he lighted upon the figure of Mary Burder whom he had jilted all those years ago at his first curacy in Essex at Wethersfield. Through discreet enquiries he learned that Mary, now well into her thirties, was still unmarried and still living with her mother at Finchingfield Park. It was to Mrs Burder, indeed, that Patrick wrote in April of 1823, after a silence of nearly fifteen years.

He informed Mrs Burder of his present circumstances, emphasizing the respectability and security of his living at Haworth, including the 'good house' which he had 'rent free', glossing over the meagreness of his salary, barely mentioning his marriage to an 'amiable and respectable lady, who has been dead for nearly two years' and saying not one word about all the children she had left behind.[1] In this initial foray of a letter Patrick Brontë's purpose was merely to get his foot, so to speak, into the Burder door, and indirectly to make contact with his old flame.

Mrs Burder took her time answering him, but when she did respond Patrick interpreted whatever she had to say as a sign of encouragement. Hence in his next assault he wrote to Mary directly, commencing with the 'very agreeable sensation in [his] heart . . . on reflecting that [she] was *still* single.' After this rather tactless beginning, Patrick dwelt on the fact that 'you were the *first* whose hand I solicited, and no doubt I was the *first* to whom you *promised to give that hand*', without mentioning why and how that promise was never fulfilled. Instead, he clearly implied that he wished now to pick up the threads he had so hastily left entangled and awry in Essex fifteen years earlier.

> However much you may dislike me now, I am sure you once loved me with an unaffected innocent love, and I feel confident ... you cannot doubt my love for you. It is now almost fifteen years since I last saw you. This is a long interval of time and may have effected many changes. It has made me look something older. But I trust I have gained more than I have lost, I hope I may venture to say I am *wiser* and better ... I have a *small* but *sweet* little family that often soothe my heart, and afford me pleasure by their endearing little ways, and I have what I consider a competency of good things of this life ... I want but *one* addition to my comforts and then I think I should wish for no more on this side of eternity. I want to see a dearly Beloved Friend, kind as I *once* saw her, and as *much* disposed to promote my happiness.

Though Patrick begged, he said, merely to visit and be received at Finchingfield Park as an '*Old Friend*', he closed his letter with: 'I cannot tell how *you* may feel on reading this, but I must say *my* ancient love is rekindled and I have a *longing* desire to see you.'[2]

Patrick Brontë's gifts as an inditer of love letters were about as scanty as those he possessed as a poet. His letter to Mary Burder was outrageously transparent, albeit ingenuously so. The connection between his rekindled 'ancient love' and his '*small* but *sweet* little family', with all 'their endearing little ways' could not be plainer. Could anyone really believe in the paradise up in Haworth which he sketched, a paradise which lacked but '*one* addition' to make it complete 'this side of eternity'?

Like Isabella Drury, Mary Burder was no fool, but her refusal was neither laconic nor peremptory. She was, as Patrick Brontë reminded her, '*still* single', and she had apparently been nursing her rancour against the architect of her state – her erstwhile, red-headed, impetuous Irish suitor – all those years since Patrick Brontë had beaten a hasty retreat from Essex. Before replying to his letter on 28 July 1823, Mary carefully 'perused ... many letters' of his written in those bygone days when Patrick had courted her, letters which she had carefully preserved for nearly a decade and a half. This 'review', she told him, excited 'increased gratitude and thankfulness to that wise, indulgent Providence which then watched over me for good and withheld me from forming in very early life ... a union ... [which] must have embittered my future days.' That said, Mary went on to congratulate herself on her single state, 'upon which you are pleased to remark', as a 'state of my choice ... a state of much happiness and comfort ... with the kindest and most indulgent of friends in a beloved Parent, Sister and brother, with a handsome competence ... teased with no domestic cares and anxieties and without anyone to control or oppose me.' Truly, she affirmed, 'My Cup overfloweth.' Still, she sympathized with her former and current suitor and 'the poor little innocents in your bereavement', and exhorted them all to look elsewhere than Finchingfield Park for comfort: 'The Lord can supply all your and their need.' As for the proposed visit of an '*Old Friend*', Mary felt unequivocally compelled to 'give a *decided* negative.'[3]

The acrimonious hostility of Mary Burder's '*decided* negative' silenced Patrick Brontë for six long months; he had anticipated, after all, nothing more serious than his greying hair or lined brow as impediments to 'rekindling' his romance with Miss Burder. And yet the wonder of the situation is that he did not give up the attempt entirely. On New Year's Day 1824, he finally replied to Mary Burder's letter of the previous July and implored her to reconsider his proposed visit to Finchingfield Park and suggested that he descend upon Mrs and Miss Burder at some convenient time during the coming spring and summer months. At the same time, Patrick flourished a few verbal daggers of his own in response to Mary's pointed, sarcastic thrusts:

> You may think and write as you please, but I *have not* the *least doubt* that if you had *been mine* you would have been happier *now* or *can* be as one in a *single* life. You would have had other and kindlier views and feelings. You would have had a *second self* ...[4]

The idea of spinsterhood as preferable to marriage and of a woman voluntarily choosing to remain single rather than becoming a wife and mother were, of course, both alien and incomprehensible to Patrick Brontë and nearly all his contemporaries, or at least to all his male contemporaries. If Maria Brontë could have participated in this correspondence from beyond the grave her allegiance might not have gone entirely to her husband. Still, the fate of an Old Maid was considered pathetic, even ludicrous. Three of the 'poor little innocents' in Haworth Parsonage were to grow up with its spectre looming ahead in their future.

There was also, of course, one of the species resident in the house. Mary Burder did not reply to Patrick Brontë's New Year's Day letter and, with her caustic rejection, the bereaved and beleaguered father appears to have ceased his efforts to remarry. Instead, he asked his sister-in-law Elizabeth Branwell – single, set in her ways, on the further side of forty and as unfond of young children as was Patrick Brontë himself – to remain with them in Haworth, and she dutifully but reluctantly consented. In no sense of the word could this arrangement be considered ideal: two stern, aloof adults, each isolated by the grip of their own private disappointment and unhappiness, and six young children, silent, fearful and preternaturally mature. The little Brontës were so cut off from any other playmates that at the only birthday party they were ever invited to, they huddled silently together and watched with bewilderment while the other children played 'hunt the slipper' and 'here we go round the mulberry bush'. Their own very different games consisted of reenacting such events as the escape of Bonny Prince Charles, during which Emily, dressed up as the prince, scrambled out of her father's bedroom window and shinned down his prize cherry tree, only to break off a branch in the process, which damage they attempted to conceal by blackening the tree's wound with coal soot.

Isolated as they were, and intimidated too by the coldness of their aunt and their father, the six children had only each other to cling to. They knew death too young, they learned helplessness and emotional starvation too early. Despite the two grown-ups who saw to their physical and educational needs, they had become with Maria Brontë's death permanent orphans. And here we glimpse already the origin of the themes of abandonment, victimization and exile which permeate all of Emily Brontë's writing.

Elizabeth Branwell appropriated the bedroom above the dining room, overlooking the graveyard, where her sister had died. She took the baby, Anne, in to sleep with her, but all the others remained crowded into the cramped, unheated 'children's study' above the entrance hall, sleeping in camp beds which were folded up during the daytime. Aunt Branwell closed her shutters, had a roaring fire lit in the fireplace and then scarcely stirred from her room for the next twenty years. Here she slept, instructed her young nieces in the basic 'household arts', and perhaps also their ABC and how to count. Here, too, she took her meals solitarily on a tray brought up by the servant while her brother-in-law also ate in lonely isolation in his study downstairs. The children had their meals across the hall or sometimes in the kitchen, unsuperintended, so that there was no one to see that they finished their vegetables before consuming baked custard or apple pudding. Not surprisingly, they all became picky, erratic eaters. They wondered what was so strange, even shameful, about eating that their aunt and father insisted upon doing it unseen and alone.

But if Aunt Branwell neglected her nieces and nephew at mealtimes her presence in the house was still pervasive and inescapable; swathed in a mauve or purple woollen shawl over a black silk dress, her head encumbered by a 'front' of false auburn curls, topped by a billowing large white cap, and her feet shod in iron pattens that clicked over the parsonage stone floors with a persistence that frayed everyone else's nerves, she ran the household, as a general might, inflexibly, indefatigably, and so punctually that the villagers said (though how they knew is a mystery) you could set your clock according to what was going on in the parsonage – needlework, lessons, baking, prayers, and so on. Aunt Branwell also rigidly enforced her brother-in-law's pyrophobia by maintaining his ban on window curtains and cotton clothing and making sure that two buckets of water were always at hand at the end of the downstairs hallway.

An eccentric, non-communicative and embittered brother-in-law and six needy young children did not in any way constitute the kind of life Elizabeth Branwell would have chosen for herself. She missed her native Penzance, its temperate climate and lively social round (she intimated to her nieces that she had been quite a belle in her youth), and she seems to have loathed everything about Haworth – the climate, the inhabitants, the countryside. Never in all her years there did she once step into the village in front of the parsonage or on to the moors behind it. Instead, she issued from the house only once a week, punctually on Sunday mornings, when she walked through the garden gate and across the crowded cemetery to the church some hundred yards away from the house to hear her brother-in-law preach. For the rest of the week, if she left her room it was to order groceries or superintend cooking in the kitchen or to read to Patrick in his study.

The monotony and uncongeniality of her lot in time soured a temperament that had never been sanguine or gay. The only remnant of her earlier years that Aunt Branwell retained was her gold snuff box which she resorted to with the shadow of a smile at such indulgence. More characteristically, she avidly read Methodist magazines and tracts and poured tea from a black china teapot inscribed in gold with Grimshaw's injunction: 'To me to live is Christ, To die is Gain.' She was strict with her already 'spiritless' nieces and positively tyrannical with the two family servants, Nancy and Sarah Garrs, who had been with the Brontës since their Thornton days. Nancy complained much later that 'Miss Branwell were ... so crosslike an' fault findin' and so close, she ga'e us, my sister ... an' me, but a gill o' beer a day, an' she gi'e it to us hersel', did Miss Branwell, to our dinner, she wouldn'a let us go to draw it oursel' in t' cellar. A pint a day, she gi'e us, that were half a pint for me an' half a pint for Sarah.'[5]

By 1824, then, it was clear that no new mother was going to join Patrick Brontë and his orphaned children at Haworth Parsonage. Aunt Branwell was installed in the front bedroom and Patrick Brontë remained immured in his study. But Nancy and Sarah Garrs, disgusted with the meagre portions of food and drink Elizabeth Branwell allotted them, left the parsonage and in their stead a fifty-three-year-old villager named Tabitha Aykroyd became the family servant. Not surprisingly, she and Aunt Branwell did not get on well, but Tabby's was a strong character which could not be easily intimidated, and she held her own against Aunt Branwell's imperious ways. Tabby was a rough, shrewd Yorkshire woman. She had been widowed for many years, was childless, and directly before coming to the parsonage she had worked at one of the neighbouring farms which surrounded the village. Aunt Branwell found Tabby's thick Yorkshire dialect grating and often incomprehensible, and Tabby must have thought Aunt Branwell's airs and parsimonious ways equally irritating.

For the children, however, Tabby's advent was a great boon. She ruled them sharply and lavished on them no caresses or soft words, but she soon felt a rough affection for them, and they as surely sensed it beneath her practical and undemonstrative exterior. She also brought to the children the worlds of the past and the supernatural. Tabby had lived in Haworth in the bygone era when packhorses with their tinkling bells brought goods to the village only once a week. 'What is more, she had known the "bottom" or valley in those primitive days when the fairies frequented the margin of the "beck" on moonlight nights ... [and] she had many a tale to tell of ... the countryside; old ways of living, former inhabitants, decayed gentry, who had melted away, and whose places knew them no more; family tragedies, and dark superstitious dooms.'[6]

Of the three elderly adults at the parsonage, Tabby, with her strange tales and special cakes and other treats, was the closest to the children. She cooked for and fed them; she created nourishment both for their pallid appetites and their hungry imaginations. But on at least one occasion, the patriarch of the household attempted to gain access to his children's minds. Patrick Brontë told Mrs Gaskell that he thought he glimpsed unusual talents and intelligence among his offspring, and in order to test this supposition, he devised a peculiar kind of experiment. 'Happening to have a mask in the house, [he] told them all to stand and speak boldly from under the cover of the mask.' The result, as he related it, was as follows:

> I began with the youngest (Anne, afterwards Acton Bell) and asked what a child like her most wanted; she answered 'Age and Experience.' I asked the next (Emily, afterwards Ellis Bell) what I had best do with her brother Branwell who was sometimes a naughty boy; she answered 'Reason with him, and when he won't listen to reason, whip him.' I asked Branwell what was the best way of knowing the difference between the intellects of men and women: he answered, 'By considering the difference between them as to their bodies.' I then asked Charlotte what was the best

book in the world; she answered 'The Bible.' And what was the next best; she answered 'The Book of Nature.' I then asked the next [Elizabeth] what was the best mode of education for a woman; she answered 'That which would make her rule her house well.' Lastly, I asked the oldest [Maria] what was the best mode of spending time; she answered, 'By laying it out in preparation for a happy Eternity.'[7]

Only Emily, among the four girls, 'spoke boldly from under the cover of the mask.' Aunt Branwell and her tracts and Methodist magazines and Grimshaw teapot had successfully inculcated a cloying feminine submissiveness and piety in the others. Anne, at the age of four, didn't want a china doll or gingerbread man, but 'Age and Experience.' Elizabeth already knew that a woman's only destiny and duty was to run her household well. The saintly Maria looked beyond the domestic sphere to the divine, while Charlotte sought knowledge both of the world to come and the natural world all about her.

Branwell, in contrast, wasn't hemmed in by feminine constraints. He unabashedly told his father that the two sexes could be differentiated by their bodies. Equally forthright was Emily's advice to whip Branwell when he was bad if reason or threats failed to curb his waywardness. Whips conjure feelings of power and domination, and already at the age of five Emily was 'a law unto herself'. Years later she would have the six-year-old Catherine Earnshaw in *Wuthering Heights* ask her father to bring her a whip as a present when he went to Liverpool. But Mr Earnshaw returned with a naughty little boy named Heathcliff instead, and Heathcliff, as he grew up, often received a thrashing, especially after his adoptive father's death. Emily herself, in fact, ate shortbread and biscuits off a small blue and white Wedgwood plate of her own which depicted a little girl in a cart wielding a whip with her brother, in harness, pulling the cart. Round the edges of the little tea plate was inscribed the rhyme 'What pleasure filled my little heart when seated in thy little cart to see thee act the horse's part, my brother.'

Patrick Brontë's mask experiment was over in a matter of minutes and the children then dispersed: Branwell perhaps went out with his father to walk to Keighley for the *Leeds Intelligencer* and the girls probably went up to their aunt's room for lessons.

Aunt Branwell did her best to instruct them, but their education was haphazard and erratic. Despite their father's occasional lessons in history, geography and arithmetic, needlework took precedence over any other kind of learning, an understandable state of affairs in those days when virtually all clothing was hand-sewn at home. Before she could even read or write Emily was given her own workbox – that indispensable nineteenth-century female possession – brimming with bobbins and pins and col-oured embroidery yarns. When she was nine she finished her first sampler of the alphabet and numbers, and the next year she produced a much more elaborate one with long embroidered passages from the Bible.

While Emily and Charlotte and Anne stitched away in Aunt Branwell's stuffy, over-heated room, now and then one of them would take a rest and read to the others, not nursery rhymes or fairy tales, for there were none in the house, but books from their father's library – Shakespeare, Byron, Wordsworth, Coleridge, Shelley and stories from *Blackwood's Magazine*. But their two great favourites were the same two classics their father had cherished in his youth: Milton's *Paradise Lost* and Bunyan's *Pilgrim's Progress*. The children possessed a set of china mugs with hand-painted scenes showing various episodes from Bunyan (the one of Pilgrim in the Slough of Despond looked uncannily like their father), and Charlotte, in particular, was so strongly affected by *Pilgrim's Progress* that when she was still very young she set off on her own pilgrimage to the paradise of Bradford, and was only just intercepted at the bottom of Main Street before it curves round to the road to Keighley.

From very early on, reading and writing were the most import-ant of all the children's activities, for throughout their eventless, monotonous lives these were their only means of escape. Books were the food which fed their brains, and writing the most important measure of their growth. Maria no doubt instructed the younger ones, because after Aunt Branwell taught them the alphabet, Maria and Elizabeth were sent by Patrick Brontë to Crofton House School at Wakefield, where Elizabeth Firth had been educated. It had a reputation for advanced educational methods and its principal was Miss Mangnall, the author of one of the standard school texts of the time, *Mangnall's Questions*.

Probably Maria and perhaps Elizabeth, too, knew how to read even before they went away to school at Wakefield. In any event, their stay there was not long, most likely because of the high school fees.

The education of his daughters was, in fact, one of the most urgent problems Patrick Brontë faced at this time. Branwell's instruction was under his father's careful and exacting supervision and consisted of a thorough grounding in the classics, history, geography and mathematics. It never seems to have occurred to Patrick Brontë that his daughters might join and benefit from their brother's lessons. The education of women was a different matter: it consisted of reading, writing and simple arithmetic, sewing, needlework, embroidery and knitting, as well as other 'household arts', and finally, if money allowed, 'accomplishments' – a smattering of French, drawing, music lessons and that quaint nineteenth-century practice of 'using the globes'. The question confronting Patrick Brontë was how all these things could be imparted to his five daughters. It had become clear that Aunt Branwell was either unequipped or unwilling to teach them to her nieces. Miss Mangnall's school at Wakefield was too expensive, as were others.

It must have seemed an act of divine providence to Patrick Brontë when he learned from the Rector of Keighley that a semi-charitable institution for the education of the children of impoverished, or at least sorely pressed, clergymen had been established by the Reverend William Carus Wilson, vicar of Tunstall, in January 1824. The Clergy Daughters School was located on the turnpike road between Leeds and Kendal, in the hamlet of Cowan Bridge, two miles from the town of Kirkby Lonsdale. Here for a mere £14 a year (plus an extra £3 for each optional 'accomplishment') the daughters of needy curates, vicars, Anglican priests and dissenting ministers could all be educated.

That they desperately needed education was indisputable. Such girls possessed no dowries and so their chances of marriage were severely compromised. Furthermore, they would be faced with destitution – perhaps even the workhouse – if, or rather when, their fathers died, as these men would be unable to leave any substantial savings behind and the church made no provision in the form of pensions or annuities for their widows and orphans. Their sons, like Branwell, would be able to follow their fathers into the church or enter the military or some other respectable profession. But the daughters of clergymen, if they failed to secure a husband, would have really only one career open to them: that of teacher or governess.

During the late winter and spring months of 1824 a succession of epidemics – whooping cough, chickenpox, and measles – passed through Haworth, including the parsonage, confining all the Brontë children to their beds. Thus it wasn't until late July that Patrick Brontë was able to send the two eldest girls, ten-year-old Maria and nine-year-old Elizabeth, to Cowan Bridge, some fifty-four miles away from Haworth. He accompanied them himself and apparently was impressed by everything he saw at the school.

It was situated in a lovely hollow, nestling at the bottom of a hill close to the River Leck, around which alder trees and willows and hazel bushes grew in profusion. The clear, swift-running stream was strewn with marble-white large stones and green pastures stretched out from its banks. The school itself consisted of a long bow-windowed eighteenth-century cottage facing the Leck. Wilson had had the cottage converted to contain the teachers' rooms and the school dining room and kitchen. At right angles to the cottage he added another long building of two stories with school rooms on the ground floor and dormitories above. Across from the school room and dormitory wing, at the other end of the cottage, was a long covered verandah where the students took their exercise when the weather prevented them from going on their daily constitutional in a long 'crocodile' of pairs of girls marching almost militarily across the surrounding hills. The school garden was hemmed in on three sides by the school buildings and ran down to the stream. Behind the school there was a single stone hut containing a privy which served the entire school population – some fifty girls and staff in the Brontës' time.

Mr Brontë spent the night at Cowan Bridge before returning to Haworth, resolved to send Charlotte and Emily as soon as they were well and strong enough to be enrolled. Charlotte joined her older sisters in August. But Emily, who had just turned six, remained at home until November, which meant that she witnessed the great Crow Hill bog eruption of 2 September. In fact she was out on the moors with Branwell, Anne and Tabby when a heralding storm engulfed the balmy early autumn weather they had walked out to enjoy. Luckily they were able to take shelter from the downpour in an abandoned stone farm-house, from which they watched with amazement and excite-ment as the violent storm swept over the hills in a gathering turbulent darkness, lashing wind and rain. The earth trembled beneath their feet and then suddenly Crow Hill bog exploded before their very eyes, hurling peat, soil and boulders into the air, down the hills to the valleys. For Emily the spectacle must have been both exhilarating and terrifying – literally 'wuthering heights'. For the rest of her life she felt both awe and a deep affinity for the harsh, rugged landscape surrounding her home. In time, it became more of a home to her than the parsonage itself, and it permeated nearly everything she ever wrote. The natural world for Emily was a realm of unpredictable, super-human forces compounded of equal parts of beauty and violence.

But from this world of natural cataclysms she too was packed off to Cowan Bridge on 25 November. In the school register she was entered after her three sisters, and her gifts, capabilities and deficiencies enumerated just as theirs had been:

Maria Brontë, aged 10 (daughter of Patrick Brontë, Haworth, near Keighley, Yorks), July 1, 1824. Reads tolerably. Writes pretty well. Ciphers a little. Works badly. Very little of geography or history. Has made some progress in reading French, but knows nothing of the language grammatically.

Elizabeth Brontë, age 9. (Vaccinated. Scarlet fever, whooping cough) Reads little. Writes pretty well. Ciphers none. Works very badly. Knows nothing of grammar, geography, history or accomplishments.

Charlotte Brontë. Entered August 10, 1824. Writes indiffer-ently. Ciphers a little and works neatly. Knows nothing of grammar, geography, history or accomplishments. Altogether clever of her age, but knows nothing systematically. Governess.

Emily Brontë. Entered November 25, age $5\frac{3}{4}$ [she was actually six and a half]. Reads very prettily and works a little. Subsequent career – governess.

Apparently Patrick Brontë did not take Emily to Cowan Bridge himself at the end of November as he had escorted the three elder girls the previous summer. Instead, he most likely put Emily in the care of a friend or trusted servant for the coach journey to the school. Thus he was unable to see how his other daughters were faring. And thus, too, he lost the opportunity of meeting the founder, prime mover and vigilant overseer of the Clergy Daughters School, the Reverend William Carus Wilson.

Even before founding the Clergy Daughters School, Wilson had a reputation in church circles for philanthropy and advanced educational theories and methods. Among the subscribers to the Clergy Daughters School were William Wilberforce and Hannah More. If it hadn't been his misfortune to have the Brontë sisters as pupils at his institution, Wilson would have rested in obscurity undisturbed, but both during his lifetime and for long after he was, to his grief and lasting shame, enshrined by Charlotte as the 'black pillar' who casts his long, fearful shadow over *Jane Eyre*: Mr Brocklehurst, whose 'straight, narrow, sable-clad shape' stands 'erect on the rug; the grim face at the top . . . like a carved mask, placed above the shaft.'[8]

The manner in which Wilson ran the school, the harsh regime he imposed, the deprivations he inflicted and, most of all, his own literary works all exposed him as a sadistic Calvinist with a fixation on torture, death, hellfire and damnation. Among his cautionary children's books was *The Child's First Tales*, written in words of one syllable for beginning readers and illustrated by crude woodcuts showing criminals being hanged, men in chains and children in coffins. Indeed, the book opened with the picture of a man suspended from a gallows and the accompanying caption: 'Look there! Do you see a man hung by the neck?'[9] Another tale related how a three-year-old little girl had a tantrum when her mother scolded her, in the midst of which God struck the child dead. As Wilson described it, 'All at once God struck her dead, no time to pray, no time to call on God to save her soul . . . Where is she now? We know that bad girls go to Hell.'[10] Another Wilson production, *The Children's Friend*, also abounded in stories of sudden death and damnation and such historical subjects as the horrors of the plague and the massacre of St Bartholomew. *Youthful Memoirs* concentrated on death-bed scenes of little children who speak in a grotesquely artificial way of their love of death. For example, when a three-and-a-half-year-old boy is asked whether he would choose death or life, he replies: 'Death for me. I am fonder of death.'[11]

In a tract written for the staff of the school, *Thoughts Suggested to the Superintendent and Ladies*, Wilson enjoined his employees to use all his 'advanced' educational methods to terrorize pupils into a state of submissive obedience. Yet in this same document Wilson articulated his vision for the Clergy Daughters School as a 'nursery for Christ's spiritual church on Earth and a nursery for Heaven.'[12]

The practical aspects of running this earthly and divine nursery were spelled out in the Prospectus of Cowan Bridge School, probably also written by Wilson. The 'Entrance Rules' included the following items:

> The terms for clothing, lodging, boarding and educating are £14 a year; half to be paid in advance ... and also £1 entrance money for the use of books, etc. The system of education comprehends History, Geography, the Use of the Globes, Grammar, Writing, and Arithmetic, all kinds of Needlework, and the nicer kinds of household arts – work such as getting up fine linen, ironing, etc. If accomplishments are required, an additional £3 a year is made for French, Music or Drawing, each.

Every pupil was required to bring with her a Bible, prayer book, workbag with necessary sewing implements, combs, brushes, umbrella, gloves and the following items of clothing:

4 day shifts	4 pairs of white cotton stockings
4 night shifts	4 pairs of black worsted stockings
6 night caps	2 nankeen tippets
2 pairs of stays	4 brown holland pinafores
2 flannel petticoats	2 white pinafores
3 white upper petticoats	1 short coloured dressing gown
1 grey stuff petticoat	2 pairs of shoes
3 pockets	

What the three pockets were meant to hold remains an enigma. They were not, in any case, visible in the school uniform all the girls wore. In the winter this consisted of purple merino dresses, brown holland pinafores, black stockings and plaid cloaks for outdoors. In the summer they donned equally plain tan-coloured nankeen frocks with matching tippets and white straw bonnets. On Sundays they exchanged this for white dresses and white muslin frills. Wilson had his hand in devising the school uniform as in every other aspect of the school. He also ordered that all the girls' hair should be cropped, and if any girl were unfortunate enough to have naturally curly hair, it would be cut especially short so that no wavy locks would escape.

The school routine was harsh and strictly regimented. At six a.m. the clang of the school bell roused the girls from whatever sweet dreams of home or family they might be immersed in. If it was winter they often had to break the ice in their china pitchers in order to wash, it was so cold in the long dormitory. Then they hastily pulled on their worsted stockings and flannel petticoats as they shivered and their teeth chattered. Between seven and eight they prayed, read, and memorized passages from the Bible and sang hymns. Then they had a breakfast of milk and porridge before commencing their lessons, which kept them busy until noon. Between twelve and one they engaged in some sort of exercise – not games or anything enjoyable, but strenuous walks outdoors, weather permitting, or in the covered verandah if it were raining or snowing. Dinner – pudding (served as a first course to take the edge off the girls' appetites), boiled beef and some sort of vegetable – was served at one, and then followed three more hours of lessons. 'Tea' at five consisted of dry bread and milk. The older girls then worked on until eight at their lessons and were rewarded for their efforts by yet more dry bread and milk at 'supper' before going to bed.

Such was the daily regime at Cowan Bridge. The girls' plight was scarcely different from that of inmates in a prison. And, as is the case in prisons, all letters and parcels sent to them were inspected, as was out-going mail. They could receive no visitors unless especially arranged for in advance, and even then, callers were not permitted to remain long.

Not even Sunday offered a reprieve; indeed, Sundays were often more miserable than school days, for on the sabbath the girls had to walk two miles to Tunstall Church in order to hear their founder and benefactor preach in his own church. In the summer this walk was undoubtedly pleasant, as it took them across open fields and spacious pastures. But in the winter it was a terrible ordeal to hike across such exposed terrain, covered with ice and snow, buffeted by knife-sharp winds against which the girls' thin shoes and plaid cloaks gave them scant protection. They arrived at Tunstall Church with benumbed, red hands and equally numb feet already swollen with chilblains. In this condition they sat on the hard wooden pew benches while William Carus Wilson preached, with the interminable verbosity of the Reverend Jabes Branderham in *Wuthering Heights*, of the horrors of one of the worlds to come. Wilson, in fact, preached two sermons at Tunstall Church on Sundays, and because of the distance between the church and the school the girls perforce remained at the church in the interval between the two services, huddled together in a gallery above the church hall, where they ate a cold supper brought along in a basket with them – a supper which was as unpalatable and unnourishing to their stomachs as were the Reverend Wilson's sermons to their souls.

Wilson's management of Cowan Bridge School amounted to a reign of hunger both literally and metaphorically. His aim was to subject the pupils to suffering in order to inure them to all carnal needs and desires, including the most basic and self-preserving one for food. The cook he hired unwittingly collaborated in this design out of slovenly carelessness rather than any wish to purify the students' souls. What food there was she managed most of the time to spoil, taint, contaminate or burn in order to render it inedible. The oatmeal was cooked to a gluey lump and usually scorched black into the bargain; greasy beef stews contained unidentifiable fragments floating in them; meat – in those days before refrigeration – was half rotten before it was cooked; puddings were made with water taken from the rain barrel, full of dust, dirt and dead leaves; milk was clotted and sour with age. Worst of all was the Saturday dinner of 'resurrection pie', consisting of all the week's left-overs taken from the dirty kitchen larder or scraped from the barely disturbed plates of the students – tainted meat and potatoes for the most part, covered with an undigestible crust made of greasy lard and flour. What little food the cook produced which was unspoiled and edible was ruthlessly appropriated and devoured by the stronger, older girls who grabbed for more than their share, leaving the little ones weak and empty-handed. The law of the jungle, the survival of the fittest, prevailed at Cowan Bridge. And over all 'pervaded morning, noon, and night ... the odour of rancid fat'[13] that steamed out of the oven in which much of the food was prepared: a stench that reached as far as the school rooms and the long dormitory, so that within the girls' stomachs hunger and nausea were continuously at war.

The little Brontës, especially the youngest, Emily, were delicate, picky eaters before coming to Cowan Bridge, and they suffered acutely from the scanty, unsavoury portions of food doled out to them. They were perpetually hungry and cold, and they suffered in other ways as well. Maria, a very clever but dreamy, absent-minded and untidy child, was hounded and capriciously punished by one of Wilson's protégés, the teacher Miss Andrews, whom Charlotte immortalized in *Jane Eyre* as Miss Scatherd, just as Charlotte enshrined her persecuted older sister as Helen Burns. But there was also a Miss Temple at Lowood School in *Jane Eyre* modelled on the kind, sensitive, generous superintendent of Cowan Bridge, Miss Ann Evans.

It is from Ann Evans, in fact, that we receive our only clear picture of Elizabeth Brontë and some of the earliest glimpses of Charlotte and Emily. Writing of the Brontës to Mrs Gaskell many years later, she said: 'Elizabeth is the only one ... of whom I have a vivid recollection from her meeting with a somewhat alarming accident, in consequence of which I had her for some days and nights in my bedroom ... [so] that I might watch over her myself. Her head was severely cut, but she bore all the consequent suffering with exemplary patience.' Charlotte, Ann Evans remembered, was a 'bright, clever child', the most talkative of the sisters. Emily, she said, was 'a darling child', the youngest of all the pupils and hence 'quite the pet nursling of the school'.[14]

Not even a school full of Miss Evanses ministering to ailing children, however, could have warded off the typhoid epidemic which descended on Cowan Bridge in the spring of 1825. Almost overnight the school was transformed from a house of starvation into a house of illness and death. Gone was the stench of rancid fat, replaced by the odours of tonics and pastilles and steaming gruel for all the heavy-limbed, feverish, listless girls prostrated by typhoid. Wilson tried to rouse them with scriptural exhortations and threats, but they remained sunk in a dull stupor by the fever, their eyes flushed, arms and legs aching, and brows burning to the touch. In vain were Wilson's injunctions to mortify the flesh in order to cleanse the spirit. Finally he had to call in a doctor who tasted the food prepared for the students and spat it out in disgust while Wilson looked on. The cook was discharged; more food supplies were ordered and fires lit in all the draughty rooms. The most acutely ill girls were sent home to die. Those who remained at Cowan Bridge were tenderly nursed by Ann Evans and the under-teachers. Lessons were suspended and the girls who remained well, like Emily and Charlotte, were left alone and free to play in the garden, skip stones in the beck and walk out on the surrounding hills, which were coming to life again after the long, cold, hard winter.

For Charlotte and Emily – playing in the garden, wading in the stream or collecting birds' feathers or cornflowers and forget-me-nots on the hills – the natural world breathed life and warmth and promises of rich red mulberries and blackcurrants in the months to come. But within doors Maria and Elizabeth were confined to their narrow iron beds, too weary and weak to respond to the patches of blue sky and billowing white clouds they glimpsed through the square dormitory windows. They did not have the 'low fever' of typhoid which was prostrating their schoolmates but instead wracking coughs which exhausted their weak bodies and an alarming shortness of breath which made them pant at the slightest exertion. As early as February it was clear that Maria had irreversibly gone 'into decline', and was wasting away from tuberculosis. She was sent home on 14 February, a skeletal, bird-like creature. All the warm fires in the world and wholesome food from Tabby's kitchen couldn't save the brave, uncomplaining little child. Awesomely, rather than grotesquely, Maria was dying with the spiritual ardour of one of the little children in Carus Wilson's tales. Less than three months after she left Cowan Bridge, Maria died on 6 May 1825, at the age of eleven.

For Emily and Charlotte, though they were still away at school, the loss of their eldest sister, their little mother, was a terrifying repetition of their real mother's death four years earlier.

Death was all about them, in the very air they breathed, and they were just at that age when children grasp the meaning of mortality and, most of all, its finality. Maria was gone; they would never see her again. She was nailed up in a wooden coffin, like the children in Wilson's gruesome picture books, and laid under the stone church floor – for ever.

Soon after Maria's death, Elizabeth was also sinking rapidly. She was sent home to Haworth on 31 May and so stricken was Patrick Brontë by Maria's death and the same awful ordeal to come which he read in Elizabeth's wan face that he rushed to Cowan Bridge the very next day and fetched home Charlotte and Emily. Several weeks later, in mid-June, when the lilacs were blooming lavender and white in the parsonage garden, Elizabeth too died and was buried with her mother and sister under the church floor.

· 3 ·

The Web of Sunny Air

Their summer of mourning gave way to a cold, wind-lashed, wet autumn. Patrick Brontë added a yard or two to his white silk cravat and retreated once again into his study, to be dislodged only for family prayers and his clerical duties. Up in her over-heated bedroom, Aunt Branwell now had only three little girls hemming table linen and pillowcases and stitching samplers. The purple heather withered out on the moors and then the first snow obliterated all memory of it. Night closed in by mid-afternoon. Chilled to the bone, Emily and the others did their lessons, ate their meals, and went to bed early, shivering under the covers – especially Emily and Charlotte, who shared a bed and clung to each other for warmth and comfort in the unheated 'children's study' above the ground-floor entrance hall.

Such was Emily's world when she and the others began in 1826 to weave, as Charlotte later put it, their 'web of sunny air' – a web of imaginary stories spun from threads of magic, royalty and castles in a land where an endless summer reigned in contrast to the cold, coarse, home-spun cloth of life in the parsonage. Most importantly, in their fantasy world, death was robbed of its finality: the children, metamorphosed into omnipotent genii, possessed the power to make any or all 'alive again' – to resurrect the dead. Loss drove them to create a counter-reality in which they could take refuge.

Emily was only eight when this imaginary world began to take shape, but it was perhaps the most decisive event of her life. For once Emily entered the 'burning clime' of their fantasy world she never forsook it, not even when she went away from home to teach or study years later, or when she was writing some of

57

her most mature poetry or *Wuthering Heights* later still. The 'web of sunny air' for Charlotte, Branwell and Anne was a childhood haven which was relinquished, however reluctantly, when they became adults. For Emily it was a way of life that she never surrendered.

The materials they used to fabricate their fantasy world were as diverse as their reading, and the only striking gap here was children's books, including fairy tales and nursery rhymes, which they had no knowledge of. Everything else which came to hand was food for their imaginations: the newspapers they read, their aunt's Methodist magazines, and the books in their father's study and those they later borrowed from the Keighley Mechanics Institute: Milton, Bunyan, Scott, Wordsworth, Coleridge, Southey and Byron. Yet though all these writers were absorbed and cherished, they could not satisfy the children's emotional needs, especially the desire for power, and the power, above all, to overcome their losses and all the other deprivations of their lives. They yearned for another world, as remote from Haworth as the antipodes, and brave, hardy conquerors of it, heroes in whom they could submerge their own insignificant identities.

The seeds of this ideal world and the characters who populated it were sown when Patrick Brontë returned from a clergymen's conference in Leeds in early June of 1826, laden with gifts for his children: a set of ninepins for Charlotte, a toy village for Emily, a dancing doll for Anne, and, most importantly, a set of toy soldiers for Branwell. Happy as they were with their own presents, Charlotte and Emily and Anne were even more fascinated with Branwell's toy soldiers, who wore painted ceremonial dress consisting of scarlet pantaloons and jackets and tall black hats. Three years later, when the adventures of the 'Young Men', as they were called, had been voluminously 'spun' out by the children, Charlotte recorded the origin of their saga:

Papa bought Branwell some wooden soldiers at Leeds. When Papa came home it was night, and we were in bed, so next morning Branwell came to our door with a box of soldiers. Emily and I jumped out of bed and I snatched one and exclaimed, 'This is the Duke of Wellington! This shall be the duke!' When I had said this Emily likewise took up one and said it should be hers; when Anne came down she said one should be hers. Mine was the prettiest of the whole, and the tallest, and the most perfect in every part. Emily's was a grave-looking fellow, and we called him Gravey. Anne's was a queer little thing, much like herself, and we called him Waiting Boy. Branwell chose his and called him Buonaparte.[1]

The Duke of Wellington – the great 'Iron Duke' – and his two sons, Lord Charles Wellesley and Arthur Wellesley, remained an obsession with Charlotte for years to come and were her chief personae and alter-egos in the on-going saga the children now initiated. In time Arthur, the Marquis of Douro, became in Charlotte's hands the wickedly Byronic Duke of Zamorna, while Charles Wellesley served as narrator and pseudonym for Charlotte's childhood writing. Branwell disguised himself as both the historical figure of Napoleon and the fictional personage Alexander Percy, also variously known as Rogue, Lord Ellrington and the Duke of Northangerland. From the very beginning Zamorna and Percy were enemies, a state of affairs that was exacerbated rather than lessened by Zamorna's marriage to Percy's daughter Mary.

Emily and Anne, for their part, both soon cast aside their childish Gravey and Waiting Boy in favour of the real-life Arctic explorers Captain Edward Parry and Captain John Ross. Emily chose Parry because of his daring polar expeditions, which she had read about in the newspapers. Parry's courage under the most extreme conditions fascinated her far more than the political and military exploits of Charlotte's Wellington or Branwell's Napoleon.

Their heroes thus settled upon, the children began weaving the web of their adventures. In 1793 their unlikely band of Wellington, Napoleon, Parry and Ross set sail on the 74-gun *Invincible* with a crew of 'twelve men, everyone healthy and stout and in the best temper'.[2] The *Invincible* and its heroes were protected by four Chief Genii (drawn from *The Arabian Nights*): Branni (Branwell), Talli (Charlotte), Emmii (Emily), and Annii (Anne), who saw to it that after many storms and other harrowing mishaps, the *Invincible* arrived safely on the West Coast of Africa, where Parry and Ross, as well as Napoleon and Wellington, adapted to the most un-Arctic tropical climate and landscape. (The young Brontës had read of Mungo Park's, Clapperton's and Denham's explorations of the Niger River as well as Parry and Ross's of the Arctic.)

As soon as the Young Men set foot on African soil they were attacked by the indigenous 'Ashantees' embodied in the form of Charlotte's ninepins. After a bloody battle, the ninepin Ashantees were routed, and in the best nineteenth-century fashion the 'Twelves' colonized the conquered territory which they divided into four kingdoms, each ruled by one of their four heroes: Wellington's Land, Parry's Land, Ross's Land, and, somewhat unaccountably, not Napoleon's but Sneaky's Land. Branwell drew a detailed map of the four kingdoms which together constituted the Great Glass Town Confederacy with the magnificent capital of Glass Town (later called Verdopolis). More than a decade before Victoria ascended the throne, the Brontë children embarked on empire-building in the steaming tropics of West Africa. Palaces were raised, including a Palace of Instruction for a thousand children with subterranean dungeons for naughty pupils; territories were annexed and wars fought in which their heroes killed thousands with impunity, for their victims could always be 'made alive again'. In the Glasstown Confederacy the sun always shone, rivers and lakes sparkled aquamarine, and snow-capped mountains crowned the horizon. It was all very, very far away from Haworth.

Beginning in 1829, three years after the advent of the toy soldiers, the children, or rather Charlotte and Branwell, who were more advanced in writing than the younger Emily and Anne, began to record the history of Glass Town – its foundation, wars, aristocratic high life, love affairs and so on – in tiny booklets of their own manufacture. Not only were the booklets minute – in some cases only slightly larger than a postage stamp – so too was the print-like handwriting in which they were transcribed or 'printed'. In many respects the Glass Town books were modelled on *Blackwood's Magazine*; at one stage, in fact, the 'publications' were entitled 'The Young Men's Blackwood's Magazine', and they contained, like *Blackwood's*, not only adventurous tales but also book reviews, political commentary, illustrations and letters to the editor.

Various reasons conspired to make the little Brontës reduce

their facsimile *Blackwood's*, 'The Young Men's Magazine', to diminutive proportions: the expense of paper, most obviously; and then, too, it seemed appropriate to scale the Glass Town chronicles to the size of the toy soldiers who were not only the cast of characters for the tales, but also 'wrote' a number of them in the first person. And finally, and perhaps most importantly, the tiny booklets with their tiny print were easily concealed and, if found, would be extremely difficult for adult eyes to decipher.

From the very beginning, then, secrecy shrouded the writing of the Brontës, a secrecy not to be fully dissolved until after Emily's death, for it was Emily above all who desired anonymity as a writer. When the children dispensed with the tiny booklets and began writing in penny or twopenny quarto-sized notebooks, they continued to use the microscopic, almost indecipherable handwriting, even when Patrick Brontë, who had noticed the incessant scribbling going on in the dining room or kitchen, gave the children a thick sixpenny notebook in which he – as it turns out vainly – inscribed: 'all that is written in this book must be in a good, plain, and legible hand.'

The Glass Town saga and the adventures of the twelve Young Men weren't the only outlets they created for their hungry imaginations. In her retrospective account, 'History of the Year, 1829', Charlotte sketched the evolution and progression of all the various fantasy worlds to date:

> Our plays were established: 'Young Men', June 1826; 'Our Fellows', July 1827; 'Islanders', December 1827. These are our three great plays that are not kept secret [that is, secret among the children]. Emily's and my bed plays were established December 1, 1827; the others March 1828. Bed plays mean secret plays; they are very nice ones.[3]

'Our Fellows', which was inspired by Aesop's *Fables*, was short-lived, and soon replaced by the far more engrossing 'Islanders', created on a bleak December evening, as Charlotte vividly recorded:

> One night about the time when the cold sleet and stormy fogs of November are succeeded by the snow storms, and high piercing nightwinds of confirmed winter, we were all sitting round the warm, blazing kitchen fire, having just concluded a quarrel with

Tabby concerning the propriety of lighting a candle, from which she came off victorious, no candle having been produced. A long pause succeeded which was at last broken by Branwell saying, in a lazy manner, 'I don't know what to do.' This was echoed by Emily and Anne.

Tabby. 'Wha ya may go to bed.'

Branwell. 'I'd rather do anything than that.'

Charlotte. 'Why are you so glum tonight, Tabby? Oh! Suppose we had each an island of our own.'

Branwell. 'If we had I would choose the Isle of Man.'

Charlotte. 'And I would choose the Isle of Wight.'

Emily. 'The Isle of Arran for me.'

Anne. 'And mine should be Guernsey.'

We then chose who should be chief men in our islands. Branwell chose John Bull, Astley Cooper and Leigh Hunt; Emily, Walter Scott, Mr Lockhart, Johnny Lockhart; Anne, Michael Sadler, Lord Bentinck, Sir Henry Halford. I chose the Duke of Wellington and two sons, Christopher North and Co. and Mr Abernathy. Here our conversation was interrupted by the to us, dismal sound of the clock striking seven and we were summoned off to bed.[4]

In 'Islanders' Charlotte remained true to her great idols, the Duke of Wellington and his two sons, but the others chose leading literary figures over the earlier Young Men political and explorer heroes. Especially interesting is Emily's enthusiasm for Sir Walter Scott (Aunt Branwell gave them Scott's *Tales of a Grandfather* as a Christmas gift in 1828), his son-in-law and grandson.

Not only did 'Islanders' have literary heroes who were prominent men of letters, they were also physically larger than life: ten miles high for Charlotte's, Branwell's and Anne's men, while, somewhat mysteriously, Emily's were only four miles high. In 1829, when Charlotte wrote her account of the inception of 'Islanders', she was thirteen, Branwell twelve, Emily eleven and Anne nine. All except Emily, however, looked much younger and were pitifully short for their years. Hence in 'Islanders' they inflate themselves into monstrous ten-mile-high giants. But Emily, who was taller than the older Charlotte and Branwell as well as Anne, was pared down to a mere four miles high. Even this early on, Emily loomed large in the family. She was not merely tall but also physically strong and brave – a presence to be reckoned with, admired and envied, and thus in this instance cut down to size.

'The Young Men', 'Our Fellows', and 'Islanders' were their 'three great plays that [were] not kept secret' among the children. But Charlotte and Emily's 'bed plays' were secret, known only to each other, and so private and precious were they that Charlotte dared not write them down: 'Bed plays mean secret plays; they are very nice ones. Their nature I need not write on paper, for I think I shall always remember them.'[5] After Tabby refused to produce a candle on those cold December evenings of 1827 and sent the children upstairs to bed at the dismal sound of the clock striking seven, Charlotte and Emily lay awake together on the narrow camp bed in the children's study. Anne still slept with Aunt Branwell, and Branwell was now in his father's room. Ever since they could remember, Charlotte and Emily had shared a bed, and now in the darkness of their little room they began to weave the secret web of their 'bed plays', murmuring to each other long into the night, creating characters, kingdoms, a whole precious universe so strange and wondrous that it remained known only to the two of them.

The bed plays were very intimate plays, for one utters in bed, in the darkness, and to the one person who is loved most in the world, all sorts of things that couldn't be said in the light of day to others, even if those others are another sister and brother. The bed plays provided a secret, shared language and world for Emily and Charlotte, and there is no indication of when or if the bed plays ever ceased. Emily and Charlotte continued to share a bed well into adulthood except for the periods when Charlotte was away from home at school or, later, as a governess. For all we know, the bed plays could have outlasted 'Our Fellows', 'Islanders' and even Glass Town.

Yet there were disagreements and divisions, no doubt, in the bed plays as well as in Glass Town. Emily chafed at the luxurious romanticism of their sister's creations and Charlotte mocked the prosaic element in Emily's. In the 'Young Men's Magazine' which Charlotte and Branwell 'edited', Charlotte wrote a satiric piece on her sister's realm in the Glass Town Confederacy entitled 'A Day at Parry's Palace'. Parry's Land, in the heart of West Africa, was a realistic and faithful replica of the Yorkshire landscape, architecture, inhabitants, customs and even food so familiar to the Brontës. Upon arriving in Parry's Land, Charlotte's reporter, Lord Charles Wellesley, was immediately struck with the 'shiftless milk-and-water beings' who live there as well as 'the changed aspect of things ... No proud castle or splendid palace towers ... No high-born noble claimed allegiance of his vassals. Every inch of ground was inclosed with stone walls ... Nasty factories with their tall black chimneys breathing thick columns of almost tangible smoke discoloured not that sky of dull hazy hue. Every woman wore a brown stuff gown with white cap and handkerchief. Glossy satin, rich velvet and costly silk or soft muslin broke not on the fair uniformity.' Parry's palace itself was an undistinguished square building of only 'moderate dimensions'. Its equally moderate grounds contained 'rows of peas, gooseberry bushes, and black, red and white currant trees', some few 'common flowering shrubs' and 'a grass plat to dry clothes on' in the garden. In 'a paddock behind the house', Wellesley found a cow 'to give milk for the family and ... butter ... and cheese.'

Sir Edward and Lady Emily Parry welcomed Lord Charles in a typically restrained Yorkshire manner and they then sat down to tea in 'complete silence'. After tea the Parrys' child 'little Eater was brought in', a disagreeable child (we never learn its sex, only that it is a glutton by its name), dressed in a greasy pinafore. A supper of coffee and 'a very few slices of bread and butter' was served several hours later, and 'this meal like the former was eaten in silence.'

The next day Wellesley described dinner at Parry's palace; it seemed that the only occurrences of any note in Parry's Land were meals. Anne's hero, Captain Ross, also attended this dinner. It began, as did dinner at the parsonage, at noon, and the menu was also the same as that at home in Haworth: roast beef and Yorkshire pudding, mashed potatoes, preserved cucumbers and apple pie. Ross, wearing a white apron, and the Parrys 'all [ate] ... as if they had not seen a meal for three weeks', and gobbled down strawberries and sweet cakes at the end of dinner. Predictably, Ross, after gorging himself, got 'extremely sick' an hour after dinner and 'no doctor being at hand, Death was momentarily expected and would certainly have ensued had not the *Genius Emily* arrived at a most opportune period when the disorder was reaching its crisis. She cured with an incantation and vanished.' By this point Wellesley was both heartily weary of and highly irritated by the Parrys, their house and atrocious table manners: 'I felt a strong inclination to set the house on fire and consume the senseless gluttons.'[6]

The mundane realism of Emily's kingdom rankled with Charlotte. But what was perhaps even more striking than the Yorkshire ambiance of Parry's Land was the centrality of food and meals and eating at Parry's palace. The meals admittedly were as spartan and mundane as the landscape, with the exception of the strawberries and sweet cakes, but the eaters of those meals were ravenous and stuffed themselves as if they hadn't had a meal in three weeks. Ross ate so much, in fact, that his indigestion threatened to be fatal until the *Genius Emily* cured him with an incantation and vanished. Charlotte's Lord Wellesley became disgusted, even nauseated, by all their gluttony.

Amusing as 'A Day at Parry's Palace' was, there were peculiar undercurrents beneath its satiric raillery. Emily was the family member who was most active in the kitchen, and in time she did all the baking for the family. At the age of eleven or twelve she was the largest of the children and probably the most well fed. Ross's attack of dyspepsia resembled those of Patrick Brontë. As for the silence which characterized the Parrys' meals, both Aunt Branwell and Patrick Brontë ate in silence behind the closed doors of their rooms. Silence and secrecy and shame are closely allied to one another, and children are quick to perceive their interconnections. Emily herself had changed in the three or four years since Cowan Bridge from a 'darling child' and 'pet nursling' to a withdrawn, shy child of few words, especially in the presence of strangers, and anyone outside the family circle was a stranger. In darkness, in bed alone with Charlotte, her tongue was loosened, especially when Charlotte promised not to record one word of the secret bed plays. But as the *Genius Emily* she uttered an incantation and vanished.

Parry's Land was a meagre, starved-looking realm in contrast to the exotic vistas of Charlotte's Wellington's Land, with its castles and palaces and fortifications, its snow-capped mountains and uncharted rivers and inland lakes. And the Parrys themselves were a morose lot compared to the glamorous nobility of Wellington's Land. In Parry's Land people stuffed themselves on heavy Yorkshire food and went to bed at seven. In Wellington's Land they attended vast multi-course banquets and danced all night or clandestinely made off in the small hours of the morning – an aristocratic gentleman on a noble steed with a veiled woman mounted behind him, her fur-trimmed cloak fluttering like moths' wings in the wind.

Though Emily and Anne were too young to do any of the actual writing of the Glass Town stories, they made their own contributions when Charlotte and Branwell read their work out loud. And so their 'web of sunny air', like Penelope's, remained in a state of perpetual creation, a counter-world to that of the parsonage. In the opening paragraphs of 'The History of the Year' Charlotte captured the tenor of their home life:

> Once papa lent my sister Maria a book. It was an old geography book. She wrote on its blank leaf, 'Papa lent me this book.' This book is a hundred and twenty years old; it is at this moment lying before me. While I write this I am in the kitchen of the parsonage, Haworth. Tabby, the servant, is washing up the breakfast things, and Anne, my youngest sister (Maria was my eldest), is kneeling on a chair, looking at some cakes which Tabby had been baking for us. Emily is in the parlour, brushing the carpet. Papa and Branwell are gone to Keighley. Aunt is upstairs in her room, and I am sitting by the table writing this in the kitchen.'[7]

It seems a hermetic existence: Aunt Branwell in her bedroom, Emily brushing the carpet, Anne, Tabby and Charlotte in the kitchen, baking and scribbling. But Papa and Branwell have gone to Keighley for the *Leeds Intelligencer* and when they return they will bring back with them all the news, especially the political news, of the day. And the *Leeds Intelligencer*, 'a most excellent Tory newspaper', as Charlotte described it, was not their only window on the world. They also read the Whig *Leeds Mercury*, and the Haworth doctor, Mr Driver, loaned them the 'high Tory' *John Bull* and the much cherished *Blackwood's Magazine*, 'the most able periodical there is', in Charlotte's estimation.[8]

It was in the pages of these newspapers and magazines that the young Brontës followed the political events transpiring in

London as avidly as they recorded those of Glass Town. For years they had kept abreast of political developments and embraced their father's Toryism. Even when they were too young to read they had breathed in the heady air of parliamentary debates and the rise and fall of governments as reported by the precocious Maria, who spent hours scrutinizing the papers. The great issue which absorbed them all now was the Roman Catholic Relief Act of 1829, formulated to end the persecution of Catholics and afford them the same civil liberties and opportunities as Protestants. In April 1829, when the Catholic Relief Bill came before Parliament, despite their Tory allegiances the whole family backed Wellington and Peel's support of it and Charlotte recorded how they awaited its fate with bated breath:

> Parliament was opened and the Great Catholic question was brought forward and the Duke's measures were disclosed and all was slander, violence, party spirit and confusion. O those three months from the time of the king's speech to the end! Nobody could think, speak or write on anything but the Catholic question and the Duke of Wellington or Mr Peel. I remember the day when the Intelligence extraordinary came with Mr Peel's speech in it containing the terms on which the Catholics were to be let in. With what eagerness papa tore off the cover and how we all gathered round him, and with what breathless anxiety we listened as one by one they were disclosed and explained and argued upon so ably and so well; and then, when it was all out, how aunt said she thought it was excellent and that the Catholics [could] do no harm with such good security. I remember also the doubts as to whether it would pass into the house of Lords and the prophesies that it would not. And when the paper came which was to decide the question, the anxiety was almost dreadful with which we listened to the whole affair: the opening of the doors, the hush, the Royal Dukes in their robes and the Great Duke in green sash and waistcoat, the rising of all the peeresses when he rose, the reading of his speech, papa saying that his words were like precious gold, and, lastly, the majority one to four in favour of the bill. [9]

The Brontë children had never met a Catholic in their lives and were never to learn that their own father's mother came from an Irish Catholic family. They had no reason, really, to care one way or another about the Catholics' plight before the passage of the 1829 bill. And yet they all were, even this early on, highly politicized. Two years later they would become even more inflamed over the first Reform Bill. Absorbing, great events were going on in Britain as well as in the Glass Town Confederacy. And it is in the Glass Town vein that Charlotte imagines and records the climactic scene when the great Duke, clad in green sash and waistcoat, made his grand entrance in the House of Lords and read his speech of precious gold before the assembled peers and elegantly clad peeresses.

In September 1829 – the autumn of the year during which they began to write up their plays in 'The Young Men's Magazine' – all the children and Aunt Branwell made a foray into the world beyond the end of Church Lane by accepting an invitation to visit Mrs Brontë's aunt and uncle, the Reverend and Mrs John Fennell, parents of Jane Fennell who had married William Morgan in the double ceremony which had also united Patrick Brontë and Maria Branwell nearly eighteen years earlier. The Fennells had moved from Woodhouse Grove to Cross Stone, some twelve miles away from Haworth.

On the face of it, it seems an ordinary enough occurrence to go to stay for a few days with elderly relatives. But these were neither ordinary circumstances nor experienced visitors. It had been three years since Emily had returned from Cowan Bridge – a long time when you're eleven years old – and her only associations with being away from home had been painful and frightening and permeated with memories of her older sisters' illnesses, sufferings and deaths. For Emily and Charlotte, too, it was fearful and dangerous to leave home, if only for a few days and at a distance of only a dozen miles. Anne and Branwell had never left home in their lives, and Aunt Branwell had scarcely stirred from the house in nine years.

But they all went to the Fennells. The weather was bad, the children were shy and homesick; they stayed inside and did lessons and drew, mostly, and Charlotte wrote her 'First Letter', as her father many years later inscribed it, dated 23 September 1829:

My Dear Papa – At Aunt's request I write these lines to inform you that 'if all be well' we shall be at home on Friday by dinner-time, when we hope to find you in good health. On account of the bad weather we have not been out much, but notwithstanding we have spent our time very pleasantly, between reading, working, and learning our lessons which Uncle Fennell has been so kind to teach us every day. Branwell has taken two sketches from nature, and Emily, Anne, and myself have likewise each of us drawn a piece from some views of the lakes which Mr Fennell brought with him from Westmoreland. The whole of these he intends keeping. Mr Fennell is sorry he cannot accompany us to Haworth on Friday, for want of room, but hopes to have the pleasure of seeing you soon. All unite in sending their kind love with your affectionate daughter, Charlotte Brontë[10]

It is a well-bred little note, written at 'Aunt's request', by a well-bred little girl whose main news is that they're coming home – to Haworth, the parsonage, Papa, and, though Charlotte doesn't say it, to Glass Town – on Friday by dinner time. For Emily the pattern may already have been established at the Fennells at Cross Stone: to leave home was to undergo an exile which provoked an overwhelming desire to return to the safe, known world of the parsonage, and dinners without adults and walks on the moors and, most of all, the excitement and adventures of the children's on-going fantasy world.

They did indeed find Papa in good health when they returned from the Fennells' in late September. However, in the opening months of the new year and the new decade, 1830, Patrick Brontë's lungs began troubling him: he became increasingly short of breath and was plagued with a wracking cough. Then lung congestion and bronchitis set in and he was confined to bed by early summer. Nine years earlier his wife had died by slow, excruciating degrees in the bedroom across the hall. And only five years back Maria and Elizabeth had panted and coughed to death in the same room and bed as their mother. Ever since they could remember, the children's father had complained about his delicate lungs. Now, once again, they crept silently about the house of illness and lay awake in bed far into the night listening to their father's paroxysms of coughing. Why shouldn't he die and leave them just as their mother and Maria and Elizabeth had?

A bizarre occurrence at the end of June seemed a portent of their worst fears. Charlotte and Tabby were alone in the kitchen one morning when a shabby old man appeared in the doorway and, without any introduction or explanation, demanded: 'Does the parson live here?' Tabby said yes, the parson did live there, but was 'too poorly in bed' to see anyone. The old man retorted: 'I have a message for him,' and when asked who sent the message, he responded: 'The Lord. He desires me to say that the bride-groom is coming and that we must prepare to meet him: that the chords are about to be loosed and the golden bowl broken; the pitcher broken at the fountain.'[11] As abruptly as he had materialized, the mad man disappeared, leaving a badly shaken Tabby and weeping Charlotte behind.

If this deranged man's prophecies did indeed come to pass, the loss to the children would be irreparable in more ways than one. After Cowan Bridge, there had been no further talk of preparing Emily and Charlotte and Anne for an independent future. They had resumed their old precocious, but highly unsys-tematic mode of education – domestic arts from Aunt Branwell, erratic lessons from their father and, most of all, their own omnivorous reading and writing. Now their father appeared to be dying upstairs and they would be left penniless orphans with only their aunt and her fifty pounds a year annuity standing between them and destitution.

Throughout the summer Patrick Brontë's life seemed to hang in the balance. When he had recovered sufficiently to return to his clerical duties, he wrote of this pain-ridden and fearful time to Mrs Franks in Huddersfield, the erstwhile Elizabeth Firth who still remained warmly concerned about the family she had refused to join by marrying Patrick: 'I had an inflammation in my lungs last summer,' he told her, 'and was in immediate and great danger for several weeks. For the six months last past I have been weak in body and my spirits have often been low. I was for about a month unable to take the church duty. I now perform it, though with considerable difficulty. I am certainly a little better; yet I fear I shall never fully recover. I sometimes think that I shall fall into a decline.'[12]

Patrick lived to tell the tale, but according to his own account, only just barely and perhaps only temporarily as well. The spectre of their father's death, an event which remained imminent for the next thirty years, haunted the house. The children huddled together; how were they to live, to care for themselves, should their father die? Patrick Brontë, almost certainly with the added stimulus of Aunt Branwell's anxiety and Mrs Franks' concern, roused himself from his gloomy ruminations on his own mortality and considered the plight of his children. Aunt Branwell may have undertaken to provide for her favourite Branwell's education; already its foundation had been firmly established by his father, and she could afford to see Branwell through to whatever profession – most probably the church or the military – he chose to embrace.

But what of Emily and her sisters? Clearly they had to be educated properly in order to support themselves as teachers or governesses. Yet Cowan Bridge had proved a disaster and there were no other charitable institutions that Patrick Brontë knew of especially designed for the daughters of impoverished and ailing clergymen. Mrs Franks wrote to her friend, Mrs Atkinson, the former Miss Frances Walker of Lascelles Hall, and her husband, the Reverend Thomas Atkinson, of the Brontë daughters' precarious situation. The Atkinsons were, in fact, old friends from the Brontës' Thornton days and also Charlotte's godparents – a wealthy, benevolent, childless couple. Mrs Franks and Mrs Atkinson decided between the two of them that Charlotte, as the eldest, should be sent away to school and that, with Mr Atkinson's blessing, her school fees would be paid by her godparents. Emily and Anne would remain at home and await the outcome of Charlotte's sojourn away at school. When Charlotte returned she would be able to instruct her sisters, or perhaps other sponsors would be forthcoming to help educate the younger girls.

There then remained the question of which school Charlotte should attend. Patrick Brontë, though grateful for the proposed school plan, was wary: no more risks were to be taken. In the end a small, new, select establishment at Roe Head, Mirfield Moor, about twenty miles from Haworth, was decided on. Mrs Atkinson's niece, Amelia Walker, was happily installed there, and Roe Head was close enough to the Franks at Huddersfield, and only a mile from the Atkinsons' parsonage at Hartshead, for Mrs Franks and Mrs Atkinson to monitor Charlotte's progress and wellbeing closely.

Well before Christmas all was decided: Charlotte was to go to Roe Head early in the new year. The prospect of her departure must have terrified Emily as much as Charlotte herself. Except for the brief period when Charlotte preceded her to Cowan Bridge, Emily could not remember a day when she had not been with her older sister, or a night when she had not shared her bed with her. What would become of the bed plays, the secret ones, as well as 'Islanders' and Glass Town? For one used to the warm presence of another it is a terrible thing to lie sleepless by oneself in bed at night. Emily would now listen alone in the middle of the night to the wailing winds of January and hear in their voices that of her sister calling, calling at the window to be let back in.

· 4 ·

Gondal

Early in the morning of 17 January 1831, Charlotte embraced Emily and the others and departed reluctantly for Miss Wooler's school in a hired, covered cart. The journey, which took nearly the whole day, was through a frozen, white, dead-of-winter landscape, like Parry's arctic world, only Parry's Land and its Chief Genius Emmii had been left behind. When Charlotte arrived at Roe Head, some five miles from Huddersfield on the Leeds-to-Huddersfield turnpike, she saw a three-storey, large Georgian house with old-fashioned bow windows in the front. And as the cart came to a halt before the front door, eight or nine students inside gathered in the window seat of one of the bow windows to peer out at the new pupil.

One of the watchers, Mary Taylor, was destined to become a life-long friend and later vividly recalled Charlotte's arrival at Roe Head: 'she looked a little old woman, so short-sighted that she always appeared to be seeking something and moving her head from side to side to catch sight of it. She was very shy and nervous and spoke with an Irish accent.'[1] We don't know what sort of first impression Charlotte made upon the headmistress of Roe Head, Margaret Wooler. There were, in fact, four Miss Woolers at Roe Head when Charlotte arrived. All four sisters were teachers, but it was the eldest who was *the* Miss Wooler of 'Miss Wooler's School at Roe Head'. Margaret Wooler was a short, stout, warm-hearted woman of thirty-nine, who looked both dignified and kindly in her embroidered white woollen dresses and long plaited hair wrapped around her head like a crown.

There were fewer than ten students at Roe Head, and lessons

73

were stimulating but not over strenuous. Miss Wooler derived her curriculum from Mrs Chapone's classic *Letters on the Improvement of the Mind*, first published in 1773, and studied by all the Wooler sisters during their school days. And they, in turn, instructed their Roe Head charges with 'Rollin for Ancient History, Mangnall's Questions for History and Biography – followed by the inescapable Hume – Lindley Murray for Grammar, Milton and Shakespeare for Poetry.'[2] But Rollin and Mangnall and Lindley Murray were liberally interspersed with play hours and long outdoor walks, or when the weather was bad the girls strolled indoors in the evening, chatting, with their arms wrapped around each other's waists.

Mrs Franks and Mrs Atkinson, it seems, could not have done better for Charlotte than to settle on Miss Wooler and Roe Head. Yet in the beginning Charlotte suffered greatly. Her spectacles and outmoded, ugly dresses made her feel self-conscious and plain. Moreover, she was initially relegated to the lowest class. None of the Miss Woolers was aware that Charlotte was the author of countless pieces in the voluminous 'Young Men's Magazine', or that she had learned large portions of the Bible, Mrs Chapone's Shakespeare and Milton, *Pilgrim's Progress* and the poetry of Wordsworth, Coleridge and Southey by heart. What was immediately clear to them was that Charlotte knew little or no grammar or geography. Her arithmetic was also deficient. She had studied nothing, in fact, systematically, and had therefore to start from scratch with students almost half her age, though fast approaching her size. Charlotte also had to endure humiliation at playtime. She was unfamiliar with the games the other girls played in the open fields and pastures surrounding Roe Head. Because of her extreme short-sightedness she couldn't even catch a ball. While the other girls played tag or hide-and-seek, Charlotte would stand stalwartly under the trees, out of the sun, and deny her misery by insisting to the others that her immobility 'was pleasanter ... pointing out the shadows [and] the peeps of sky '[3]

About a week after Charlotte had come to Roe Head, another new pupil, named Ellen Nussey, belatedly arrived. It was the recreation hour, in the afternoon, when the newcomer went into the empty, as she thought it, schoolroom. She approached one of the bow window seats to watch her future schoolmates outdoors playing an energetic game of 'French and English' when she noticed Charlotte, 'a silent, weeping, dark little figure by the large bay window.' Ellen hastily introduced herself, somewhat formally, as 'Miss Nussey', and, the ice thus broken, both girls confessed their mutual homesickness.

Together Ellen and Mary helped to comfort Charlotte in her grief and longing for Emily and home. Ellen provided sympathy, emotional warmth and unwavering constancy. Mary, on the other hand, was quick to perceive Charlotte's intelligence and breadth of knowledge and talents. Mary, in fact, grasped all these things long before the Miss Woolers did. She later told Mrs Gaskell how Charlotte

> would confound us by knowing things out of our range altogether. She was acquainted with most of the short pieces of poetry that we had to learn by heart: would tell us the authors, the poems they were taken from, and sometimes repeat a page or two and tell us the plot ... She used to draw much better and more quickly than anything we had seen before, and knew much more about celebrated pictures and painters. Whenever an opportunity offered of examining a picture or cut of any kind, she went over it piecemeal with her eyes close to the paper, looking so long that we used to ask her 'What she saw in it?' She could always see plenty and explained it very well. She made poetry and drawing ... exceedingly interesting to me.[4]

Charlotte also impulsively admitted Mary into the secret, sacrosanct world of Glass Town. Mary was puzzled by Charlotte's tiny, print-like handwriting, and when questioned about it Charlotte told her the truth: she and her sisters and brother all wrote in that peculiar way for 'their magazine. They brought out a magazine once a month, and wished it to be as like print as possible. She told me ... a tale out of it. No one wrote in it and no one read it but herself, her brother, and her two sisters.' Charlotte explained how at home they all 'made out' histories and characters and stories and recorded them in the 'Young Men's Magazine'. At first Charlotte promised to show Mary some of the magazines, but when Mary bluntly observed that it all sounded 'like growing potatoes in a cellar', Charlotte ruefully agreed and then retracted her promise and 'would never be persuaded to change her mind.'[5] As close as Charlotte became to Mary and Ellen, they could never replace Emily or Anne or Branwell. Mary was excluded from Glass Town; Ellen didn't even know it existed.

Within a month of her arrival at Roe Head, by dint of double lessons and incessant application, Charlotte escaped from the lowest class, and by the end of her first half-year she had risen to the position of the top student in the school – 'the first in everything but play'.[6] She had, in fact, almost too much opportunity for diligence. Miss Wooler's flexible schedule and free play periods meant that Charlotte could fill up all the interstices in the day with extra study. 'When her companions were merry round the fire or otherwise enjoying themselves during the twilight', Charlotte would be kneeling at the window, poring over a book in the waning light, so that her schoolmates accused her of seeing in the dark.[7]

The little free time Charlotte allowed herself she spent in learning more about her two new friends. Ellen Nussey came from a large, genteel, Tory, Church of England family. She embodied all the conservative and conventional values Charlotte was also drawn to, or at least felt she should embrace. But, unlike Charlotte, Ellen could afford to be complacent; though her mother was widowed and Ellen was the youngest of thirteen children, six of whom were still at home, Ellen knew she would never be called upon to earn her own living as a schoolteacher or governess. She merely had to wait, in the best nineteenth-century fashion, for a husband to materialize. And with her teacups, embroidery hoops, handwoven hair bracelets, and curling papers, this is precisely what Ellen Nussey did for months, years and decades to come.

Mary Taylor's family were dissenters, cloth manufacturers ('trade' to Ellen's 'county') and Radicals. With Mary, Charlotte hotly debated the Reform Bill, first brought before Parliament in 1831, which was designed to extend the franchise to the industrial middle class and more equitably distribute the electoral system. 'We [were] ... furious politicians', Mary told Mrs Gaskell. Charlotte 'knew the names of the two ministries: the one that resigned, and the one that succeeded and passed the

Reform Bill. She worshipped the Duke of Wellington, but said that Sir Robert Peel was not to be trusted; he did not act from principle like the rest, but from expediency ... She said she had taken an interest in politics ever since she was five years old. She did not get her opinions from her father – that is, not directly – but from the papers, etc., he preferred.'[8]

In fact, Patrick Brontë supported the Reform Bill, but for purely pragmatic reasons: reform was in the air and had to be contained and curbed since it was clear it could not be suppressed altogether. He endorsed the bill as a 'moderate' concession to the public clamour for political change because he thought it would forestall more extreme measures and avert revolution. Mary Taylor championed the bill as a harbinger of far more comprehensive reform, and it is possible, perhaps even likely, that Emily did too. In both her poetry and *Wuthering Heights* Emily always sided with revolutionaries, and the oppressed. Charlotte, along with her hero the Duke of Wellington, violently opposed the bill. Exiled and smothered as she felt herself to be at Miss Wooler's, she wrote home to Branwell that 'I had begun to think that I had lost all the interest which I formerly used to take in politics, but the extreme pleasure I felt at the news of the Reform Bill's being thrown out by the House of Lords ... convinced me that I have not yet lost *all* my penchant for politics.'[9]

Charlotte received weekly bulletins from home, full of the latest news of London, Haworth, the parsonage and Glass Town, and in May Branwell walked the whole twenty miles to Roe Head and back to visit her. But Charlotte's excitement and joy at Branwell's brief visit vanished as soon as she lost sight of his receding figure on the turnpike road. For the hour or so of happiness they had shared she paid heavily with loss of appetite, racing thoughts, insomnia and, when she did sleep, disturbing dreams. It was only her scanty appetite, however, which was apparent to her schoolmates and Miss Wooler. At Roe Head Charlotte refused to eat meat and consumed only the tiniest portions of other foods. As Ellen described it, Charlotte's 'appetite was of the smallest; for years she had not tasted animal food; she had the greatest dislike to it; she had something specially provided for herself at the midday repast.'[10]

While Charlotte was away at school, Emily and Anne grew weary of Branwell's management of the Glass Town Confederacy. He was obsessed with complicated political feuds and military affairs and spent hours and days on espionage, plots, arms and fortifications. With Charlotte gone the human dimension of Glass Town evaporated. Emily boldly decided to secede and took Anne with her. Parry's and Ross's Lands were left to Branwell and his warring armies, and Emily and Anne emigrated to the other side of the world, to an island kingdom in the north Pacific which they named Gondal. The only remnant of Glass Town which they carried with them was the huge Palace of Instruction with its dungeon and one thousand students and other prisoners.

Gondal, in fact, was not just at the antipodes from Glass Town; it constituted in many ways a counter-world to it. Emily was now thirteen and Anne eleven. They were fully capable not only of imaginatively creating their own 'web of sunny air', but also of recording its chronicles, histories, biographies and poetry, though unfortunately only the Gondal poems, not its prose, have survived. But from the poetry, and also from references to their island kingdom in Emily and Anne's later diary papers, we know a great deal about Gondal and the extent to which it diverged from Glass Town. Glass Town was located in tropical West Africa, while Gondal, in the north Pacific, possessed the same climate and landscape as Yorkshire: extremely cold and wind-blasted winters, balmy flower-scented springs, and azure-skied summers.

There were other dramatic contrasts between Glass Town and Gondal. Charlotte and Branwell's realm was a Tory, male-dominated, highly politicized, militaristic land. Charlotte saw to its aristocratic high life and romantic intrigues, while Branwell raised palaces, monuments and fortifications and orchestrated armies and their unceasing wars. It was at about this period, in fact, that the neighbouring kingdom of Angria was created. Branwell's armies, under the leadership of Arthur Wellesley, Duke of Zamorna, conquered a large expanse of land to the east of Glass Town which Branwell and Charlotte named Angria, and which soon supplanted Glass Town as the major arena of their imaginations.

Gondal was another affair entirely. It was a female-dominated, royalist world. Emily was inspired by Princess Victoria, who was less than a year younger than Emily, and destined soon to become Queen. In Gondal strong-willed women sovereigns ruled tyrannically, took and disposed of lovers and husbands at will, and died violently in the desolate Gondal landscape of heath-covered moors. Armed outlaws and rebels also stalked the moors, while enchained prisoners languished in dank, dark dungeons and proclaimed their inner freedom and righteousness and cursed their captors with their dying breaths.

When Charlotte returned to the parsonage in July for the summer holidays, she came back bearing all three prizes which Miss Wooler awarded for scholastic achievement plus the highest accolade of the silver medal, reserved for the most outstanding girl in the school. She came home weary and frail, but also triumphant. Yet crossing the threshold of home, Charlotte left all thought of lessons and prizes behind her. In the midst of her joyful reunion with Emily, Anne and Branwell, she pressed them for the latest news of Glass Town.

It came as a shock. Charlotte was confounded by Emily's secession and creation of Gondal. Perhaps she tried to revive the secret bed plays at night; perhaps she even succeeded. Nevertheless, Emily had left her for Gondal, a seething, violent land ruled over by a beautiful, ruthless queen named Augusta Geraldine Almeda. Emily and Charlotte now dwelt on opposite sides of the world.

In the autumn of 1831 Charlotte returned to Roe Head, leaving Angria and Gondal, Branwell, Emily and Anne all behind again. This second departure was easier to bear than the first and so, too, was Charlotte's second sojourn at Roe Head. She was the top student in the class, she now enjoyed rather than slaved at her studies, and she had her two school friends, Mary Taylor and Ellen Nussey. By the end of the school year, in the spring of 1832, Charlotte had completed Miss Wooler's full course of study after only eighteen months at Roe Head. She was ready to go back home and polish her attainments by instructing her sisters; then she, and later Emily and Anne as well, would have to seek a position as a teacher or governess away from Haworth.

On the face of it, life back in Haworth was outwardly as calm and eventless as ever. In July Charlotte wrote to Ellen Nussey, with whom she had begun a regular correspondence, 'you ask me to give a description of the manner in which I have passed every day since I left school: this is soon done, as an account of one day is an account of all. In the morning from nine o'clock till half-past twelve, I instruct my sisters and draw, then we walk till dinner, after dinner I sew till tea time and after tea I either read, write, do a little fancy work or draw, as I please. Thus in one delightful, though somewhat monotonous course my life is passed.'[11] Mary Taylor, who was also a regular correspondent, but did not preserve Charlotte's letters, may have had a different and fuller account from her of life at the parsonage in the months after Charlotte returned from Roe Head. The truth was that 'after tea time', they were all 'growing potatoes in the cellar' again. Both Angria and Gondal were flourishing and at this stage, though the two realms were separate, writing went on communally at the dining room or kitchen table, and Charlotte and Branwell were aware of the latest developments in Gondal just as Emily and Anne were up to date on Angria.

In September of 1832 Charlotte made her first visit to Ellen Nussey's home, the Rydings, near Birstall. Branwell escorted her there and declared he was leaving Charlotte in paradise after he surveyed the large, battlemented house and its spacious chestnut-filled park and rookery. When Charlotte came home she brought a basket of apples as a gift from Ellen to Emily and Anne, whom Ellen, of course, had not yet met.

It was nearly a year before Charlotte could return Ellen's hospitality and invite her to Haworth. The weather was bad and then, too, a visitor to the parsonage was such a rare occurrence that it took some time getting used to the idea. At last in June of 1833 Charlotte wrote to Ellen saying that her father and aunt had decided that the time was ripe for Ellen's eagerly awaited and 'long promised visit', and in early August Ellen arrived in Haworth. The Brontës' was such an insular household and so aloof from everything outside its walls that Ellen's unprecedented visit (no one other than relatives had ever come to stay before) marked an epoch of sorts in the family history. Everyone went out of their way to welcome her warmly, and Emily vacated her bed with Charlotte for Ellen and moved into the servants' back room.

Ellen was initially a bit dismayed at the 'scant and bare' aspect of the house, so different from her own home: curtainless windows, stone floors, and unpapered walls stained a dove-coloured tint. Plain hair-seated chairs and mahogany tables and book shelves comprised most of the furniture. As for the inmates of the house, she found Patrick Brontë 'very venerable with his snow-white hair and powdered coat-collar', and voluminous cravat. Ellen soon grasped that 'he was considered something of an invalid and always lived in the most abstemious and simple' way, while his 'manner and mode of speech' possessed 'the tone of high-bred courtesy'.[12] Aunt Branwell was equally arresting with her false auburn curls, billowing caps and clicking pattens. In her own way, she was as eccentric as her brother-in-law, but she could also 'be lively and intelligent and tilt arguments against Mr Brontë without fear.'[13] Anne, with her wavy light brown hair, clear, transparent complexion and violet-blue eyes, was her aunt's favourite and 'still pursued her studies, and especially her sewing, under the surveillance of her aunt.'[14]

But it was the fifteen-year-old Emily – who now had begun 'to have the disposal of her own time', while Anne remained tied to her aunt's apron strings – who made the strongest impression on Ellen. 'Emily had by this time acquired a lithesome, graceful figure ... [and] was the tallest person in the house except her father. Her hair, which was naturally as beautiful as Charlotte's, was in the same unbecoming frizz, and there was the same want of complexion. She had very beautiful eyes – kind, kindling, liquid eyes, but she did not often look at you; she was too reserved. Their color might be said to be dark grey, at other times dark blue, they varied so. She talked very little.'[15] A less idealized picture of Emily at fifteen describes her as 'a tall, long-armed girl, full grown, elastic of tread ... thin [and] loose-jointed ... not ugly but with irregular features and a pallid, thick complexion ... She talked very little. No grace or style in dress belonged to Emily, but under her awkward clothes her natural movements had the lithe beauty of the wild creatures that she loved. She was a great walker, spending all her leisure on the moors.'[16]

Household life in the parsonage was not altered on Ellen's

account. She awoke to the sound of Patrick Brontë shooting his pistol out of his bedroom window, ate the usual fare of Scotch porridge for breakfast and simple joints and milk puddings for dinner, and sewed with the others in aunt's bedroom and read in the evenings. After Patrick Brontë and Aunt Branwell retired to bed at nine, Ellen walked about the small dining room table with Charlotte, Emily, and Anne, arm in arm, just as she and Charlotte had done at Miss Wooler's.

But the happiest times during Ellen's visit were when the four girls, accompanied by the dog Grasper (whom Aunt Branwell disliked and only 'admitted to the parlor at stated times'), left the parsonage and its two elderly inmates behind and walked out on the moors. A favourite destination was a waterfall they called 'the meeting of the waters', about two miles from the parsonage. Once out of doors, Emily cast off her reserve, and on arriving at the falls, 'half reclining on a slab of stone, [she] played like a young child with the tadpoles in the water, making them swim about and then fell to moralizing on the strong and the weak, the brave and the cowardly, as she chased them with her hand.'[17]

These excursions to 'the meeting of the waters', or even further and higher up to the deserted old stone farmhouse, Top Withins, also unleashed a streak of exuberant mischievousness in Emily. Ellen described how she became 'a child in spirit for glee and enjoyment', and found particular delight in 'leading Charlotte where she would not dare to go of her own free will. Charlotte had a mortal dread of unknown animals, and it was Emily's pleasure to lead her into close vicinity, and then tell her how and what she had done, laughing at her horror with great amusement.'[18]

The endless, eerily beautiful landscape of heath and heather-covered moors surrounding Haworth answered a profound inner yearning for release in Emily. Though the largest of her family, she desired the freedom and exhilarating sensation of personal smallness and insignificance which she discovered in the beauty and immensity of nature on the moors. Walking to Pondon Kirk, the huge outcropping of rock which she called Penistone Crag in *Wuthering Heights*, Emily encountered only the most hardy and tenacious animal and plant life: merlins, ousels, lapwings and grouse in the air, and furze, bracken, ling and bilberry covering the slopes of the moors underfoot like the closely shorn wool of browsing sheep. The stunning silence of these high spaces was rarely broken by the harsh cries of hawks or the whistling of a sudden gale sweeping over the hills from the west. Heather effaced peat bogs, and the rarity of trees, rocks and other land-marks made it perilously easy to lose one's way.

Despite Charlotte's fear of strange animals and her own reluc-tance to climb rocks and cross streams that Emily negotiated with grace and ease, no one better understood and explained Emily's love and need for her natural environment. Charlotte later described how:

> The scenery of these hills is not grand – it is not romantic; it is scarcely striking. Long low moors, dark with heath, shut in little valleys, where a stream waters, here and there, a fringe of stunted copse ... it is only higher up, deep in among the ridges of the moors, that Imagination can find rest for the sole of her foot; and even if she finds it there, she must be a solitude-loving raven – no gentle dove. If she demand beauty to inspire her, she must bring it inborn: these moors are too stern to yield any product so delicate. The eye of the gazer must *itself* brim with a 'purple light,' intense enough to perpetuate the brief flower-flush of August on the heather, or the rare sunset-smile of June; out of his heart must well the freshness, that in latter spring and early summer brightens the bracken, nurtures the moss, and cherishes the starry flowers that spangle for a few weeks the pasture of the moor-sheep. Unless that light and freshness are innate and self-sustained, the drear prospect of a Yorkshire moor will be found as barren of poetic as of agricultural interest; where the love of wild nature is strong, the locality will perhaps be clung to with the more passionate constancy, because from the hill-lover's self comes half its charm.

> My sister Emily loved the moors. Flowers brighter than the rose bloomed in the blackest of the heath for her; out of a sullen hollow in a livid hill-side her mind could make an Eden. She found in the bleak solitude many and dear delights; and not the least and best loved was – liberty.[19]

Before Ellen ended her visit to the parsonage, they arranged to meet the following month for a day expedition to nearby Bolton Abbey. This excursion, however, was thrown into doubt when Emily fell seriously ill in late August. Charlotte wrote to Ellen that 'Emily has been very ill; her ailment ... erysipelas in the arm, accompanied by severe bilious attacks, and great general debility: her arm was obliged to be cut in order to remove the noxious matter which had accumulated in the inflamed parts.' But by the appointed Bolton Abbey date Emily's health was 'almost perfectly reestablished'.[20]

As planned, then, on a brilliant September morning Branwell, at the reins of a rickety dog cart, set off with Charlotte, Emily and Anne for the Devonshire Arms at Bolton Bridge where they had agreed to rendezvous with Ellen. All were in the highest spirits until they arrived at Bolton Bridge and found Ellen waiting for them at the inn seated in a fashionable carriage which also held several of Ellen's fashionable friends. Instantly the occupants of the shabby dog cart fell silent and resentfully braced themselves for 'that fiercest of all ordeals ... a meeting with strangers.' The adventure was ruined; in the company of Ellen's friends the Brontës could not enjoy the ruins of the old abbey, the beauty of the landscape or the rare freedom from their home routine. Branwell was silenced by mortified pride, Charlotte, Emily and Anne by painful shyness. All day they 'clung to each other or to [Ellen] ... scarcely venturing to speak above a whisper and betraying in every look and word the positive agony which filled their hearts' when confronted with strangers.[21]

Emily's behaviour at Bolton Abbey was more remote, even hostile, than her sisters'. She was always loath to leave home, even for a day's holiday, precisely because she feared the kind of confrontation Ellen inflicted upon them by bringing along her fashionable friends. Emily dreaded and hated strangers, and never seems to have felt the slightest need for change, variety, travel or new faces. From an early age she was obsessed with control, but at this period Emily focused it on her environment rather than her body. She refused social activities the way Charlotte rejected food at Roe Head. Gondal and its ever-increasing cast of characters, along with her sisters and brother, satisfied Emily's hunger for human contact, a hunger which had never been great.

The following winter of 1834 was one of the worst in living memory, with day after day of freezing cold, sleety rains and high winds. The number of deaths in Haworth rose alarmingly and Patrick Brontë was hard-pressed to write funeral sermons, never a congenial occupation for one with his morbid cast of mind. (The only task he disliked more was performing marriage ceremonies.) Confined to the house by the severe weather, Emily and the others listened to 'the passing and funeral bells so frequently tolling and filling the air with their mournful sound – and when they were still, the "chip chip" of the mason as he cut the grave stones in a shed close by.'[22]

The household kept to its usual routine: lessons, sewing, housework, drawing, family prayers, and the three daily punctuation marks of breakfast, dinner and tea. Baking day, laundry day, and the Sabbath were the only distinguishing days of the week. No one called. But Gondal and Angria throve and grew; the bitter weather and the monotony of their daily routine scarcely mattered as long as Emily and Anne and Charlotte and Branwell were imaginatively living in the north Pacific and West Africa.

In 'My Angria and the Angrians', written during this year, Charlotte created a wonder spoof on all of them. The tale was narrated by her favourite, Lord Charles Wellesley, and was set, of course, in Africa, though the scenery was decidedly English. Wellesley met up with one Patrick Benjamin Wiggins, an obvious caricature of Branwell, who was realistically described as 'a low, slightly built man'. Branwell was sensitive about his small stature and particularly the fact that his younger sister, Emily, was taller than he. Wiggins was dressed in 'a black coat and raven grey trousers, his hat placed nearly at the back of his head, revealing a bush of carroty hair so arranged that at the sides it projected almost like two spread hands', and perched across his Roman nose was a pair of spectacles.

In fairness, though, Charlotte had Patrick Benjamin Wiggins describe his three sisters, Charlotte Wiggins, Jane Wiggins (Jane was Emily's middle name) and Anne Wiggins, in equally unflattering terms. 'Are they as queer as you?' Wellesley asked, and Patrick responded: 'They are miserable silly creatures not worth talking about. Charlotte's eighteen years old, a broad, dumpy thing, whose head does not come higher than my elbow. Emily's sixteen, lean and scant, with a face about the size of a penny, and Anne is nothing, absolutely nothing.'[23] In 'My

Angria and the Angrians' Charlotte dwelt on her own and her brother's and sisters' size, and, however satirical her portrayal, she gave a faithful picture of them all. Branwell was short and slight. At eighteen Charlotte was still 'stunted', but no longer slender. Instead, she had become 'broad, dumpy'. Emily, in contrast, was 'lean and scant', a description close to other contemporary accounts of her as 'lithesome' and 'angular'. And Anne was dismissed as 'absolutely nothing'.

On 24 November 1834, Emily Brontë took up her pen and wrote in an uncharacteristic vein – speaking not through the mouthpiece of one of her Gondal characters of momentous events in her imaginary kingdom, but rather in her own voice of the goings-on at the parsonage that Monday morning. She wrote at the kitchen table while she was supposed to be helping Anne and Charlotte and Tabby prepare dinner.

> I fed Rainbow, Diamond, Snowflake, Jasper pheasant (alias). This morning Branwell went down to Mr Driver's and brought news that Sir Robert Peel was going to be invited to stand for Leeds. Anne and I have been peeling apples for Charlotte to make us an apple pudding and for Aunt nuts and apples. Charlotte said she made puddings perfectly and she was of a quick but limited intellect. Taby [sic] said just now 'Come, Anne pilloputate' (i.e. pill [sic] a potato). Aunt has come into the kitchen just now and said 'where are your feet Anne?' Anne answered, 'on the floor, Aunt.' Papa opened the parlour door and gave Branwell a letter saying, 'here, Branwell, read this and show it to your Aunt and Charlotte' – The Gondals are discovering the interior of Gaaldine. Sally Moseley is washing in the back kitchen.
>
> It is past Twelve o'clock. Anne and I have not tidied ourselves, done our bedwork or done our lessons and we want to go out to play. We are going to have for Dinner Boiled Beef, Turnips, potatoes and applepudding. The kitchin [sic] is in a very untidy state. Anne and I have not done our music exercise which consists of b major. Taby said on my putting a pen in her face, 'Ya pitter pottering there instead of pilling a potate' [sic] . I answered, 'O Dear, O Dear, O dear I will directly.' With that I get up, take a knife and begin pilling. Finished pilling the potatoes. Papa going to walk. Mr Sunderland expected.
>
> Anne and I say I wonder what we shall be like and what we shall be and where we shall be if all goes on well in the year 1874 –

in which year I shall be in my 57th year. Anne will be in her 55th year Branwell will be going in his 58th year and Charlotte in her 59th year. Hoping we shall all be well at that time we close our paper.

Emily and Anne[24]

Throughout this bulletin from the parsonage kitchen runs the thread of food, cooking and meals. Emily begins by saying that she's fed her pet birds, Rainbow, Diamond, Snowflake and Jasper, all of whom were kept in the small peat room behind the dining room and across from the kitchen. Emily and Anne have been peeling apples for the 'perfect' apple pudding Charlotte will make for dinner. Other dishes to be served are boiled beef, turnips and potatoes. Emily, in fact, should be peeling potatoes with Anne rather than writing, and she interrupts her diary paper in the second paragraph when Tabby rebukes her for not 'pilling a potate'. They are also preparing apples and nuts for Aunt Branwell who sticks her head into the kitchen and makes sure Anne doesn't have her feet on the stove fender. What with the apple and potato peelings, nut shells and turnips, the kitchen 'is in a very untidy state'. And Emily seems supremely happy and comfortable, scribbling in the midst of it all, at the kitchen table.

In the same paragraph with the apple and potato peelings and the servant Sally Moseley's laundry in the back kitchen, we learn that 'The Gondals are discovering the interior of Gaaldine.' The world of Gondal had grown and developed considerably since its inception in 1831. The major figures of Augusta Geraldine Almeda, her lovers, Amadeus, Lord Alexander of Elbe (who may at one juncture have become her husband), Alfred Sidonia and the guitar-playing, exotic Fernando de Samara, had all been established. And so, too, had the Byronic Julius Brenzaida, lover of the raven-haired, beautiful A.G.A. (the acronym Emily used for her heroine's name) as well as the equally beautiful, despotic Rosina. In addition to his amorous exploits, Brenzaida was also a fearless military leader. It was he, in fact, who led the Gondal forces in their conquest of Gaaldine, a large island in the South Pacific.

The real and the mundane, and the imaginary and sublime

jostled one another in Emily's 1834 diary paper. Peel is going to stand for Leeds, Anne and Emily have not yet made their beds though it is past noon, Papa has received a letter that might interest Branwell, Charlotte and their aunt. And then there is the future. Where will they all be, and what will they all be some forty years hence, in 1874, 'if all goes on well'? Emily is sanguine about the future; she closes her bulletin 'Hoping we shall all be well at that time'.

In the present, meanwhile, Abraham Sunderland, the organist of Keighley Parish Church, whom Patrick Brontë had procured to give the children music lessons, is 'expected', and Emily and Anne have not done their music exercise of B major. The previous May a new organ had been consecrated at Haworth Church and Mr Sunderland had coached Branwell, who for a while served as the Haworth organist. Now Mr Sunderland was giving Emily and Anne piano lessons as well. By this time the family had acquired a small upright piano, which was installed in Patrick Brontë's study. Charlotte couldn't play because of her short-sightedness, but Branwell, Emily and Anne all studied under Mr Sunderland. Handel, in particular, was a great family favourite, but they also played other fashionable continental composers such as Bellini, Czerny, Diabelli and Weber. Despite Emily's neglect of her piano practice recorded in the diary paper, she learned to play with precision and brilliance. When Patrick Brontë was feeling particularly melancholy or unwell, he summoned Emily in the evenings to play for him. The additional expense of Emily's and Anne's music lessons was justified by the fact that it would give them another marketable 'accomplishment' as teachers or governesses.

So, too, would drawing lessons, though it was on Branwell's, rather than his sisters', account that Patrick Brontë engaged the Leeds artist William Robinson to instruct his children this same year. In June of 1834, Patrick Brontë took Charlotte and Branwell to the Annual Exhibition of the Northern Society for the Encouragement of Fine Arts at Leeds, where they were greatly impressed by Robinson's portraits, and also by the sculpture of Joseph Leyland, later to become one of Branwell's close friends. For some time Branwell's future had been uncertain. His situation was the opposite of his sisters': he was indecisive over the choice, rather than constrained by the lack, of opportunities available to him. The family now felt he was far too gifted to choose either the military or the church as a profession. Instead, all agreed Branwell must seek his fame as well as livelihood in one of the arts. But which should claim him – literature, music or painting? He had already shown an extraordinary precocity in all of them. It was probably the Leeds exhibition and Robinson's portraits in particular which inspired Branwell to settle on painting.

Natural ability, everyone believed, he possessed in abundance. What he required now was rigorous training. Robinson was hired by Patrick Brontë to give Branwell (and his sisters) lessons at two guineas a visit, a considerable sum, given Patrick Brontë's limited income. The whole family concentrated their hopes and dreams and money on what they were confident would be no gamble, but rather a brilliant professional future for Branwell. William Robinson's lessons were meant to be the first step towards this glorious end. Robinson had studied under Sir Thomas Lawrence at the Royal Academy in London, and by 1834 he was an established portrait painter of considerable repute whose subjects included the family hero, the Duke of Wellington, as well as the Duke of York and Princess Sophia. The plan was for Branwell to follow in Robinson's footsteps and proceed, in time, as Robinson had, to the Royal Academy in London.

Before Patrick Brontë engaged Robinson, Branwell had already begun to dabble in oils, and all the children had been drawing ever since they were old enough to hold a pencil or chalk. The white-washed walls of Charlotte and Emily's small room were copiously decorated with pencil sketches, of faces, animals and flowers, sketches which reached higher and higher towards the ceiling as they grew taller. Charlotte and Branwell spent hours copying engravings by such romantic painters as John Martin and Henry Fuseli, whose extravagantly detailed and enormous vistas had a profound influence on the landscapes of Glass Town. Emily copied illustrations from Thomas Bewick's *British Birds* with remarkable patience and fidelity, as shown in her careful 1829 drawings of the 'Winchat' and 'Ring Ousel'. But as she grew older, Emily turned more and more to the subjects and scenes around her, drawing 'from the life'. While

Charlotte continued to wear out her eyes minutely duplicating the elaborate engravings of keepsake albums, Emily sketched the birds and cows and moor sheep she saw outdoors, hastily capturing them on pencilled scraps of paper. And she painted striking watercolour portraits of her favourite pets: the large merlin hawk Hero, Anne's black and white spaniel Flossie, and Emily's own dogs, Grasper and, later, Keeper.

It was while Branwell was still studying under Robinson at Haworth, during 1834 and 1835, that he produced his most enduring works, not so much on account of their technique, for there is much to criticize in their execution, but rather because of their subjects – his three sisters. The first painting is the so-called 'pillar portrait' of Charlotte, Emily and Anne. The central 'pillar', which separates Charlotte from Emily, was painted over a likeness of Branwell himself which he blotted out either because the painting was too congested with the four of them squeezed into a vertical canvas or, more likely, because he was dissatisfied with his self-portrait. Branwell may have preferred to efface himself with a pillar rather than risk self-exposure as the slight, carrot-haired, bespectacled young man Charlotte captured in words in her Patrick Benjamin Wiggins caricature.[25]

But Branwell did not idealize his sisters in the painting. Mrs Gaskell dismissed it as 'not much better than sign-painting as to manipulation.' But the 'likenesses', she judged, were 'admirable' by the striking resemblance to Charlotte, who many years later held the painting in front of herself for Mrs Gaskell to inspect. Certainly Charlotte's broad forehead, full cheeks and rather square jaw tally with her own description of herself as 'dumpy'. Anne appears, as Ellen Nussey described her, gentle and delicate, with something of a receding chin and dreamy-looking eyes. Emily is the tallest of the group, but no one looking at the pillar portrait would describe her face as being 'about the size of a penny'. Her nose seems abnormally large and her face too full for the lean, lithe young girl others described. But what is most arresting about Branwell's likeness of Emily in the pillar portrait is her blank, unfocused gaze, compressed lips and slightly jutting-out chin; all conspire to give her not just an impenetrable air, but also one bordering on hostility. She appears at once both unapproachable and subtly contemptuous.

The Emily in Branwell's 'profile portrait' is another creature altogether. Emily's profile is actually a surviving fragment of another group painting of the three sisters and Branwell which was destroyed at some point after Charlotte's death.[26] Compared to the pillar portrait, it is a masterpiece, for it goes beyond literal, photographic realism to capture the essence of its subject. In contrast to Emily's vacant stare in the pillar portrait, here we find her averted eyes gazing out at a hidden vista beyond the ragged edges of the canvas fragment. The thick complexion which Ellen noted is rendered by Branwell as a translucently pale face, flushed rose on the cheeks, above marble white neck and shoulders. Her dark hair curls around her temples and waves under at the nape of her neck. The collar bone stands out distinctly, and her head leans slightly forward as she looks straight ahead. It is a haunting portrait, in part because we cannot see Emily whole here. One half of her face is hidden, like the dark side of the moon, and we cannot follow her gaze and glimpse what she clearly sees.

While the young Brontës were studying music and art as well as scribbling away at Angria and Gondal at the dining room or kitchen table, the *Leeds Intelligencer* and *Mercury* and *John Bull* were all bringing exciting news from the hurly-burly of the political 'world without'. In her 1834 diary note of 24 November Emily had included the information that Branwell had just returned from the home of the local doctor, Mr Driver – the only home Branwell and his father visited regularly in the village – with the news that Sir Robert Peel was going to stand for Leeds. Ten days earlier, on 14 November, Melbourne's Whig government had collapsed, to the Brontës' great joy, and George IV had called on their beloved Wellington to form a new government. The Tories, however, were not destined to remain in power for long. Wellington relied on Peel to unite them, but in April 1835 Peel's ministry fell in the face of Lord John Russell's Irish bill. Elections were called for in May and June.

The Haworth campaign was rowdy, and Patrick Brontë and his son were in the thick of it. As Tories, along with Mr Driver, a few prosperous farmers, and the Heatons of Pondon Hall – the only 'genteel' family in the immediate vicinity – they were a beleaguered minority. When Patrick Brontë spoke on the 'Blue' hustings in front of the Black Bull, he was jeered and shouted down by the crowd, local men who had downed more than a pint or two at the Bull before gathering to hear the parson speak. Branwell was enraged at such disrespectful treatment of his father, and leapt to the podium and screamed at the unruly mob: 'If you won't let my father speak, *you* shan't speak.' Branwell's indignation and fury were repaid by the assembly burning an effigy of him. In the end, the whole family was bitterly disappointed. Lord Melbourne was returned to power and securely remained there for the next six years.

Several months after the election, in the summer of 1835, Branwell felt confident enough to begin making plans for entering the Royal Academy in London. He had been receiving instruction from Robinson for nearly a year, and it was probably Robinson himself who considered Branwell sufficiently prepared to go to the Academy. Accordingly, Branwell wrote to the Royal Academy Secretary expressing his desire to become a probationary student that autumn. The problem facing the family now was the same one, only writ larger, which they had confronted when Charlotte went to Roe Head three years earlier: how were they to subsidize Branwell's dream, a dream they all endorsed, of studying in London? Though the Academy charged no fees, Branwell would have to be maintained in London for the normal three-year course of study. Once again, a godmother – this time, Branwell's, Mrs Firth, the stepmother of Mrs Franks (the former Elizabeth Firth who had been so helpful in placing Charlotte at Roe Head) – came to the rescue, at least partially, by pledging to contribute to Branwell's training at the Royal Academy. No doubt Aunt Branwell, who doted on her nephew almost as much as she did on Anne, also agreed to help out financially.

No voice, not even an internal one, protested or questioned why it was Branwell, rather than the equally (or even more) gifted Emily or Charlotte, who was the chosen one destined for fulfilment, excitement and acclaim as an artist. Branwell was among the elect simply because he was a male. His sisters were, by the very nature of things, expected to scrimp and save and work so that their brother's brilliant future could be realized.

There was no question, then, of the necessity of sacrifice. The only uncertainty was over how and where it should be enacted. Which martyrdom would be the best for Charlotte and Emily and Anne as they tried to look ahead during the summer of 1835? With her prizes and silver medal from Miss Wooler's, and her studies and art lessons in the three years since she had left school, Charlotte was more than adequately qualified to take up a position as a teacher or governess. Her employment would lighten the financial burden at home, and even though her wages would be small (governesses were notoriously underpaid), she would be able to save something to contribute to Branwell's support. It was also time that Emily began thinking about the future. She had had the 'disposal of her own time' for long enough. It was necessary for her now to receive more training so that she could follow Charlotte's lead.

Both Charlotte's and Emily's immediate needs for employment and instruction were conveniently met by Miss Wooler's offer of a teaching position to Charlotte and a place as a student to Emily, whose school fees would be deducted from Charlotte's salary. Two of Margaret Wooler's sisters had married since Charlotte's days at Roe Head, and at the same time the number of pupils had increased, so new teachers were badly needed. Miss Wooler's offer seemed, in fact, a heaven-sent one. Charlotte would be returning to a familiar, known world, and no additional expenditure would be required for Emily's education. Even more importantly, the Roe Head plan meant that Emily would not have to be sent off to school on her own. By this time she had become so reserved and even, at times, forbidding that it was clear she would never 'mix' if she went away from home alone; it was difficult to imagine her tolerating an alien environment with strangers at all.

Yet, ideal as this arrangement seemed, Charlotte wrote of it to Ellen in early July with a note of foreboding. 'We are all about to divide, break up, separate', she reported, emphasizing the fragmentation of the family with the three forceful verbs, 'divide', 'break up' and 'separate'. 'Emily', she continued, 'is going to school. Branwell is going to London, and I am going to be a Governess. This last determination I formed myself, knowing that I should have to take the step sometime, and "better sune

as syne," to use the Scotch proverb and knowing also that Papa
would have enough to do with his limited income should
Branwell be placed at the Royal Academy and Emily at Roe
Head. Where am I going to reside? you will ask ... at a place
neither of us are wholly unacquainted with, being no other than
the identical Roe Head mentioned above. Yes, I am going to
teach in the very school where I myself was taught – Miss Wooler
made me the offer and I preferred it to one or two proposals of
Private Governess-ship which I had before received. – I am sad,
very sad, at the thoughts of leaving home but Duty – Necessity –
these are stern mistresses who will not be disobeyed.' Yet Charlotte also conceded that she and Emily were fortunate. 'Since I
must enter a situation, "my lines have fallen in pleasant places" –
I both love and respect Miss Wooler.' Most of all, she told Ellen,
'the idea of being together' with Emily 'consoles us both'.[27]

Patrick Brontë wrote at the same time of the 'break up' of his
family to Mrs Franks in Huddersfield, and asked her once again
to keep an eye on Charlotte and now Emily as well at nearby
Roe Head, and to alert him if anything was amiss. Cowan Bridge
still loomed large in his memory, and then, too, along with
Charlotte, he must have had great anxieties about his most
difficult daughter, Emily, and how she would fare at Miss
Wooler's. He also rather proudly informed Mrs Franks that
Branwell was to go to the Royal Academy in London, while
'dear little Anne,' he said, 'I intend to keep at home for another
year under her aunt's tuition and my own.'

As for himself, nothing was changed. To the erstwhile Elizabeth Firth who refused his proposal thirteen years earlier, he
complained that he was as physically run-down and socially
starved as ever, and harked back to their good old days in
Thornton: 'My ... health is generally but *very* delicate, yet
through a gracious Providence, and with great care, I am for the
most part able to perform my various ministerial duties; indeed,
I have never been well since I left Thornton ... In this place I
have received civilities and have, I trust, been civil to all but I
have not tried to make friends, nor have I met with any whose
mind was congenial with my own.'[28]

On 29 July 1835, the day before Emily's seventeenth birthday,
she and Charlotte set off from Haworth in the same covered cart

which had carried Charlotte through a frozen winter landscape, frightened and alone, to Roe Head more than four years earlier. The countryside now was a deep, verdant green: it was a midsummer's Gondal landscape which surrounded them, but, as Emily's grim face and rigid, thin form beside Charlotte made all too clear, the cart was bearing them further and further away from Gondal and Angria, to an indefinite exile at Miss Wooler's 'Palace of Instruction'.

· 5 ·

Hunger Strikes

The covered cart carrying Emily and Charlotte to Roe Head didn't arrive at Miss Wooler's until the close of the golden July afternoon. As they rolled up the drive, dusk was falling, turning the garden and rolling hills damp and cold with night mist. The students – more than a dozen now, some of whom were younger sisters of Charlotte's former schoolmates – gathered, as before, in one of the large bow window seats to observe the new arrivals. Yet here was a quandary: which was the new teacher and which the new pupil? Both wore old-fashioned, drab dresses, and though the taller one looked older, her stricken face and confusion upon entering the house made it clear she'd never been in it before. The smaller one, in contrast, walked in with a sense of familiarity and a brave show of self-possession.

Miss Wooler, as stout and energetic as ever, warmly welcomed Emily and Charlotte, a kindness Charlotte was grateful for and could return with real feeling. But Emily refused to thaw; except for a few softly and hesitantly uttered monosyllables, she remained silent. They were ushered up to the dormitory, where they deposited their boxes, and found to their great relief that they were to share a bed together, just as they did at home. Then the bell rang for tea. Weary and hungry as they were after a twenty-mile journey from Haworth, once they were seated along with all the others in the dining hall, Charlotte and Emily could scarcely swallow a thing. Impossible to eat and drink in a strange place, surrounded by all the other girls who chattered and ate and sneaked surreptitious, wondering glances at the queer new-comers.

Somehow the rest of the evening passed. After tea came the

October Emily was back at the parsonage, and Anne was sent almost immediately to Roe Head to replace her thin, ailing sister.

Within days of returning home, Emily's frail body and flagging spirits both dramatically improved. Not only did she resume eating, she began at this point to take an active role in the kitchen. The sullen, silent girl who had sent her plates back untouched at school, now, according to Mrs Gaskell, 'took the principal part of the cooking upon herself'.[3] The kitchen became the most important and most comfortable room in the house for Emily, the inner sanctum of the parsonage where she could most freely be herself. Here she read and wrote at the kitchen table where she also peeled potatoes and kneaded the bread dough with a German book propped up behind the bread board. Soon she took all the family baking upon herself. And she also continued her education on her own, studying French as well as German, and filling up many of the lamentable gaps in geography, history and grammar which her brief sojourn at Miss Wooler's had so mortifyingly exposed. Left to her own devices, Emily could manage superbly: studying, 'making out' and writing up Gondal, drawing, sewing, cooking and eating. But she had to be left well alone to do all these things. Privacy, even secrecy, was necessary for her to consume – books, knowledge and food.

With Anne gone to Roe Head, Aunt up in her bedroom and her father closeted in his study, privacy was the prevailing atmosphere at Haworth Parsonage with all its closed doors inside and the fortress of gravestones surrounding it outdoors. And yet Emily was not quite as alone as she expected when she returned home from Miss Wooler's in October of 1835. Much to her surprise, Emily found Branwell had anticipated her own retreat, and was back home after an even shorter exile in London than hers at Roe Head.

Branwell's assault on the 'world without' had also proved a fiasco. What exactly happened to him in London remains something of a mystery, for there is no trace of this disaster in Charlotte's letters, and the only explanation Mrs Gaskell could obtain from Ellen Nussey was a cryptic 'conduct or want of finances'. But Branwell himself shed a good deal of light on his London misadventures in an autobiographical Angrian piece

recreation hour round the fire with Miss Wooler; then one of the girls read from some edifying work of literature as the others stitched in the lamplight. Soon it was time for evening prayers, and after prayers they trooped up to the dormitory to laugh and gossip and wind up their hair in curling papers before going to bed.

Then, at last, came silence and darkness. A terrible darkness for Emily and Charlotte, locked in each other's arms in their bed at the end of the long dormitory. Charlotte tried to rouse and cheer her sister in soft whispers, but Emily remained rigid and unresponsive. No bed plays could be created and indulged in here. Nor sleep perhaps either. Charlotte feared for the morrow; she had every reason to. Bells would chop it up into temporal chunks for study, for exercise, for prayer, for meals. Granted it was a relaxed, congenial, humane regime, presided over by the kind and capable Miss Wooler. Neither their minds nor their bodies would be overtaxed; both the lessons and food would be nourishing and palatable. Instead of languishing in one of the dungeons of Gondal or Angria, Charlotte and Emily were only under house arrest at Miss Wooler's. Yet the chains which bound them were no less chafing and strong for being invisible.

It had been more than ten years since Emily had gone away from home to Cowan Bridge School where she had been the coddled 'pet nursling' of the school. The day after she arrived at Roe Head, on 30 July 1835, she turned seventeen and was one of the oldest students at the school. In the decade between Cowan Bridge and Roe Head, Emily had had intervals of regular music and art lessons, but she had received no other systematic education besides the lessons Charlotte gave her and Anne. For several years before coming to Roe Head, Emily had had the 'free disposal' of her own time, and, whatever the Miss Woolers of the world might think, she had not wasted it. She had been reading and writing continuously; she had created Gondal, an entire universe of her own, and recorded its history, written the biographies of its rulers and prominent (or notorious) inhabitants, composed poetry about it and illustrated it.

But like Charlotte's in 1831, Emily's knowledge of geography and grammar left much to be desired. She didn't know the answers to Miss *Mangnall's Questions*; she hadn't 'improved' her

mind along Mrs Chapone's lines. Though the tallest girl in th
school and among the eldest, Emily was put into one of the lowe
classes to remedy her deficiencies, and was humiliated to b
working alongside girls nearly half her age. As an apprentic
'under teacher', Charlotte, too, was relegated to the younge
pupils, but she took over the very bottom class of little girls and
was given the tedious job of drilling the rudiments of the alphabe
and numbers into their immature, wandering minds.

It was in their early days at Roe Head, in the midst of these
students so much younger than they, that Emily and Charlotte
conceived their life-long dislike of small children. They, after all,
had never really been children themselves; the very furthest back
that their minds could reach was their mother's last illness, when
the servants remarked how 'spiritless' and unchildlike the young
Brontës all were. Patrick Brontë had always treated and talked
to his children as if they were adults. They had been raised
on an adult diet of religion, politics, books, illness and death.
Deprived as they themselves had been of a childhood, Emily and
Charlotte were unable to comprehend and participate in those
of Miss Wooler's students. They found the other girls silly, noisy,
cruel, petty and every bit as odd and unapproachable as the
pupils found them.

For much of the day at Roe Head Emily was separated from
Charlotte as she toiled away in her junior class while Charlotte
instructed her own small charges. Meals, the recreation period,
and in bed at night were their sole times together, and only
during the last were they alone. They should have looked forward
to their rare periods together and been buoyed by them so that
they could return strengthened to their respective classes and
isolations. But soon their snatched moments of intimacy turned
into ones of dismay, anxiety and struggle.

Emily hated the school and did nothing to conceal her antipathy. She spoke to no one other than Charlotte, and even with
Charlotte she talked only when absolutely necessary. In addition
to being silent and withdrawn, Emily was barely eating and
growing thinner and thinner and more and more languid and
unresponsive each day. The acts of speaking and eating were
strangely intertwined in Emily's life. She would often substitute
one for the other: words for food or food for words. Or she would

withhold one for the other: silence for fasting or fasting for speech.
At Roe Head, in the late summer and autumn of 1835, she
refused, as far as possible, to eat or speak. But her refusal of food
was, in fact, a kind of utterance. By pushing her plate away at
breakfast, dinner and tea, day after day, she was clearly, if
silently, speaking her mind: *I hate it here. I will not eat. I want to
go home. I refuse to grow up, to grow big. I will make myself ill, starve
even, unless I am released.*

In a very short time Emily was drifting beyond even Charlotte's influence and reach, the only things which tethered her
at all to Miss Wooler's. When Charlotte tried to encourage Emily
to rally, to persevere, to eat, Emily denied that anything wa
wrong with her, and when Charlotte would not stop harassin
, Emily refused to argue any further and scarcely acknov
ledged Charlotte's pleading. This behaviour, of course, was ago
izing for Charlotte, and it opened the floodgates of memory
the illnesses and deaths of Maria and Elizabeth. When all l
appeals to Emily failed, Charlotte finally turned to Miss Woo
and urgently pressed her to send Emily home. Miss Woo
readily complied; she found Emily's conduct both perverse
inexplicable: Emily refused to talk, she barely ate, and she
making but scant progress in her studies. Emily was a misf
Roe Head and, as Miss Wooler admitted many years later
'did not care for Emily, and was not sorry to lose her.'[1]

Charlotte's account of Emily's painful period at Roe
was also written many years later, but time did not tempe
anguish with which she described Emily's crisis at s
'Liberty was the breath of Emily's nostrils', Charlotte
'without it, she perished. The change from her own hom
school, and from her own very noiseless, very seclude
unrestricted and inartificial mode of life to one of disci
routine (though under the kindliest auspices), was what sh
in enduring. Her nature here proved too strong for for
Every morning when she woke, the vision of home and th
rushed on her. Nobody knew what ailed her but me. I kn
too well. In this struggle her health was quickly brok
white face, attenuated form, and failing strength thr
rapid decline. I felt in my heart she would die if she di
home, and with this conviction, obtained her recall.'[2]

entitled 'Charles Wentworth's Visit to Verdopolis'. In the early autumn of 1835 Branwell made the two-day coach journey to London (this was before the railway reached as far north as Leeds) and took lodgings at the Chapter Coffee House in Paternoster Row, where his father had stayed when he visited London during the years before his marriage. Branwell was well prepared. In addition to the funds provided by his family and his godmother, Mrs Firth, he carried letters of introduction from Robinson and others, and after a close and long study of London street maps, he knew the city better than most natives, down even to small tracks and byways.

But issuing from the Chapter Coffee House the morning after his late-night arrival, Branwell was overwhelmed by the great Babylon of his dreams. Instead of making his way to the Royal Academy at Somerset House on the Thames, he wandered the streets in a daze. His feverish roaming took him to the Houses of Parliament, Westminster Abbey, St Paul's, the Tower, the Elgin Marbles and all the other wonders of the British Museum, and, perhaps most traumatically, to the National Gallery, where he met, face to face, the great masterpieces of Reynolds, Gainsborough and Lawrence, among others. The seemingly unbreachable gulf between these paintings and the specimen drawings Branwell had brought in his portfolio to present at the Academy Schools may have been his undoing. He recoiled before works of genius he could never hope to rival, and he never presented himself at the Academy at all. Instead, he wandered down to the Embankment and spent hours leaning over the bridge, gazing at the river rushing past him far below.

Branwell did not leap into the Thames. Instead, he spent his evenings drowning his keen sense of failure, cowardice and insignificance at the Castle Tavern in High Holborn. When his money ran out, scarcely a week after leaving Haworth, he took the coach home, his pockets empty, and his letters of introduction and portfolio of drawings lost or forgotten. To his shocked aunt and father he fabricated a tale of being robbed by 'sharpers' before he had even reached the city.

For the next two years, with the exception of holidays, Emily and Branwell were at home together with their aunt and father while Charlotte and Anne continued at Miss Wooler's. Thrown together as they were, it is not surprising that they became closer to each other than they'd ever been. Branwell's disastrous visit to London nurtured this intimacy, for both he and Emily had returned to the parsonage under a cloud, though their feelings about their returns were very different. Branwell was shaken and humiliated, while Emily felt triumphant and free. And there were other, more fundamental differences between Emily and Branwell. In contrast to his sister's great reserve, Branwell was so garrulous and high-spirited that he was habitually summoned to entertain strangers at the Black Bull. Not that such summonses were often necessary; at the age of eighteen, Branwell was already spending most of his evenings drinking and holding forth with the village men at the Bull. He was the one family member who mingled with the villagers. Not the least impressive of his gifts was his ambidexterity, which enabled him to write with both hands at once. Some of his admirers in the village even maintained that he could simultaneously pen Latin with one hand and Greek with the other.

Yet there was a dark, frightening underside to Branwell's personality. His exuberance, charm and good will could, at a moment's notice, give way to raving anger and violence, culminating in uncontrollable fits. These may have been epileptic seizures, rather than emotional outbursts, but whatever their cause, they quite naturally terrified his family, with the result that his father and aunt and sisters all took pains not to excite or cross Branwell for fear of inadvertently sparking off a fit. Hence Patrick Brontë and Aunt Branwell dared not question Branwell's tale about robbery and sharpers when he returned from London.

By November, the unexpected and partially inexplicable homecomings of Emily and Branwell had receded into the past. Emily reimmersed herself in Gondal and Branwell in Angria, for, close as they became during this season of shared failure, they didn't unite or collaborate in their writing. To a certain extent, they kept each other abreast of recent developments in Angria and Gondal, and communicated them, too, by letter to Charlotte and Anne at Roe Head. But the 'web of sunny air' was permanently rent, and Emily remained in the north Pacific, on the other side of the world from Branwell in West Africa.

Emily was contented. She helped her aunt run the household, managed the kitchen on her own, walked out on the moors in all but the most bitterly cold and wet weather, and 'made out' Gondal and wrote during the lulls in the day when the bread was rising or the kettle put on to boil. She wrote even more in the evening, when she was relieved of her daily domestic chores, and after her father and aunt retired to bed at nine. From very early on, Emily was a poet of the night, and a devotee of the stars and moon. One early storm-tossed lyric opened with,

> High waving heather, 'neath stormy blasts bending
> Midnight and moonlight and bright shining stars
> Darkness and glory rejoicingly blending
> Earth rising to heaven and heaven descending
> Man's spirit away from its drear dongeon sending
> Bursting the fetters and breaking the bars.[4]

At night, alone, Emily sat at the kitchen or dining room table and wrote with her small oil lamp beside her while the moon poured a river of light through the window and high winds rattled the glass. Or she sat on her narrow camp bed up in her tiny bedroom and wrote with her lap desk perched on her knees. Through her bedroom window she looked out across all the gravestones, and up to the moon and the star-speckled heavens. Or she gazed at the unreflecting, thick pall of darkness which enshrouded the house when fog or snow obliterated all points of light in the sky.

Often Emily's night poems provided an atmospheric setting for violent or cataclysmic events in Gondal. But not all, perhaps not even most, of Emily's poetry was devoted to her imaginary kingdom. 'The Nightwind', for example, described the very intimate, seductive power of night in the form of a dialogue between Emily and the caressing, enveloping voice of the night wind:

> In summer's mellow midnight,
> A cloudless moon shone through
> Our open parlour window
> And rose trees wet with dew

> I sat in silent musing,
> The soft wind waved my hair:
> It told me Heaven was glorious
> And sleeping Earth was fair.
>
> I needed not its breathing
> To bring such thoughts to me,
> But still it whispered lowly,
> 'How dark the wood will be!' ...
>
> 'O come,' it sighed so sweetly ...
>
> 'Have we not been from childhood friends?
> Have I not loved thee long?
> As long as though hast loved the night
> Whose silence wakes my song.'[5]

In 'Stars' Emily addressed the stars just as intimately, in the tones and accents of a lover:

> All through the night, your glorious eyes
> Were gazing down in mine,
> And with a full heart's thankful sighs
> I blessed that watch divine! ...
>
> Thought followed thought – star followed star
> Through boundless regions on,
> While one sweet influence, near and far,
> Thrilled through and proved us one.[6]

The prevalence of night, darkness, the wind, moon and stars in Emily's poetry was partially due to the prosaic fact that she wrote most freely in the evening, often far into the night, when her aunt and father were asleep and Branwell out at the Black Bull. Then a deep silence descended on the house. Emily put away the day's lessons and cares, and let her imagination range,

> On a windy night when the moon is bright
> And the eye can wander through worlds of light.[7]

Night and darkness conferred a sense of liberation – 'bursting the fetters and breaking the bars' – and aroused passion: the passion of star-crossed 'demon' lovers in Gondal and the exhilaration Emily experienced out on the moors. The immensity of the dark, heather-covered moors, in fact, seemed a reflection of the cloudless night sky above. The darkness of night, like fasting, made Emily feel she transcended the demands and even all awareness of her body. She became a 'space-sweeping' or 'chainless soul' governed by a "God of Visions" who delivered her from the 'shattered prison' of her body. At night, alone, Emily was also absorbed or lost in the process of writing. Her poems were the product of this absorption and self-forgetfulness; she herself was merely the transcribing medium.

Branwell was also writing a good deal of poetry during the winter of 1835-6, but his motivation and aspirations had little if anything in common with Emily's. The Royal Academy failure still haunted him. Branwell now decided that his true métier was literature, not art, and he attempted to embark on this new career by firing off a series of letters to the old family favourite, *Blackwood's Magazine*, letters which extolled his own poetic gifts and generously offered them to *Blackwood's*.

By early December, Branwell's first two letters had failed to elicit a response. In the meantime, James Hogg, a regular contributor to *Blackwood's*, a poet who had belonged to the Byron and Shelley circle, had died. Hogg's death spurred Branwell to write a third letter which opened with 'Sir – Read what I write', and concluded: 'You have lost an able writer in James Hogg, and God grant you may gain one in Patrick Branwell Brontë.'[8] But *Blackwood's* remained invulnerable to Branwell's epistolary assaults. Several months later he sent them the manuscript of a long, lugubrious poem entitled 'Misery' and commanded: 'Read now at last' and 'CONDEMN NOT UNHEARD.'[9] Further silence. Branwell then discharged his final volley: 'Do you think your Magazine so perfect that no addition to its power would be either possible or desirable? Is it pride which actuates you – or custom – or prejudice? Be a man, Sir!'[10] Branwell apparently thought he could storm *Blackwood's* the way Zamorna had Angria. But *Blackwood's* was unassailable, and Branwell's effusions remained unpublished.

After Emily left Miss Wooler's and Branwell had returned to Haworth with his Royal Academy dream collapsed, Charlotte sank into a deep depression at Roe Head. The trauma for her of

Emily's and Branwell's failures was great. Her sacrifice, her submission to the stern mistresses of duty and necessity, had achieved nothing. Instead of helping to support and contribute to the wellbeing and futures of the two people she loved most in the world, Charlotte was now drudging and suffering at Miss Wooler's to no end, really other than Anne's education, which Charlotte could just as well impart to her at home.

Charlotte's only haven at Roe Head was 'the world below', as she called it, or the 'world within' in Emily's phrase. For the next two years she 'made out' Angria whenever she could snatch a moment from the tedious school routine. These moments were few, but such crumbs of memory and desire and imaginative escape forestalled, for a time at least, her own collapse. By the summer of 1836, however, her sense of balance was shaken. She absented herself more and more from tea and other meals; she started or cringed at the slightest noise, her hands trembled, headaches engulfed her, and, as Charlotte herself put it, 'my spirits felt worn down to a degree of desperate despondency.'[11]

One balmy, sunshiny August morning, seated at her desk at the head of the schoolroom with the students ranged in front of her, bent over their exercises, Charlotte could bear it no longer. She snatched pencil and paper, closed her eyes tightly to annihilate all sight of the students and schoolroom, and began to scribble furiously:

> I am just going to write because I cannot help it ... encompassed by bulls ... all wondering why I write with my eyes shut – staring, gaping long their astonishment. A.C. on one side of me, E.L. on the other and Miss W[ooler] in the background, stupidity the atmosphere, school-books the employment, asses the society ... All this day I have been in a dream, half miserable and half ecstatic, miserable because I could not follow it out uninterruptedly and ecstatic because it showed almost in the vivid light of reality the ongoings of the infernal world. I had been toiling for nearly an hour with Miss Lister, Miss Marriott and Ellen Cook, striving to teach them the distinction between an article and a substantive. The parsing lesson was completed, a dead silence had succeeded it in the school-room and I sat sinking from irritation and weariness into a kind of lethargy. The thought came over me am I to spend all the best part of my life in this

wretched bondage forcibly suppressing my rage at the idleness, the apathy and the hyperbolical and most assinine stupidity of those fat-headed oafs and on compulsion assuming an air of kindness, patience and assiduity? Must I from day to day sit chained to this chair, prisoned within these four walls, while these glorious summer suns are burning in heaven and the year is revolving in its richest glow, and declaring at the close of each summer's day, the time I am losing will never come again?[12]

As she scribbled with her eyes screwed shut, suddenly Angria flooded Charlotte's raw, exposed consciousness:

Then came on me rushing impetuously all the mighty phantasm that we had conjured from nothing to a system strong as some religious creed. I felt as if I could have written gloriously – I longed to write ... if I had had time to indulge it I felt that the vague sensations of that moment would have settled down into some narrative better at least than anything I ever produced before. But just then a Dolt came up with a lesson. I thought I should have vomited.[13]

Now, like Emily before her, Charlotte found her imprisonment at Miss Wooler's insupportable – literally nauseating. As far as she could, she shut her eyes and her mouth to it, speaking and eating as little as possible. She imaginatively fled to Angria and also to home, for the Roe Head diary is as full of yearning for Emily and Branwell as it is for the 'world below'. On storm nights she imagined Emily listening to the same sobbing wind back in Haworth. And when Charlotte wrote of home, her mind focused on the small bedroom above the downstairs hallway and the narrow bed she shared with Emily, the room where they created the secret bed plays together. 'Pen cannot portray the deep interest of the scenes, of the ... train of events I have witnessed in that little room with the low narrow bed and bare white-washed walls – twenty miles away.'[14]

Charlotte described the bedroom and bed she shared with Emily in terms that recall a nun's cell: physically it was small and bare, but sacred, saving things happened there. Angria and Gondal were like religious creeds to Charlotte and even more to Emily, for the only God Emily ever recognized was her 'God of Visions'. Angria and Gondal conferred meaning on Charlotte and Emily's cramped, empty lives, they promised a better world, they made the present, dreary one bearable, they were, above all, what Charlotte and Emily lived on and for. But the great difference between this shared spiritual foundation of their imaginary worlds was that it brought self-transcendence, peace and satiation to Emily while it provoked a terrible guilt and yet more inner conflict within Charlotte. It was during this period at Roe Head that Charlotte began calling Angria 'the infernal world', 'the world below' and 'the burning clime', and her deepening depression came to assume a religious coloration.

In her crisis Charlotte turned not to Emily, but to simple, pious, self-righteous Ellen Nussey, who, of course, had no inkling of Charlotte's addiction to 'making out'. During the autumn and winter of 1836 Charlotte became fixated on the idea of living with Ellen, as if her friend's mere proximity would keep at bay the 'evil' thoughts and fantasies which tortured her. She wrote to Ellen in early December, saying that

> If I could always live with you and daily read the bible with you ... I trust, I might one day become better, far better, than my evil wandering thoughts, my corrupt heart, cold to the spirit and warm to the flesh will now permit me to be ... my heart is a real hot bed for sinful thoughts ... I know not how to pray, I cannot bind my life to the grand end of doing good ... I forget God and will not God forget me?[15]

Why, in extremity, did Charlotte turn to Ellen rather than Emily or even Mary Taylor? Mary would no doubt have told Charlotte to pull herself together and embark on some positive course of action leading to financial and emotional self-sufficiency. Never would she have nourished the morbid dependence that Ellen actually encouraged. Nor would Emily. But Emily's role in the psychological crisis Charlotte was enduring was a highly ambiguous one. Charlotte longed for a life together with Ellen full of devotional activities, but she longed no less for Emily and their small, private room and bed and all the fantasies and imaginary dramas they conceived together there.

Yet Charlotte must have doubted Emily's spiritual state even more than her own, for Emily's religious beliefs were amorphous and mysterious even to her family. But they knew that her peculiar faith was highly unorthodox and thus worlds away from Ellen Nussey's. During a visit to the parsonage, Mary Taylor recalled that one evening she told Charlotte and Emily how someone had pumped her for her religious views and she had retorted: ' "that that was between God and me." Emily (who was lying on the hearth rug) exclaimed, "That's right."' It was all, Mary said, she 'ever heard Emily say on religious subjects'.[16] Emily was the only Brontë daughter who was exempted from teaching Sunday school and who did not attend church regularly. And then we have Emily's own verdict on conventional religions in a poem written some years later:

> Vain are the thousand creeds
> That move men's hearts, unutterably vain,
> Worthless as withered weeds
> Or idlest froth amid the boundless main.[17]

Nor does religion fare well in *Wuthering Heights*. The crusty old servant Joseph's Calvinism reduces him to a grotesque caricature; the Reverend Jabes Branderham in Lockwood's dream is mocked for his interminable hellfire sermonizing. Even more tellingly, the village church at Gimmerton falls into disuse and ruin in the course of the novel, so that by the time Lockwood visits its graveyard at the end, it is little more than a pile of rubble. Growing up in the isolated parsonage of an evangelical clergyman, Emily nevertheless remained immune to conventional religious doctrine along with so much else in her environment.

Charlotte came home from Roe Head for the Christmas holidays of 1836 and her depression was soon allayed by practical demands on her time and energy. The servant Tabby – now well into her sixties – fell on an icy village street just a day or two after Charlotte's return and broke and dislocated one of her legs, with the result that she was confined to bed, a complete invalid. Aunt Branwell wanted neither the trouble nor the expense of caring for Tabby at the parsonage and persuaded her brother-in-law that she should be removed to her sister's cottage in the village. When Emily and Charlotte and Anne were told of this plan, they protested: 'Tabby had tended them in their childhood; they, and none other, should tend her in her infirmity and age.'[18] This argument, however, fell on deaf ears; their aunt and their father insisted that Tabby should be sent to her sister, and there was no further discussion of the matter.

Yet it was far from being settled. At teatime Emily and Charlotte and Anne did not touch their meals. The next morning, at breakfast, they also refused to eat. Dinner, too, was completely ignored. At last Aunt Branwell and Patrick Brontë were forced to acquiesce in the face of this hunger strike. Tabby was allowed to stay at the parsonage. Emily and Charlotte and Anne took over all the housework themselves as well as the extra labour of caring for Tabby. Where words had failed, fasting carried the day – an important lesson that Emily, who may have been the one to propose the strike, well knew. It was a lesson which was simplicity itself. One need never be entirely powerless and devoid of control. If worse comes to worse, one could simply refuse to eat. Then even the most parsimonious and unbending will be forced to relent.

Tabby stayed and Charlotte began mastering the new arts of blackleading the stove and ironing the linen without scorching it. Emily remained in charge of the kitchen, and did all the cooking. And, at night, they wrote once again at the dining room table, though Emily in Gondal and Charlotte in Angria still dwelt on opposite sides of the world.

Other developments during the Christmas holidays also conspired to separate them. Charlotte's guilt over 'making out' and writing had been so thoroughly banished that when Branwell announced that he was going to seek Wordsworth's opinion of his poetry Charlotte decided to do the same with the Poet Laureate, Robert Southey. She wrote Southey a meek but imploring letter, confessing her dream of becoming a poet and enclosing several of her poems for him to read.

Emily had nothing to do with Charlotte and Branwell's letter-writing campaign and their ambition to turn Angria into a public and marketable commodity. As Emily wrote later in one of her best-known poems,

> Riches I hold in light esteem
> And Love I laugh to scorn
> And lust of Fame was but a dream
> That vanished with the morn – [19]

Emily wanted no role in Charlotte's germinating dream that writing might deliver them all from the servitude of teaching. But then Emily, for a time at least, had already escaped from the prison of the school room.

When the holidays ended, Charlotte had to return to Roe Head, shortly after writing her letter to Southey. Then she had to wait nearly two months before receiving a response from him. Branwell never had any sort of reply from Wordsworth, to whom he had written in the same intemperate and presumptuous vein as his letters to *Blackwood's*. 'Surely in this day when there is not a *writing* poet worth a sixpence, the field must be open, if a better man can step forward', Branwell wrote, reminding the ageing Wordsworth of his poetic aridity. Not surprisingly, as Wordsworth told Southey, he was 'disgusted' with Branwell's letter and ignored its closing command of '*return* me an *answer*'.[20]

Whether Charlotte was more fortunate than Branwell because Southey eventually wrote to her is questionable, for Southey replied, as he told a friend, with 'a dose of cooling admonition to the poor girl ... [and her] flighty letter'. He admitted that Charlotte possessed, 'in no inconsiderable degree, what Wordsworth calls the "faculty of verse"'; but this was merely a preamble to his major advice for the 'poor girl'. 'Literature', he told Charlotte, 'cannot be the business of a woman's life, and it ought not to be. The more she is engaged in her proper duties, the less leisure will she have for it, even as an accomplishment and recreation. To these duties you have not yet been called, and when you are you will be less eager for celebrity. You will not seek in imagination for excitement, of which the vicissitudes of this life, and the anxieties from which you must not hope to be exempted, be your state what it may, will bring with them but too much.'

Charlotte's most exposed nerve was touched when Southey went on to warn her that 'the day dreams in which you habitually indulge are likely to induce a diseased state of mind; and in proportion as all the ordinary uses of the world seem to you flat and unprofitable, you will be unfitted for them without becoming fitted for anything else.'[21]

Charlotte had sought some sort of sanction for her writing, but no less than the Poet Laureate of England had told her to

extinguish all ambitions of becoming a writer. And in her reply
to his letter Charlotte vowed: 'I trust I shall never feel ambitious
to see my name in print; if the wish should rise, I'll look at
Southey's letter, and suppress it.' Southey's advice should have
crushed her, but instead Charlotte savoured every stringent,
silencing word of it. His letter, she told him, 'is consecrated; no
one shall ever see it but papa and my brothers and sisters.'[22] This
promise indicates that she showed the letter to Emily and the
others. It must have confirmed Emily's estimate of the futility of
Charlotte's and Branwell's appeals to Southey and Wordsworth,
and her disdain for the whole idea of becoming professional
writers.

While Charlotte and Anne were away at Miss Wooler's –
recently moved from Roe Head to Dewsbury Moor, some two
or three miles away – back in Haworth Emily was blithely
ignoring Southey's strictures on women and literature and producing a great deal of poetry, much of it devoted to the on-
going turbulent world of Gondal. In a characteristic night poem,
however, she described the self-sufficient serenity and contentment of her eventless, dream-laden life at home at the parsonage:

> All day I've toiled, but not with pain,
> In learning's golden mine;
> And now at eventide again
> The moonbeams softly shine.
>
> There is no snow upon the ground,
> No frost on wind or wave;
> The south wind blew with gentlest sound
> And broke their icy grave.
>
> 'Tis sweet to wander here at night
> To watch the winter die
> With heart as summer sunshine light
> And warm as summer day.
>
> O may I never lose the peace
> That lulls me gently now ...

> True to myself and true to all
> May I be faithful still,
> And turn away from passion's call,
> And curb my own wild will.[23]

At the end of the school term Charlotte and Anne returned home for the summer holidays. The lilacs and columbine were in bloom in the garden where Emily and Charlotte and Anne often sat and read and wrote in the afternoon sun and flower-scented air. 'Love is like the wild rose-briar', as Emily later wrote, 'The wild rose-briar is sweet in spring, / Its summer blossoms scent the air.'[24]

On 20 June 1837 Victoria ascended the throne; a queen now ruled England, a fact which plainly contradicted Southey's notions of a woman's proper sphere. Six days later Emily and Anne wrote their second diary paper, which they agreed to open four years later on 30 July, Emily's birthday:

> Monday evening June 26 1837 A bit past 4 o'clock. Charlotte working in Aunt's room, Branwell reading Eugene Aram to her – Anne and I writing in the drawing room – Anne a poem beginning 'Fair was the evening and brightly the sun' – I Agustus-Almeda's [sic] life, 1st v. 1–4th page from the last – fine rather coolish ... grey cloudy but sunny day. Aunt working in the little room ... Papa – gone out. Tabby in the kitchin [sic] – the Emperors and Empresses of Gondal and Gaaldine preparing to depart from Gaaldine to Gondal to prepare for the coronation which will be on the 12th of July. Queen Vittiora [sic] ascended the throne this month. Northangerland in Monceys Isle – Zamorna at Eversham. All tight and right in which condition it is to be hoped we shall all be on this day 4 years at which time Charlotte will be 25 and 2 months – Branwell just 24, it being his birthday – myself 22 and 10 months and a peice [sic] Anne 21 and nearly a half. I wonder where we shall be and how we shall be and what kind of day it will be then – let us hope for the best.

Following these lines are a hasty pen-and-ink sketch of Emily and Anne writing at the dining room table, and then a postscript, squeezed into the bottom and side of the sheet of paper, apparently inspired by Aunt's poking her head into the parlour to see what her nieces are up to:

Aunt. come Emily, it's past 4 o'clock. Emily, yes Aunt. Anne, well, do you intend to write in the evening? Emily, well, what think you? (we agree to go out 1st to make sure, if we get into a humor we may stay in.) I guess that this day 4 years we shall all be in the drawing room comfortable, I hope it may be so. Anne guesses we shall all be gone somewhere together comfortable, we hope it may be either.[25]

A little more than a month after Emily and Anne wrote their diary note, the restorative, happy summer idyll at Haworth came to an end for Charlotte and Anne when they returned to Dewsbury Moor. Charlotte wrote to Ellen in late August: 'I am again at Dewsbury Moor engaged in the old business teach-teach-teach.'[26] Soon after their return to Miss Wooler's, Anne's health began to fail. She caught a cold that settled in her lungs, already vulnerable on account of her chronic asthma. She grew pale and weak, feverish, unable to eat, and plagued by a relentless, wracking cough. In addition, Anne's illness brought in its wake a deep religious depression, very similar to that which had tormented Charlotte the year before. Anne became haunted by the conviction of her own sinfulness, of the darkness and evil she believed she harboured in her soul. She felt estranged from God, an outcast, one of the lost, destined for Hell.

A doctor was called in to see to Anne's physical state, and he apparently found it far less serious than Charlotte imagined. Then Anne herself begged to see a clergyman, and a Moravian minister, the Reverend James La Trobe, was summoned to heal Anne's aching, fearful heart and mind. He, too, judged her to be over the worst. But neither the doctor's not the minister's encouraging prognoses allayed Charlotte's anxieties. Remembering Cowan Bridge and Emily just two years earlier at Roe Head, Charlotte confronted Miss Wooler with her fears for Anne's life and demanded that Anne be sent home.

Miss Wooler demurred, and pointed out that both the doctor and Reverend La Trobe had said that Anne was out of danger. Miss Wooler's complacency enraged Charlotte, and she accused her of callousness and neglect. Miss Wooler was stunned by the vehemence of Charlotte's attack and the next day wrote of it to Patrick Brontë. He immediately summoned home both Charlotte and Anne; the Christmas holidays were almost upon them in any case. Charlotte remained incensed with Miss Wooler, and as she packed her own and Anne's things, resolved never to return to Dewsbury Moor. But an emotional farewell, tinged perhaps with contrition on both sides, overruled Charlotte's resolve. Before departing for Haworth she promised Miss Wooler that she, but not Anne, would return to Dewsbury Moor at the beginning of the new year.

Outwardly the Christmas holidays of 1837 were quiet enough. No castles in the air devoted to literary fame were erected, no beseeching, hopeful letters were written to editors and famous poets. Tabby's health was restored and she was active once again in the household. With Charlotte and Anne home from Miss Wooler's, and their physical and mental wellbeing swiftly recovered, all seemed, in Emily's phrase, 'tight and right'. Yet there were subtle, barely perceptible, unarticulated but nevertheless important changes or shiftings in the relationships among the four Brontë children, who, in fact, were all nearly adults now.

Branwell was spending more and more time outside the household; he became passionately interested in pugilism, joined the Masons and rose through their ranks to hold various offices, was a member of the local Temperance Society (despite his almost nightly attendance at the Black Bull) and chaired meetings of the Haworth Operative Conservative Society.

While Branwell was becoming more involved in village life, Emily had by this time completely withdrawn from the world beyond the parsonage. She had been home from school, pursuing her idiosyncratic, solitary life, for more than two years, with the result, as Mrs Gaskell described it, that 'Emily was impervious to influence; she never came in contact with public opinion, and her own decision of what was right and fitting was a law for her own conduct and appearance with which she allowed no one to interfere.'[27] In a rare moment of insight, Ellen Nussey later commented that Emily was 'a law unto herself and a heroine in keeping to that law.' Emily's imperviousness to influence, her waywardness and wilfulness, were evident in both trivial and large matters. Her clothes, for example, announced her independence and eccentricity at a glance. She persisted in wearing large, leg-of-mutton sleeves which had been out of fashion for more than a decade, while her skirts hung down straight from the waist, without any petticoats beneath, thus accentuating her tall, lanky body. No doubt the unfashionable, free-hanging skirts made for easy walking; the puffed-up sleeves, however, served no purpose. By refusing to teach Sunday school and attending church only irregularly, Emily effectually cut herself off from everyone outside her home. She would even retreat to the kitchen at the postman's bell or to the parlour when the butcher's boy or baker's man appeared at the kitchen door.[28]

Even with her sisters, Emily was sometimes inaccessible. A triangle of sorts now began to take shape among the three of them. According to Mrs Gaskell, Emily's 'love was poured out on Anne, as Charlotte's was on her'.[29] There is no doubt that Charlotte loved Emily more than anyone else in the world, but it was a passionate, possessive love and Emily the most elusive, and freedom-demanding of love objects. Charlotte, as she showed over and over again, wanted to protect, interpret and control Emily, 'her bonnie love', as she called her in letters when they were apart. Emily, not unexpectedly, often found Charlotte's love smothering. Charlotte wanted to drag her into the glare of the 'world without' – to school, to work, and, in time, to publish. And so a pattern of underlying struggle emerged between them. Meanwhile, Emily turned to her collaborator in Gondal, the docile, undemanding Anne, for intimacy. For her part, Anne apparently accepted her assigned family role as the insignificant little sister – 'nothing, absolutely nothing' – as Charlotte caricatured her in the Patrick Benjamin Wiggins sketch. But, as events would show, Anne was not the cipher that her sisters and brother took her to be.

At the end of January Charlotte reluctantly went back to Miss Wooler's, but, almost as soon as she arrived at Dewsbury Moor, she fell ill with all the old familiar symptoms. She couldn't sleep or concentrate or eat. Her nerves were so strained and painfully sensitive that 'she would turn sick and trembling at any sudden noise and could hardly repress her screams when startled.'[30] A doctor was summoned who pronounced Charlotte's state dangerous and urged her to return home at once. Like Emily and Anne before her, for Charlotte illness was the only route back to freedom and her body the only weapon to gain it. By May she was back at Haworth.

The late spring of 1838, then, found all four Brontë children at home together again, but they knew this reunion could only be short-lived. They had to put their separate failures behind them and try to fashion some sort of future for themselves. Branwell was the first to make a move. After *Blackwood's* and Wordsworth's silence over his poetry, he had reverted to his artistic ambitions and resumed his studies with William Robinson. Shortly after Charlotte's return from Miss Wooler's, Branwell departed for Bradford with the intention of establishing himself there as a portrait painter. Bradford, of course, was not London. It was not even Leeds. But there were interesting faces to paint there and, what is even more important, the money to commission them to be painted, and the competition would be less keen in Bradford than in Leeds or York. The plan was not brilliant, but it seemed moderately promising.

Branwell set himself up at No. 3 Fountain Street in Bradford in the home of the Kirby family. Mr Kirby was a porter and ale merchant (perhaps an entirely too appropriate landlord for Branwell), and he and his wife were among Branwell's first subjects. Other commissions came his way, and Branwell also formed important friendships with the sculptor Joseph Leyland and the painter John Hunter Thompson. Every weekend he would take the coach, or in good weather walk ten miles, home to Haworth, and deliver glowing reports of his new life in Bradford to his family. Both Emily and Charlotte visited him at the Kirbys' at least once during the summer of 1838. But they did not see, nor did Branwell tell his family, that the good life and bright lights of Bradford consisted of more than painting flattering portraits of well-to-do woollen manufacturers. Branwell began to spend more and more time at pubs with his stimulating circle of bohemian friends. It was also probably at Bradford that he began to experiment with opium in the form of laudanum, and shifted his hero worship from Wordsworth to Coleridge and De Quincey.

Branwell's apparent success in Bradford was a great relief to his family. But it was also, to his sisters, something of a reproach. They were a financial drain on the family; their father's health was as frail as ever, and they were not yet adequately prepared to take care of themselves were he to die. After several false starts,

Branwell now seemed to be making his own way in the world. They must rouse themselves to do the same.

By the end of the summer Charlotte felt sufficiently recovered to return once again to Miss Wooler's. Anne had only been home for eight months, while Emily had not stirred from the house for three years. Anne's health was still delicate. Emily's, in contrast, was hearty and robust from eating the wholesome food she cooked for the family and her long, strenuous walks on the moors. Either she or Anne would have to remain at the parsonage with their father and aunt and, given their respective conditions, it seemed better for Anne to stay at home a bit longer.

But how would Emily manage if she went away again, and went away, moreover, entirely on her own? Emily had spoken to no one outside the household for three years. She had shaped her own daily life to accommodate her domestic chores, but these still allowed her a great deal of freedom: to read and write and dream whatever and whenever she wished. She had grown used to walking out on the moors, alone, in all weathers. She was accustomed to preparing her own food and, when the others were away, eating it alone in the dining room while her father and aunt also took their meals in solitude. Her dress was bizarre; she disliked children, and seemed to prefer animals to humans for company. All this did not bode well for Emily's chances in the 'world without' she shunned with a mixture of fear and disdain.

And yet in September of 1838 Emily left home to take up a position at a school at Law Hill some eight miles from Haworth. Less than a month later Charlotte wrote to Ellen, 'Emily is gone into a situation as a teacher in a large school of near forty pupils, near Halifax. I have had one letter from her since her departure; it gives an appalling account of her duties – hard labour from six in the morning until near eleven at night, with only one half-hour of exercise between. This is slavery. I fear she will never stand it.'[31]

· 6 ·

Governesses

Despite Charlotte's gloomy predictions and anxieties, Emily did in fact 'stand it' at Law Hill for the better part of the school's annual session. When she came home briefly at Christmas time Emily discovered that Charlotte herself had broken down at Dewsbury Moor and returned to the parsonage for good; it was Charlotte's failure, not Emily's, this time around. During the holidays, Charlotte and Emily had more than enough time and freedom to discuss Emily's situation at Law Hill. But there is no way of knowing whether Emily divulged all the details of her 'hard labour' from six in the morning until eleven at night, or whether she fleshed out the panicked, cramped account of her 'slavery' that she had sent to Charlotte in her first – now lost – letter from Law Hill.

Virtually everything concerning Emily's time at Law Hill has, in fact, been lost. Even her precise dates there are unsure.[1] If Emily did confide in Charlotte while she was at home, Charlotte was silent about her sister's plight in all her subsequent letters. Anne just glancingly mentioned Emily's time as a teacher in her 1841 diary paper – 'Emily has been a teacher at Miss Patchett's school and left it' – while Emily didn't mention it at all in her corresponding diary note.[2] Miss Elizabeth Patchett, who founded and ran the school at Law Hill and lived to a ripe old age, long after the Brontës had written their books and all died, refused ever to discuss her former employee. She was deeply offended by Mrs Gaskell's publication of Charlotte's letter with its allegations of 'hard labour' and 'slavery'. Rather than defending or explaining her treatment of Emily, Miss Patchett kept a resolute silence. Charlotte's letter and Anne's brief allusion to Emily's time there are the only contemporaneous accounts which have survived.

But long after even Elizabeth Patchett had died, a Mrs Watkinson of Huddersfield, who was at Law Hill during 1838 and 1839, recalled that Emily 'could not easily associate with others and her work was hard ... she was not good at needlework and ... was untidy and fond of day-dreaming.' More vividly, Mrs Watkinson remembered that one day Emily – with what exasperation and suppressed fury can only be imagined – informed her class that the house dog was dearer to her than any of the students.[3]

Given Emily's qualifications, it is surprising that she acquired her uncongenial appointment in the first place. Unlike Charlotte, she had virtually no formal education and no teaching experience whatsoever. The lot of governesses at the time was appalling: work days of sixteen or eighteen hours, endless teaching and marking of exercise books, and oceans of needlework should the poor governess ever find a moment to call her own. If she wasn't cramming her pupils' heads with the answers to *Mangnall's Questions* or the more rudimentary elements of the alphabet or arithmetic sums, she was darning their stockings, hemming their handkerchiefs and turning their collars. And she endured all this for something between £15 and £25 a year (laundry amounting to £4 or £5 to be deducted). Yet the competition for governess posts was keen. When Emily went to Law Hill there were more than 20,000 governesses in England working under these conditions and for this pay. Hundreds more were unemployed. One beleaguered employer had 810 applicants for a position which paid £15 a year.[4] By 1841 the plight of governesses and teachers without work had become so desperate that a Governesses Benevolent Institution was founded to 'afford assistance privately and delicately to ladies in temporary distress'. It was promptly besieged with appeals for help far beyond the Institution's means. For one annuity of only £20 it received hundreds of requests.[5]

Emily, then, was extremely fortunate to get her position at Miss Patchett's. Most likely she had Charlotte to thank for it. Once Charlotte realized that Emily's resolve to go out and teach was, like so much else about her, unbending, she must have spoken to Miss Wooler, and asked her to forget for the moment her own misgivings about Emily and help her find a job. Miss

Wooler may have been reluctant but she was able to comply. Through a family connection she learned that Maria Patchett, a schoolmistress who had helped run her sister's school at the village of Southowram near Halifax, had recently married, leaving Elizabeth Patchett in need of an assistant teacher. For Law Hill was a large boarding academy, with forty students and a full range of accomplishments, including horseback riding – one of the few pleasurable skills and occupations Emily acquired there. Miss Wooler probably contacted Miss Patchett before Miss Patchett even had time to advertise and learn that there were literally hundreds of better-qualified women than Emily Brontë eager to take up the post at Law Hill.

Despite the long hours and paltry wages, there was much to interest Emily there. The landscape was sustaining and familiar, for Southowram was only eight miles from Haworth. It was perched among the hills surrounding Halifax, swathed in a black industrial fog. Looking down on Halifax from an altitude of almost 1000 feet, Southowram nestled in a circle of hills and was exposed to glorious sunrises and sunsets throughout the year. The school consisted of a main house, Law Hill, and a number of large outbuildings and barns scattered about the grounds which gave way to vistas of moorland on three sides. The school house itself was not impressive – a rectangular box-like three-storey structure devoid of any architectural embellishment, but within two miles of Law Hill there were other imposing houses which could engage the imagination as well as the eye, and Emily became familiar with them.

Waterclough Hall, with the same initials as Wuthering Heights, stood barely a mile from Law Hill. It possessed a strange history which resonated in a curious way with Hugh Brunty's Irish tales of his own life and that of his vengeful uncle, Welsh Brunty. Waterclough Hall had belonged to the Walker family since the seventeenth century; by the 1720s its inhabitants numbered one John Walker, his wife, four children, two married and two maiden sisters. Walker farmed his land and was also a prosperous woollen manufacturer. Though he had two sons of his own, he adopted and favoured his nephew, a rascal named Jack Sharp. Walker trained Sharp to take over the thriving family woollen business, which in due course Sharp did and along with it Wateclough Hall as well. By the time John Walker died in 1771, Jack Sharp was in full possession of the Walker estate. But not legally. After a good deal of protracted negotiation and bad feeling on all sides, John Walker's rightful heir, his son, also named John Walker, managed to oust Sharp from Wateclough Hall. Before vacating it, Sharp in retaliation first destroyed most of the Hall's fixtures and heirlooms, and then carried off whatever he could of its furniture, plate, silver and linen, leaving a virtually empty and badly damaged house behind him. The Sharp proceeded to build his own home, Law Hill, as close as he legally could to John Walker's seat. Sharp named his new house after the hill from which, it must have seemed to the Walkers, it mockingly looked down on Wateclough Hall.

But Sharp's carefully nursed wrath at the Walkers was not yet appeased. He apprenticed a Walker cousin named Sam Stead, the son of one of old Mr Walker's sisters, to his woollen business. Sam Stead was as dubious a character as his so-called benefactor but far less clever. He was also given to drinking and gambling, and was thus putty in Jack Sharp's hands. In a short time and with no apparent motive other than causing further pain and injury to the Walkers, Jack Sharp worked Sam Stead's complete degradation with drink and gaming.

To think of Jack Sharp as anything other than a most unsavoury rogue would seem inconceivable, yet Emily's understanding of this bit of ugly local history was anything but conventional. We can see very clearly in Jack Sharp's history the lineaments of Heathcliff's and in that of the hapless Sam Stead, Hareton Earnshaw's. The surname of Hareton, Catherine and Hindley derived from Law Hill too, for one of the female staff during Emily's time there was named Earnshaw.

There were also two other houses in the district of Law Hill which influenced the novel Emily was to write eight years later. High Sunderland Hall was a much more palatial affair than Wateclough Hall or Law Hill and of far greater antiquity. It dated even further back than Wuthering Heights, to the thirteenth century. During Elizabethan times the Hall had been fortified with an elaborate, impregnable stone shell, decorated with ornate carvings and Latin inscriptions. Most impressive, however, was its fantastically ornamented gateway, which was remarkably similar to the 'grotesque carvings . . . a wilderness of crumbling griffins and shameless little boys' adorning the door of Wuthering Heights.[6]

Close to High Sunderland Hall and Law Hill was a third manor house, the fifteenth-century Shibden Hall, a sprawling building with dark, gleaming, wood-panelled walls inside, open beamed ceilings and huge fireplaces similar to those in Wuthering Heights. In Emily's day the 'master' of Shibden Hall was a strange spinster heiress named Anne Lister, who always wore black and habitually dressed in men's clothes, so that it was sometimes difficult for strangers to tell if Miss Lister was a man or a woman.

We can discern, then, the seeds sown in Emily's imagination at Law Hill and identify the influences on her novel. But Emily didn't wait until she came to write *Wuthering Heights* to distil her experience at Law Hill. While still at the school she found the environment inspiring. She wrote more than a dozen poems during her six-month stay at Law Hill despite her 'hard labour', taxing schedule and the demands of the indulged and intellectually stunted daughters of the local gentry and wealthy Halifax businessmen whom she taught. Most of Emily's Law Hill poems were Gondal narratives. It would seem that all the constraints and demands at Miss Patchett's actually unleashed Emily's creative energy: she had to escape the stifling atmosphere of the female seminary, and the only haven for her distracted, weary mind was the 'world within'.

One of the most moving of Emily's Law Hill poems, written in early December, when she had been at the school only two months, described the process of her imaginative release and also its inevitable termination. She wrote in the deserted schoolroom, at the end of the day:

> A little while, a little while,
> The noisy crowd are barred away;
> And I can sing and I can smile
> A little while I've holyday!
>
> Where wilt thou go, my harassed heart?
> Full many a land invites thee now;

And places near and far apart
Have rest for thee, my weary brow.

She was torn between the twin harbours of home and Gondal.
Both beckoned; both reveries of Haworth and immersion in
Gondal proffered escape from Emily's hated teaching duties. But
both, too, yielded only fleeting 'holydays'.

Could I have lingered but an hour
It well had paid a week of toil,
But truth has banished fancy's power;
I hear my dungeon bars recoil –

Even as I stood with raptured eye
Absorbed in bliss so deep and dear
My hour of rest had fleeted by
And given me back to weary care.[7]

Many of the Law Hill poems, like Emily's earlier poetry, were
written at night when her pupils were in bed and her needlework
at last put aside. She wrote even further into the night away at
school than she had at Haworth, and often she opened her poems
with descriptions of the wind and rain-buffeted landscape outside
her window. 'The night is darkening round me, / The wild winds
coldly blow', one poem began, and another:

Loud without the wind was roaring
Through the waned autumnal sky;
Drenching wet, the cold rain pouring
Spoke of stormy winters nigh.[8]

At Law Hill, Emily stayed awake later and later, writing by
the dim light of a single candle, alone in the schoolroom or at the
far shadowy end of the dormitory where she had her curtained-off
bed. She wrote, as she explained in another poem, because

Sleep brings no joy to me,
Remembrance never dies;
My soul is given to misery
And lives in sighs . . .

Sleep brings no strength to me
No power renewed to brave

I only sail a wilder sea,
A darker wave.

Sleep brings no friend to me
To soothe and aid to bear;
They all gaze, oh, how scornfully
And I despair.[9]

The title of this lyric, 'A.G.A.' – the initials of the Gondal heroine Augusta Geraldine Almeda – indicated that it was a Gondal poem. But the insomnia, uncontrollable memories and abiding sense of isolation all reflected Emily's own experience at Law Hill. The poetry she wrote there was imbued with certain recurring, powerful themes – imprisonment, above all, and then exile, the anguished separation of lovers, and the transitory balm of deliverance. All spoke of a mind haunted by loss and isolation. In Emily's Law Hill poems, in fact, we glimpse a far more profound picture of her during her period away at school – the only time she was away from home alone – than Miss Patchett's uncomprehending and bitter recollections could have afforded.

Day after day through the autumn and winter, Emily toiled. Time assumed an unprecedented languorous dimension. Days seemed to expand to the duration of weeks or months, and weeks and months became years or even decades. Before spring arrived Emily's 'health was broken'. She had all the same symptoms she'd experienced at Roe Head three years earlier, but more severely, because at Roe Head she had only had to endure passively her imprisonment in an alien environment, while at Law Hill she had to participate in it actively, preparing lessons, maintaining order in a schoolroom of noisy, undisciplined pupils, and then sewing and mending until eleven p.m. or later. Emily had decided of her own volition to take up a teaching post and she was determined to 'stand it', whatever the consequences to her mental and physical health. But her body revolted against her resolution. As the Law Hill poems show, with all their captured prisoners languishing in dark, cold dungeons, Emily felt incarcerated and powerless at school, and, as she had done at Roe Head, she turned her frustration and rage at her helplessness against herself by again refusing to eat.

First depression destroyed her appetite, and then fasting

became a solace and reward in and of itself. Emily's light-headedness and weakness conferred an air of unreality and inconsequence on her daily chores. Her dreamy abstraction became habitual. When she stood before a class it was as if she were looking down a telescope the wrong way; her students receded into a blurred background; their voices came to her as if from a great distance. Hunger and semi-starvation induced these symptoms and distorted perceptions, and they also exacerbated her insomnia and inability to concentrate. By late February it was clear that Emily was close to breakdown, or at least clear to everyone around her. She had become weak, thin and haggard, her movements slow and uncertain, her voice muted and almost unintelligible. Miss Patchett, who had grown increasingly alarmed at the strange behaviour of her young assistant over the months, must have felt she had no choice but to dismiss Emily. Lost in her own thoughts, sleep-walking through her duties and lying awake half the night, Emily was in no position to assess her own condition. Furthermore, she would have done anything rather than resign from her hard-won and resolutely endured position.

Just how Miss Patchett unburdened herself of Emily is not known. There must have been a painful, awkward scene with Miss Patchett making solicitous noises about Emily's health, and Emily, most likely, uttering nothing in response to her employer's sympathetic but nevertheless decided dismissal. By March of 1839 Emily was back home at Haworth.

Within weeks of Emily's return, Anne took up a post as governess in a private family: that of Mr John Ingham of Blake Hall, close to Miss Wooler's school at Dewsbury Moor. Once again their old schoolmistress interceded on behalf of the Brontë sisters and helped Anne secure her position just as Emily was floundering in hers. Charlotte was almost as worried about Anne's ability to 'stand it' at Blake Hall as she had been over Emily's staying power at Law Hill. She worried, especially, about Anne's stutter, which she feared Mrs Ingham would think due to lack of intelligence rather than a speech impediment. And then Anne had always been considered, as she herself wrote in her first novel, *Agnes Grey*, 'as a *child*, and the pet of the family ... all combined to spoil me ... by ceaseless kindness to make too helpless and dependent – too unfit for buffeting with the cares and turmoils of life.'[10]

It was with great relief, then, that Charlotte wrote to Ellen Nussey in April of Anne's contentment with her situation at Blake Hall and her two young charges. Of herself, Charlotte confessed, 'For my own part, I am yet wanting a situation – like a housemaid out of a place', and then jestingly described how she occupied herself with domestic chores at home. 'I've lately discovered that I've quite a talent for cleaning – sweeping up hearths, dusting rooms – making beds, etc. So if everything fails – I can turn my hand to that.' 'I won't be a cook – I hate cooking', she added, indicating how she had relinquished the kitchen entirely to Emily. And Charlotte asserted, too, that she would never be 'a nursery maid – nor a lady's maid far less a lady's companion – or a mantua-maker – or a straw bonnet maker or a taker in of plain work – I will be nothing but a housemaid.'[11]

As Ellen already knew, however, less than a month earlier Charlotte had been offered the opportunity to be a great deal more than a housemaid, straw bonnet maker, lady's companion or nursery maid. Nothing less than the ultimate feminine destiny of marriage had been within her reach, and Charlotte had almost immediately spurned it. Her suitor was Ellen's older brother, Henry Nussey, five years Charlotte's senior, a Cambridge graduate, a curate at Donnington on the east coast of Sussex, who needed a wife to occupy and take care of the large rectory he inhabited (the vicar was not resident), and to direct and teach in the school he wished to establish.

Charlotte Brontë was not Henry Nussey's first choice. He had already offered his hand to the daughter of his former vicar, the Reverend Mr Lutwidge, but, as he recorded in his diary, in mid-February 1839 Henry 'received a letter from Mr L— senr. with a negative to my wishes', to which Henry piously added: 'Thy will, O Lord, be done.' Yet it seems Henry Nussey was not, after all, content to submit to God's will in the matter. Shortly after receiving the Reverend Lutwidge's 'negative', he wrote to Mary Lutwidge herself, but this direct assault on the object of his desires was as unsuccessful as his initial proposal. Once again, he 'received a decisive reply from M.A.L.'s papa; a loss, but I trust a providential one. Believe not her will, but her father's.

All right, but God knows best what is good for us.' Almost as an afterthought Henry then jotted a reminder to himself to 'Write to Yorks. friend: C.B.'[12]

Unfortunately his proposal to the second candidate on his list, 'C.B.' or Charlotte Brontë, is lost, but we can probably assume that it was nearly as transparent and ungratifying as had been another curate's, Patrick Brontë's proposal to Mary Burder, sixteen years earlier. And like Mary Burder, Charlotte Brontë did not hesitate to give 'a *decided* negative' to her suitor. On 5 March she wrote Henry Nussey a long explanation of her unequivocal refusal. 'In forming this decision, I trust I have listened to the dictates of conscience more than those of inclination. I have no personal repugnance to the idea of a union with you, but I feel convinced that mine is not the sort of disposition calculated to form the happiness of a man like you.' Charlotte believed that the most suitable wife for her closest friend's brother would be one whose 'character should not be too marked, ardent, and original', a rather oblique way, perhaps, of Charlotte congratulating herself for possessing these qualities. Furthermore, the future Mrs Nussey 'should be mild, her piety undoubted, her spirits even and cheerful, and her *personal attractions*' – underlined in the letter – 'sufficient to please your eyes and gratify your pride. As for me,' she continued, 'you do not know me' – not literally, of course, for they had met several times at the Nussey home. What Charlotte meant was that 'I am not the serious, grave, cool-headed individual you suppose; you would think me romantic and eccentric; you would say I was satirical and severe.' Furthermore, Charlotte bravely confessed she would 'never, for the sake of attaining the distinction of matrimony and escaping the stigma of an old maid, take a worthy man whom I am conscious I cannot render happy.'[13]

Could the creator of Zamorna and Percy, the worshipper of the Duke of Wellington and disciple of Byron, attach herself to the cautious, self-serving prig we find in the pages of Henry Nussey's diary? Would anyone today waste a moment on this document, which he kept, he said in its pages, for the edification of posterity, if he had not proposed to Charlotte Brontë and been refused? When her 'decided negative' arrived in Donnington on 8 March, Henry Nussey recorded its verdict with pious resignation:

'Received an unfavourable reply from C.B. The will of the Lord be done.'

Charlotte's refusal of Henry Nussey was an act of tremendous courage. No one and nothing in her world, other than Emily, would have comprehended it. Charlotte was plain, she was as penniless as a woman of her rank could be, she was temperamental and nervous and intelligent, none of which made her attractive on the marriage market. Nine out of ten twenty-three-year-old young women in 1839 would have snapped up Henry Nussey and his comfortable rectory and school plans without a twinge of conscience. But Charlotte possessed both integrity and awareness of her own self-worth; she was too honest to marry Henry Nussey, and, though not vain or proud, she also knew she was too good for him. Above all, she could not marry a man she did not love. She had nothing to look forward to other than the genteel poverty of governessing and the social stigma of an old maid, but still she said 'no' to security, respectability, comfort, financial wellbeing and companionship. And she did so with the full knowledge that such an opportunity in all likelihood would never come her way again. As she put it to Ellen, perhaps overestimating the odds, 'Ten to one I shall never have the chance again, but *n'importe*.'[14]

Yet, astonishingly, Charlotte *did* have another 'chance' just several months later, in the summer of 1839. One fine day in August, a former curate of Patrick Brontë's, a Mr Hodgson, visited the parsonage with his own curate, an ebullient, handsome, young Irishman named David Bryce, fresh from Dublin University. On her home territory Charlotte was far more relaxed than when she met strangers outside, and she soon thawed in David Bryce's company. He was 'witty – lively, ardent – and clever too'; Charlotte's tongue was loosened and she talked freely, though when Mr Bryce became over familiar and expansive towards evening and began 'to season his conversation with something of Hibernian flattery', she cooled down considerably. They parted, however, on good terms.

Three days later Charlotte was puzzled to receive a letter addressed to her in an unfamiliar hand, and then astounded to read its contents. It was, as she told Ellen, 'a declaration of attachment – and proposal of Matrimony ... expressed in the ardent language of the sapient young Irishman!' Charlotte, however, did not pause any longer to reject Mr Bryce than she had Henry Nussey. She could not reciprocate David Bryce's infatuation, for that is how she viewed it – as an impulsive crush rather than a genuine case of love at first sight. It is just as well that she saw things in this light, for six months later the lively, high-spirited David Bryce died suddenly from a ruptured blood vessel, and it seemed to Charlotte that all her hopes of marriage died with him. She wrote fatalistically to Ellen that 'I'm certainly doomed to be an old maid ... I can't expect another chance – never mind, I made up my mind to that fate ever since I was twelve years old.'[15]

Undoubtedly Emily had also given over all thought of marriage at an early age, if she ever considered it at all. Emily, however, would never have the chance to prove her indifference because no man ever proposed to her. Indeed, with one or two exceptions, she scarcely conversed with any man other than her father and brother. And yet even more than Charlotte, Emily had a profound understanding of passionate love and the obsession, anxiety, jealousy and possessiveness which make it seem a cosmic kind of affliction. Gondal was dominated by the unappeasable appetites of star-crossed lovers, especially Augusta Geraldine Almeda and her various paramours. And, of course, *Wuthering Heights* is the most cataclysmic love story in the language, and Heathcliff and Catherine mythic figures of romance. Love, as Emily portrayed it, was an all-consuming, violent and almost always destructive passion. It also invariably existed outside of marriage. The great mystery of Emily's life is how she was able to fathom as she did the nature of human love. We know that she read Byron and Shelley and Scott and Goethe and some of the French Romantics as well. But the knowledge she had of love – of its relentless fury and redemptive joy – cannot be traced to literary influences. It came from within, from her own urgent desires, from her capacity to imagine with the utmost clarity and empathy something she had never seen, never known, and never would see or know. Yet if her life had not been so barren and solitary her writing probably would not have been so rich and powerful. The paradox of genius is that it creates plenty – in Emily's case plenty with a vengeance – out of nothing.

It is unclear whether Charlotte told Emily, as well as Ellen, of her two proposals of marriage; she may have been too ashamed of her suitors to do so. Henry Nussey, in particular, would have elicited a sneer from Emily. On the other hand, Emily would have whole-heartedly endorsed Charlotte's categorical rejection of both offers. Yet over the more fundamental issue of marriage – the question of whether or not it was a woman's highest and best destiny – they would have differed. Charlotte's was the conventional view; she was unable or unwilling to think of love outside marriage, just as she refused to contemplate the prospect of marriage without love. In this Charlotte was a product of the social and religious world she inhabited. Emily, in contrast, was 'a law unto herself and a heroine in keeping to that law'. No social or religious forms bound her. Love, for her, was essentially an amoral power, like an immutable force of nature. It had its own time and seasons and was no respecter of artificial human creations such as matrimony.

Having rejected marriage, Charlotte had to seek a new governess position, no easy task, as she soon found out. She began answering advertisements for governesses shortly after Emily returned from Law Hill. Branwell, too, returned home in the spring of 1839, having failed, after a year in Bradford, to establish himself as a portrait painter. He came back laden with debts and much the worse for wear from drink and opium, and it soon became obvious that he was in no hurry to seek another means of livelihood. Nor did it seem likely that Emily would leave home again to teach. Her health was still precarious after her six months of 'slavery' at Miss Patchett's; her sojourn at Law Hill, in fact, had proved to everyone how unsuited Emily was to be a governess. And yet what else, given her circumstances, could she ever hope to be? For the time being, this underlying question was ignored, and Emily lapsed back into her familiar routines of life in the parsonage. Anne, meanwhile, was still at the Inghams'.

In May Charlotte finally received an offer of a temporary position with the family of John Benson Sidgwick at Stonegappe, some four miles from Skipton. But before going to Stonegappe, Charlotte paused to take stock of her life. She was now twenty-three years old. She had been living, writing, dreaming, even breathing, the air of Angria for more than ten years, almost as long as she could remember. After a great deal of soul-searching, she decided she must give it all up, abandon the fantasy world which had nourished and sustained her for so long, buoyed her during periods of homesickness and depression, and been the chief joy of her life at home with her sisters and brother. She wouldn't renounce writing, as Robert Southey had exhorted her to do, but she would relinquish the heady empire of her imagination. Hence she sat down to write a formal valediction, which she entitled 'Farewell to Angria'. It marked a milestone in her life, and her initiation into adulthood:

I have now written a great many books, and for a long time have dwelt on the same characters and scenes and subjects. I have shown my landscapes in every variety of shade and light which morning, noon, and evening, the rising, the meridian, and the setting sun, can bestow on them ... My readers have been habitu-ated to one set of features, which they have seen now in profile, now in full face, now in outline, and again in finished painting – varied but by the change of feeling or temper or rage; lit with love, flushed with passion, shaded with grief, kindled with ecstasy; in meditation and mirth, in sorrow and scorn and rapture; with the round outline of childhood, the beauty and fulness of youth, the strength of manhood, and the furrows of thoughtful decline; but we must change, for the eye is tired of the picture so oft recurring, and now so familiar.

Yet do not urge me too fast, reader: it is no easy theme to dismiss from my imagination the images which have filled it so long; they were my friends and my intimate acquaintances, and I could with little labour describe to you the faces, the voices, the actions of those who peopled my thoughts by day, and not seldom stole strangely even into my dreams at night. When I depart from these I feel almost as if I stood on the threshold of a home and were bidding farewell to its inmates. When I strive to conjure up new inmates I feel as if I had got into a distant country where every face was unknown, and the character of all the population an enigma which it would take much study to comprehend and much talent to expound. Still, I long to quit for awhile that burning clime where we have sojourned too long – its skies flame, the glow of sunset is always upon it. The mind would cease from excitement and turn now to a cooler region where the dawn breaks grey and sober, and the coming day for a time at least is subdued by clouds.[16]

The 'Farewell to Angria' was a poignant, brave document and also a cry from the heart; Charlotte was bidding farewell to nothing less than her childhood. And in doing so, though neither she nor Emily guessed it at the time, Charlotte was passing into an alien region where Emily would never belong, never willingly follow. For at the very same time that Charlotte was renouncing Angria, Emily was immersing herself more than ever in Gondal. And she would remain faithful to and dependent upon her imaginary world for the rest of her life. No guilt ever wracked her, nor no sense of responsibility to the 'grey and sober', clouded vistas of adulthood.

In early June Charlotte wrote home to Emily about her miserable existence at the Sidgwicks'. 'Dearest Lavinia', she began, using one of the pet names they had devised for each other; 'I have striven hard to be pleased with my new situation. The country, the house, the grounds are ... divine.' But Charlotte's lovely surroundings and the steady unfurling of one glorious summer day after the next were all lost on her because 'there is such a thing as seeing all beautiful around you ... and not having a free moment or a free thought left to enjoy them. The children are constantly with me, and more riotous, perverse, unmanageable cubs never grew.'[17]

The lack of time to call her own and the demands of little Mathilda and John Benson might have been endurable if Charlotte had been treated with more than aloof, perfunctory civility by her employers. In another letter to Emily, Charlotte complained that Mrs Sidgwick 'did not know' her: 'she cares nothing in the world about me except to contrive how the greatest possible quantity of labour may be squeezed out of me, and to that end she overwhelms me with oceans of needlework, yards of cambric to mend, muslin nightcaps to make, and, above all things, dolls to dress ... I now see more clearly than I have ever done that a private governess has no existence, is not considered as a living and rational being except as connected with wearisome duties she has to fulfil.' After complaining so openly to Emily,

Charlotte begged her to say nothing of her unhappiness to the others, for 'they will think I am never satisfied, wherever I am. I complain to you because it is a relief, and really I have had some unexpected mortifications.'[18]

It was, in fact, as much Charlotte's wounded pride as her overworked mind and body which suffered at Stonegappe. Visitors came and went – the 'stir of grand folks' society', as she wrote to Emily – and if they noticed her at all, they did so, Charlotte believed, as if she were one of the fixtures of the establishment – something necessary, admittedly, just as food in the larder or coals in the cellar were necessary in order to eat and keep warm, but otherwise entirely unremarkable and certainly uninteresting. If Charlotte construed the Sidgwick family and friends and house and lovely grounds as the various ingredients of a story – a novel, say – it was clear that she, the plain little governess, was a very minor character, part of the background really, sitting in a corner of the parlour in her severe black dress and white collar unadorned by any brooch.

Charlotte continued to confide her great unhappiness to Emily, and 'Lavinia', in turn, wrote Charlotte sustaining letters during this summer of exile. In July Charlotte dashed off a note in response to Emily's last message of courage and love:

> Mine bonnie love, I was as glad of your letter as tongue can speak: it is a real genuine pleasure ... a thing to be saved till bedtime, when one has a moment's quiet and rest to enjoy it thoroughly. Write when you can. I could like to be at home. I could like to work in a mill. I could like to feel mental liberty. I could like this weight of restraint to be taken off. But the holidays will come. *Corragio*.[19]

By the time the holiday did arrive, Charlotte and Mrs Sidgwick had reached an understanding that Charlotte should not continue at Stonegappe. Her health was deteriorating: she had begun to suffer alarming bouts of palpitations and shortness of breath in addition to low spirits, insomnia and loss of appetite. Illness, once again, was the great liberator. Shortly before Emily's birthday, at the end of July, less than two months after coming to Stonegappe, Charlotte departed for home.

· 7 ·

Dividing Seas

The self-absorbed, self-sufficient rhythm of Emily's long summer days was disrupted by Charlotte's return. They were almost perpetually together now – out in the garden picking currants, at dinner and tea, writing at the dining room table together in the evening, sharing their bed once more in the 'children's study'. Anne was still working as a governess with the Ingham family at Blake Hall. Branwell was home but not much in evidence. For a great deal of the day he was out and about, hunting, boxing, attending Masonic meetings, and during the evenings he was invariably to be found in his three-cornered chair at the Black Bull. Aunt Branwell was still up in her bedroom, her windows latched against the warm, fresh breezes outdoors. Patrick Brontë was either closeted in his study or out making his parish rounds. On 30 July 1839 Charlotte and Emily celebrated Emily's twenty-first birthday in the evening after their father and aunt had gone to bed. As usual, they were left on their own together.

But not left entirely alone. Though the other human inhabitants of the house remained aloof, companionship of a different sort was easily found. In the past year or so Emily had stealthily – because of her aunt's disapproval – added to the parsonage's non-human population. Out in the garden by day, and tucked into the peat room behind the dining room at night, were Emily's two pet geese, Victoria and Adelaide, named in honour of the young Queen and her mother. A merlin hawk had also joined the household; Emily had found him out on the moors, wounded and unable to fly, brought him home, nursed him back to health, taming him in the process, and named him Hero. There was also Anne's kitten, quickly metamorphosing into a cat, little Black

Tom. And, finally, there was the dog Grasper's far more imposing successor, a great bull-mastiff named Keeper.

Keeper – a fiend of a dog – could roar and spring like a tiger and was answerable only to Emily. Emily, in fact, trained him to growl, bark and jump on command; he terrified everyone else. A large, tawny, muscular, bristle-haired animal, as Emily drew him, Keeper wore a heavy engraved brass collar. Despite his size and ferocity, however, he was given to dainty ways. He was fond of lounging on snowy white bed counterpanes and only desisted when Emily pummelled his eyes until they bled, a punishment no one else could have inflicted without running the risk of a counter-attack. Dealt with at Emily's hands, Keeper cowered and whimpered.

On another occasion Emily extricated him from a tumultuous fight with several other village dogs which drew a crowd of spectators to Church Lane and no small measure of amazement when the parson's elusive daughter darted from the house at the commotion and abruptly terminated the battle with her bare hands, aided by a box of pepper which she liberally applied to the eyes and noses of the snarling, snapping dogs. It may have been on this occasion or another close in time to it, for Charlotte was a witness, that Emily was bitten by a rabid dog, or at least a dog suspected of having rabies because of his wild behaviour and frothing mouth. After the mad dog had run off in the direction of the moors, Emily examined her wound and discovered that the dog's teeth had broken her skin and she was bleeding. Then, without a word to anyone, she walked into the kitchen where Tabby was pressing clothes and cauterized her open wound with a hot iron full of red, glowing coals.

Dog fights, the discovery of an abandoned bird's nest on the moors, the arrival of the latest number of *Blackwood's Magazine*, the outbreak of another civil war in Gondal – such was the tenor of Emily's life at home during the summer of 1839. For her, the eventless, even current of days, the unvarying routine of parsonage life and its seclusion, of animal companions rather than human visitors, of a calm disturbed by nothing greater than a dog fight, was – because of its freedom and self-sufficiency – an ideal existence. She kept house, she cooked, she walked out early and late, she drew, she read, she wrote.

For Emily this was enough, but not for Charlotte, largely because Gondal was still flourishing while Angria had become a renounced, lost world. Angria was submerged, like Pompeii, under the lava of conscience, its history and poetry and legends all written in a dead tongue. Charlotte soon became restless at home, so when Ellen Nussey invited her to go to the sea in mid-August, she leapt at the opportunity. In her imagination Charlotte had sailed the Atlantic to the turbulent west coast of Africa, braving hurricanes and pirates and shipwreck. But in life she had never seen an ocean, indeed never seen any body of water larger than the Stanbury village reservoir and the tumbling 'meeting of the waters' waterfall on the path to Top Withins.

Ellen had been advised to go to the sea 'for her health', and perhaps Charlotte invoked her own palpitations and shortness of breath to persuade her father and aunt to allow her to go with Ellen to the coast. It was, of course, unseemly then for two young women to travel about England unchaperoned, especially on that new tornado of speed and smoke and noise, the railway. But Charlotte's entreaties were successful; less than a month after coming home to Emily, she went with Ellen on a four-week holiday to the coastal resort of Burlington (later renamed Bridlington) and the smaller town of Easton several miles inland where friends of the Nusseys lived. Emily wasn't invited, nor would she have wanted to go. Undoubtedly she was happy to recover her self-contained privacy while Charlotte was away.

The sea had a profound, intoxicating effect on Charlotte. Accompanied by Ellen, she approached the bluffs of Burlington with intense expectation. Then, at the first glimpse of the endless expanse of deep, green-blue water, rimmed by a collar of foamy breakers on the shore, she signalled Ellen to withdraw, to leave her alone, so that she could gaze alone at the ebb and flow of the delicate white waves, the glassy, undisturbed water further out, flecked by sunlight or large pools of deep shadow cast by stray, drifting clouds overhead. Here Charlotte found in the natural world something commensurate with her most intense longings and desires. Now she understood Emily's need for the ocean of moors at home and how exile from them at Roe Head or Law Hill had made Emily ill.

Charlotte had been prepared to surrender herself to the sea

not only by her Angrian adventures, but also by the poetry of William Cowper, that strange, sad eighteenth-century poet whose preoccupation with the individual sensibility and melancholy endeared him to the Brontës. The sea, storms and shipwreck resound through Cowper's poetry as images of human isolation and powerlessness. His most famous poem, 'The Castaway', was loved and known by heart by Emily and Charlotte, especially its closing stanza:

> No voice divine the storm allay'd,
> No light propitious shone;
> When snatch'd from all effectual aid,
> We perished, each alone:
> But I beneath a rougher sea,
> And whelm'd in deeper gulphs than he.

Though she had never been to the sea herself, Emily, too, in her own way was as drawn to it as Charlotte. But Emily had no need to travel to Burlington or Scarborough or Yarmouth to see the ocean. For her, the sea was more a state of mind than a geographical expanse of water. She saw the sea in the night sky 'while gazing on the stars that glow / Above in the stormless sea'. The stars shone down from their watery heaven, and Emily

> ... was at peace, and drank your beams
> As they were life to me
> And revelled in my changeful dreams
> Like petrel on the sea.[1]

Emily likened the moors as well as the night sky to the sea, especially in a poem which she wrote shortly after Charlotte's seaside holiday with Ellen Nussey. Emily's theme was estrangement and it was the 'desert sea', evoking both the moors and the ocean, which served as a barrier between two who have loved and been as one, but are so no more:

> Let us part, the time is over
> When I thought and felt like thee
> I will be an ocean rover,
> I will sail a desert sea.[2]

When Charlotte returned from Burlington, she found Emily

more involved than ever in Gondal, and unsympathetic to Charlotte's resolve to seek another governessing position. They were drifting apart: Emily was driven more and more in upon herself and her own interior world, while Charlotte felt duty-bound to set sail upon the waves of the real world and meet all its demands, contingencies and also perhaps – a persistent voice of hope still whispered – rewards. Emily would have none of this. She would be a solitary 'ocean rover'; she would 'sail a desert sea'.

Throughout the autumn and winter of 1839 Charlotte continued to reply to advertisements for governess positions, while Emily kept everything in the parsonage running smoothly after Tabby had fallen ill with a large ulcer on her leg. It was clear that Tabby's convalescence would be a prolonged one. Anne was at Blake Hall, Charlotte would be off as soon as she found an employer, and even Emily's stamina at home would not enable her to run the household and nurse Tabby at the same time. Aunt Branwell once again urged the solution of Tabby going to her sister's cottage in the village, and Emily and Charlotte reluctantly agreed. There was no talk of another hunger strike. Instead, Emily and Charlotte devoted themselves with a vengeance to all the household chores, as Charlotte wrote to Ellen: 'Emily and I are ... busy as you may suppose – I manage the ironing and keep the rooms clean – Emily does the baking and attends to the kitchen – we are such odd animals that we prefer this mode of contrivance to having a new face among us ... I excited Aunt's wrath very much by burning the clothes the first time I attempted to iron, but I do better now. Human feelings are queer things – I am much happier black-leading the stove – making the beds and sweeping the floors at home, than I should be living like a fine lady anywhere else.'[3]

Anne returned at Christmas from Blake Hall for good, to everyone's surprise. 'Gentle Anne' had been dismissed by Mrs Ingham for tying her two pupils to the legs of the nursery table so that she could get on with her work. The Ingham children had been wild charges – placid and obedient in their parents' presence, but holy terrors when left alone in Anne's hands.

It was over Christmas, too, that Branwell decided to follow his sisters' lead – despite their unhappy experiences – and try to earn his way as a tutor. With his sound classical training, he easily secured a post with the Postlethwaite family of Broughton House, Broughton-in-Furness, some ten miles from Ulverston. Emily, Charlotte and Anne spent most of the holiday 'shirt-making and collar stitching' in preparation for Branwell's departure on New Year's Day, 1840, a propitious date for a new beginning. But when Branwell broke his journey to Ulverston at Kendal, where he spent the night, he fortified himself in his old familiar way. He wrote to his Haworth friend, the sexton John Brown, that he lodged at the Royal Hotel in Kendal and bade 'farewell to old friend whisky ... ordered whisky-toddy as hot as hell ... I gave sundry toasts that were washed down at the same time till the room spun round and the candles danced in our eyes.' The next morning he found himself 'in bed with ... a bottle of porter, a glass and a corkscrew.' With a throbbing headache and queasy stomach, Branwell roused himself and set off for the Postlethwaites.[4]

Compared to his sisters' governessing positions, Branwell's situation as a tutor entailed far less work and a considerably larger salary. Mr Postlethwaite was a retired magistrate and large landowner. Branwell's two pupils, he told John Brown, were 'fine, high-spirited lads' of twelve and ten and a half. Once the day's lessons were over, Branwell was in possession of his own time, and there was nothing to keep him captive at the Postlethwaites'. Branwell, in fact, did not lodge with his employers, but instead with the local surgeon. Thus the Post-lethwaites and their guests had no opportunity to patronize Branwell, but they wouldn't have done so even if they had had the chance. Branwell, when he chose, could be the most charming and admirable of young men. And, as he wrote to John Brown, he spared no efforts to win over the Postlethwaites. 'What am I? That is, what do they think I am? A most calm, sedate, sober, abstemious, patient, mild-hearted, virtuous, gentlemanly phil-osopher – the picture of good works, and the treasure house of righteous thoughts. Cards are shuffled under the table cloth, glasses are thrust in the cupboard if I enter the room. I take neither spirits, wine, nor malt liquours. I dress in black and smile like a saint or martyr. Everybody says "What a good young gentleman is Mr Postlethwaite's tutor!"'[5]

For several months Branwell carefully cultivated this admirable persona and devoted his free time to translating Horace's Odes, which he sent to Hartley Coleridge, the son of Samuel Taylor Coleridge, at Ambleside, for criticism. And in May, Branwell took a short holiday from the Postlethwaites and visited Hartley Coleridge, and received encouragement both for his translations and for some original poetry he had brought along. Hartley Coleridge's approbation reawakened Branwell's old dream of professional authorship.

This brief period of responsibility and productivity was not to last. Branwell soon found his light teaching duties and the strain of being a paragon of gentlemanly conduct tiresome. Ulverston boasted four pubs, and Branwell began to frequent all of them. His landlord, Dr Gibson, had a bevy of attractive young daughters, and Branwell shifted his energies from impressing the inmates of Broughton House to charming these young ladies. In June, after six months at the Postlethwaites', Branwell was dismissed on the grounds of irresponsibility and drunkenness.

During Branwell's period at Ulverston, the parsonage had not been devoid of a young masculine presence. The previous August Patrick Brontë had acquired a new curate. For the most part, Emily and Charlotte and Anne found their father's clerical assistants a dreary lot, and this combined with their own extreme shyness had ensured that nothing more than a distant, nodding acquaintance had ever existed between Patrick Brontë's curates and his daughters. But when William Weightman took up his duties as the new curate, Emily thawed, Charlotte was charmed, and Anne, in the end, fell in love.

William Weightman was twenty-five when he came to his first curacy at Haworth, with a brand new M.A. in classics from Durham University. He was a handsome young man with a ruddy complexion, blue eyes and curling auburn hair. Almost too handsome, perhaps, for a man; hence Charlotte's mocking nickname for him of 'Miss Celia Amelia'. But Willie Weightman's good looks were just one facet of his overall charm and attraction. He was also kind, generous and sensitive – to the surprise not only of the Brontës but also the parishioners of Haworth, who were accustomed to Patrick Brontë's unflagging but nevertheless gruff ministrations. Weightman was clever and articulate too, with interesting, well-thought-out and well-argued views on political, ecclesiastical and literary subjects. But most of all, Willie Weightman had a sense of humour. For the first time within memory the dining room of the parsonage rang with laughter while Aunt Branwell pursed her lips upstairs and Patrick Brontë smoked his clay pipe and digested his dinner across the hall. When, if ever, had they last joked, bantered, hurled facetious epithets and ludicrous nicknames at each other? Haworth Parsonage had been variously a house of death, a house of hunger, a house of study, exertion, and duty, of plans, hopes and dreams. But never, not even when they had all been 'spiritless children', had it been a house of laughter, high spirits or fun.

When Ellen came to visit in February of 1840 the Weightman influence had become pervasive. By then, too, Emily and Charlotte had discovered that Weightman was not as flawless as he first seemed. He was, in fact, fond of making female conquests, and he almost immediately trained his charms on Ellen. The Brontës knew, however, that Weightman was 'attached' to a young lady back in his native Appleby while at the same time he was casting about himself in Haworth for other objects to charm off their feet. Perceiving this fickleness, Charlotte retreated emotionally from the handsome young curate, no doubt with relief, and teasingly demoted him to Miss Celia Amelia.

During Ellen's February visit she was the cynosure of Weightman's attentions, so much so that Emily was deployed to accompany Ellen and Weightman on their walks on the moors, an office that earned her Willie's sobriquet of 'the Major'. 14 February approached while Ellen was still at the parsonage and Weightman was amazed to learn that the Brontë sisters had never received valentines. He immediately set about writing several original specimens addressed to 'Fair Ellen', 'Fond Love', and 'Soul Divine'. He then walked eight miles to Bradford to post them so that Aunt Branwell and Patrick Brontë would not easily guess who the anonymous, amorous sender was.

Shortly after the valentine adventure, Weightman was scheduled to give an evening lecture on the classics at the Keighley Mechanics Institute, and he invited Emily, Charlotte, Anne and Ellen all to attend. Aunt Branwell objected to the lateness of the hour and Patrick Brontë gloomily predicted inclement weather, for there was no means of getting to Keighley in the evening other than by foot. At last, however, the elders grudgingly agreed to the outing when Weightman himself promised to escort his guests to Keighley and back home again. The classics lecture was one of the very few cultural events they had ever attended. After his performance, Weightman was as good as his word: he and another clergyman walked back to Haworth in the moonlight with Charlotte, Emily, Anne and Ellen. On the threshold of the parsonage, Charlotte impulsively invited the young men to come in and warm themselves up. They all sat up past midnight laughing and talking and drinking coffee in the kitchen while up in her room Aunt Branwell fumed over the late-night visitors.

Willie Weightman was not content with captivating only one of Charlotte's friends. When Mary Taylor came for a visit in June, he tried, without success, to enchant her over the chess table. Mary had no need of 'the Major's' protection to keep Weightman at bay. By this time Charlotte had become rather disenchanted with their handsome young curate and warned Ellen not to 'set your heart on him ... he is very fickle.'[6] It seems that the whole time Weightman had been playing court to Ellen, he was carrying on a correspondence with an 'enamorata' in Swansea; and while attempting to charm Mary Taylor, he was dispensing ardent letters and verses to Caroline Dury in Keighley. Charlotte was not exaggerating when she told Ellen that 'he has scattered his impressions far and wide', and is 'a thorough male-flirt ... [who] will never want for troops of victims amongst young ladies.'[7]

In May of 1840 Anne accepted a new governessing position with the family of the Reverend Edmund Robinson at Thorp Green, near York. Anne, then, was prevented from following the complicated amorous career of Weightman, with the result that, in the end, she herself became what Charlotte called one of his 'victims'. When Anne returned home in December for the Christmas holidays, she and Weightman fell in love. Charlotte wrote to Ellen how 'he sits opposite to Anne at church sighing softly and looking out of the corners of his eyes to win her attentions – and Anne is so quiet, her look so downcast – they are a picture.'[8]

Yet to dismiss Willie Weightman as a kind of innocent clerical

Don Juan would be to do him an injustice. He was as energetic in his parish duties as he was in pursuit of love, and he was particularly kind and generous to the old and infirm, the sick and the dying. Anne later drew upon this sensitive side of Weightman's personality for the gentle curate hero, Edward Weston, in her first novel, *Agnes Grey*. No doubt it was Weightman's kindness and generosity as well as his sense of humour which drew him to Emily. He was the only man outside of the family who ever befriended 'the Major'.

Weightman, too, proved a faithful friend to Branwell and a far more beneficial one than the sexton John Brown and Branwell's cronies at the Black Bull. Weightman and Branwell went hunting together and discussed the classics and literature and art. And after Branwell was dismissed from the Postlethwaites in June of 1840, Weightman must have helped him find his feet again. For by the end of August Branwell had found and accepted another appointment – not as an artist or writer or even tutor. Instead, Branwell was to become part of the vanguard of the future by accepting a post as 'Assistant Clerk in Charge' at the newly opened Sowerby Bridge station of the Manchester-Leeds Railway. Sowerby Bridge was just two miles from Halifax. For selling tickets, keeping the accounts and managing the one-room station when the senior clerk was absent, Branwell's salary was £75 per annum, more than three times what his sisters could ever hope to earn as governesses.

Branwell was installed at Sowerby Bridge by early September 1840, at the beginning of the decade of railway fever which swept through Britain and permanently transformed the face and life of the nation. But very little of the glory which the railway brought in its wake came to rest at Sowerby Bridge. Branwell, who had aspired to the Royal Academy, bombarded magazine editors with his verse, painted portraits and translated Horace, had come to this – an assistant clerkship in a tiny provincial railway station. Charlotte did not attempt to hide her disillusionment with Branwell when she wrote to Ellen of his new position: 'A distant relation of mine, one Patrick Boanerges, has set off to seek his fortune in the wild, wandering, adventurous, romantic knight-errant-like capacity of clerk on the Leeds and Manchester Railroad. Leeds and Manchester, where are they?

Cities in a wilderness – like Tadmor, alias Palmyra – are they not?'[9] Eight months later Branwell was transferred to Luddenden Foot station and promoted to 'Clerk in Charge' with a handsome annual salary of £130. But Charlotte remained sceptical. Of this, the only success of her brother's various professional endeavours, she observed with doubt to Emily 'as you say, it *looks* like getting on at any rate.'[10]

Perhaps it was Branwell's dismaying professional descent – from aspiring artist and poet to railway clerk – that motivated Charlotte once again to make a gesture towards their old dream of becoming writers. She had written very little since bidding farewell to Angria, but either she produced a new prose story or reworked an old Angrian piece and sent it off to William Wordsworth, the very poet who had refused to answer any of Branwell's appeals for criticism on his poetry four years earlier. To his credit, Wordsworth did reply to Charlotte's letter and though his response has not survived, he apparently read Charlotte's story with some care. Unlike Robert Southey, Wordsworth did not unequivocally discourage Charlotte from writing. And yet he did not give her positive encouragement either, most likely because he could not tell whether Charlotte – who had signed her letter 'Charles Thunder' – was 'an attorney's clerk or a novel-writing dress-maker'. Charlotte, nevertheless, was grateful for the few crumbs of hope Wordsworth's letter contained and wrote to him, 'I am very obliged to you for your kind and candid letter, and on the whole I wonder you took the trouble to read the demi-serious novelette.'[11]

Emily, meanwhile, still dwelt in Gondal and was deaf to the advice of poet laureates and ageing Romantic poets – if she was aware of such advice. And while her sister was undergoing her solitary creative famine, Emily was producing a vast amount of poetry and prose. Between 1839 and the end of 1841, she wrote upwards of fifty poems and verse fragments which have survived, as well as Gondal prose works which are lost. And many of Emily's poems during this period are among her best. Her method of composition was piecemeal but careful. She would scribble first drafts on any scraps of paper which came to hand, while in the midst of tidying the parlour or peeling potatoes or kneading bread in the kitchen, for her head was often full of phrases of verse, metaphors, images, scenes or Gondal events. In the evenings, after her father and aunt retired, Emily would take out her lap desk and systematically rework and revise the fragments of verse she had jotted down in the course of the day. Sometimes these would evolve into much longer poems, or the scraps of poetry would inspire entirely new works and be dispensed with. The scraps of poems were like the ingredients of the fragrant brown bread or currant-flecked rice pudding she prepared for dinner: some were polished and perfected; others were refined out of recognition, amalgamated with other fragments into something entirely different from their original constituents. By 1844, when a poem was rendered complete she would carefully transcribe it into one of her two wine-red, leather-bound manuscript notebooks. Emily was not only devoting almost all of her spare time to writing, she was also clearly becoming more and more convinced of her vocation as a poet. And this vocation – her sense not only of poetic calling but also of commitment – brought with it a disdain for and rejection of the world beyond Haworth in which her sisters and brother were attempting to find a footing.

In early March 1841 Charlotte secured a position with the family of Mr John White of Upperwood House in the village of Rawdon just six miles from Bradford. Mr White was a wealthy woollen manufacturer and Charlotte's pupils were a girl of eight and a boy of six, 'wild and unbroken' children, Charlotte wrote to Ellen, 'but apparently well disposed.' Her salary was a paltry £20 per annum, £4 of which was deducted for laundry.

On the very same day that Charlotte left home for the Whites, Emily wrote what was to become one of her most famous poems, an explanation, even an apologia, for the life she had chosen and would always remain faithful to:

> Riches I hold in light esteem
> And Love I laugh to scorn
> And lust of Fame was but a dream
> That vanished with the morn –
>
> And if I pray, the only prayer
> That moves my lips for me

Is – 'Leave the heart that now I bear
And give me liberty.'

Yes, as my swift days near their goal
'Tis all that I implore –
Through life and death, a chainless soul
With courage to endure![12]

'A Chainless Soul' articulated a valediction as well as an apologia, and marked a milestone for Emily much as did Charlotte's 'Farewell to Angria'. In her poem Emily was saying goodbye to the affairs of the world, including the 'stern necessity and duty' of earning her own way in it. Even more importantly, she announced her contempt for such absolutes as wealth, love and fame, and her unwavering quest for personal liberty. She had chosen a solitary path for herself that few, if any, would comprehend.

But the rewards of her choice were captured in a characteristic night poem written several months after 'A Chainless Soul'. At night or out on the moors, Emily could undergo trance-like states – provoked perhaps by hunger and fasting – during which she would lose all sense of her individuality and even of her own body. These extraordinarily intense and pleasurable 'spells' were less akin to religious experiences than to the release and exhilaration of sexual communion when the self is merged with a desired presence or being beyond itself.

Aye, there it is! It wakes tonight
Sweet thoughts that will not die
And feeling's fires flash all as bright
As in the years gone by!

And I can tell by thine altered cheek
And by thy kindled gaze
And by the words thou scarce dost speak
How wildly fancy plays.

Yes I could swear that glorious wind
Has swept the world aside,
Has dashed its memory from thy mind
Like foam-bells from the tide –

And thou art now a spirit pouring
Thy presence into all –
The essence of the Tempest's roaring
And of the Tempest's fall –

A universal influence
From thy own influence free;
A principle of life, intense,
Lost to mortality.

Thus truly when that breast is cold
Thy prisoned soul shall rise,
That dungeon mingle with the mould –
The captive with the skies.[13]

In poem after poem Emily thus reaffirmed her position. Her
'chainless soul' could not bear restraint. Charlotte's was a 'prisoned soul', however, at the Whites. She couldn't settle to her
work or reconcile herself to her situation. Her dissatisfaction
wasn't due, as it had been at the Sidgwicks, to a tedious workload
or unfriendly, insensitive treatment. Nor was she merely homesick. Her restlessness, uneasiness and vague but deep discontent
all stemmed from her separation from Emily, a separation which
was as much emotional or psychological as it was geographical.

By the time Charlotte returned home at the end of June for a
three-week holiday, she had already formulated a plan that
would bring Emily back to her and unite them once again.
Rather than going out to teach in private families or schools,
Charlotte decided that she and Emily and Anne should establish
their own school, 'The Miss Brontë's Establishment'. Charlotte
had just missed Anne, who had returned to the Robinsons or, as
Charlotte put it, back 'to the land of Egypt and the house of
bondage', on 30 June. This meant that Charlotte and Emily
were again alone together at the parsonage. Charlotte almost
immediately unveiled her dream that they should open their
own school and never be parted again.

Emily, of course, baulked at the very idea of the Miss Brontës'
Establishment. For Charlotte and Anne it would be liberating
because it would release them from demanding and patronizing
employers. But for Emily it would mean the end of freedom. Yet

Patrick Brontë's birthplace: a two-room cottage in Imdel, County Down, Northern Ireland

Patrick Brontë as a young man

Haworth Parsonage and church drawn by Mrs Gaskell

The parsonage in the time of the Brontës

Aunt Branwell's teapot

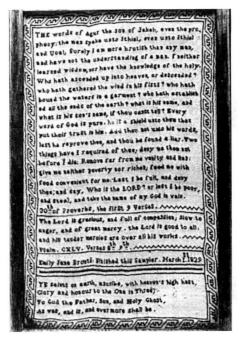

*Sampler painstakingly stitched by Emily Brontë
when she was ten*

Cowan Bridge School in 1824 when the Brontë daughters attended it

The Reverend William Carus Wilson

Ellen Nussey as a girl drawn by Charlotte Brontë

Roe Head School drawn by Charlotte Brontë

Keeper drawn by Emily Brontë

Hero drawn by Emily Brontë

Emily and Anne's June 1837 diary note written by
Emily, who sketched herself from the rear

Law Hill School

The garden of the Pensionnat Heger, Brussels

Constantin Heger in later life

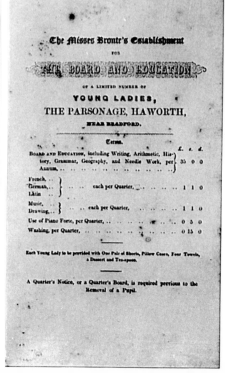

Prospectus for the Misses Brontë's Establishment

Pen-and-ink drawings by Branwell Brontë of
himself which he sent to his friend
J. B. Leyland

Top Withins farmhouse on the moors above Haworth

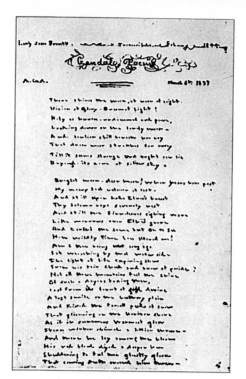

The first page of the Gondal Poems
manuscript book

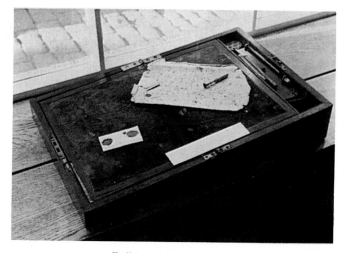

Emily's rosewood writing desk

The 'pillar portrait' of Anne, Emily and Charlotte Brontë by Branwell Brontë

The 'profile portrait' of Emily by Branwell Brontë

The recently discovered 'gun group' photograph of the oil painting by Branwell Brontë (c. 1834), of which only the 'profile portrait' survives

Arthur Bell Nicholls

A photograph of Charlotte Brontë, probably taken during her honeymoon in 1854

Patrick Brontë c. 1856 after the deaths of all his children

to reject the school idea out of hand, Emily knew, would be selfish. And so she and Charlotte debated the matter, back and forth, pro and con, evening after evening after their father and aunt had gone to bed. By the middle of July, Emily had agreed to the idea, and she and Charlotte discussed the matter with Patrick Brontë and Aunt Branwell. Their father offered encouragement and their aunt the even more tangible promise of funds with which to start up their school.

On 19 July Charlotte wrote to Ellen of the scheme as if it were the product of her own and Emily's united mind: 'There is a project hatching in this house, which both Emily and I anxiously [wish] to discuss with you ... to come to the point [it is] ... our, *id est*, Emily, Anne and myself commencing a school.' 'The project', Charlotte told Ellen, 'is yet in its infancy, hardly peeping from its shell', but she went on later in the letter to discuss such practical concerns as whether the £150 they could expect from Aunt Branwell would be adequate 'to establish a respectable ... school and to commence housekeeping' – for theirs would be a boarding establishment, like Miss Wooler's. Charlotte also wondered whether Ellen thought Burlington on the sea might be an advantageous location for their venture.[14]

By Emily's twenty-third birthday, 30 July, Charlotte had returned to the Whites. The extent to which she had won over Emily to the school plan is evident in Emily's 1841 diary paper, in which it is a major theme:

A PAPER to be opened
when Anne is
25 years old,
or my birthday after
if
all be well.
Emily Jane Brontë. July the 30th, 1841.

It is Friday evening, near 9 o'clock – wild rainy weather. I am seated in the dining-room alone, having just concluded tidying our desk boxes, writing this document. Papa is in the parlour – aunt upstairs in her room. She has been reading *Blackwood's Magazine* to papa. Victoria and Adelaide are ensconced in the peat-house. Keeper is in the kitchen – Hero in his cage. We are all stout and hearty, as I hope is the case with Charlotte, Branwell, and Anne, of whom the first is at John White, Esq. Upperwood House, Rawdon; the second is at Luddenden Foot; and the third is, I believe, at Scarborough, inditing perhaps a paper corresponding to this.

A scheme is at present in agitation for setting us up in a school of our own; as yet nothing is determined, but I hope and trust it may go on and prosper and answer our highest expectations. This day four years I wonder whether we shall still be dragging on in our present condition or established to our hearts' content. Time will show.

I guess that at the time appointed for the opening of this paper, we i.e. Charlotte, Anne, and I, shall be all merrily seated in our sitting-room in some pleasant and flourishing seminary, having just gathered in for the midsummer holyday [*sic*]. Our debts will be paid off, and we shall have cash in hand to a considerable amount. Papa, aunt, and Branwell will either have been or be coming to visit us. It will be a fine warm summer evening, very different from this bleak look-out, and Anne and I will perchance slip into the garden for a few minutes to peruse our papers. I hope either this or something better will be the case.

The Gondalians are at present in a threatening state, but there is no open rupture as yet. All the princes and princesses of the Royalty are at the Palace of Instruction. I have a good many books on hand, but I am sorry to say that as usual I make small progress with any. However, I have just made a new regularity paper! and I mean *verb sap* to do great things. And now I must close, sending from far an exhortation, 'Courage, courage,' to exiled and harassed Anne, wishing she was here.[15]

Charlotte had convinced Emily to acquiesce in the school venture, even to hope that it would 'prosper and answer our highest expectations', but the diary paper showed how superficial Emily's commitment really was. Far more vivid than the chimera of the school was Emily's evocation of home life, including the location of all the animal as well as human inhabitants, and a closing report on the unstable political situation in Gondal. And even in the passages devoted to the proposed school, Emily made no mention of pupils or lessons. Instead, she imagined herself and Charlotte and Anne merrily seated in the sitting-room of their 'pleasant and flourishing seminary, having just gathered in for the midsummer holyday' – that is, when all the students had departed for home.

Anne also referred to the school plan in her corresponding diary paper, written at Scarborough, where she had accompanied the Robinsons. But Anne's laconic reference merely reported 'we are thinking of setting up a school of our own, but nothing definite is settled ... yet, and we do not know whether we shall be able to or not.'[16]

Meanwhile, back at the Whites, Charlotte received a letter from Mary Taylor which drastically changed the hopes and plans she had been nursing for the past several months. Mary's younger sister, Martha Taylor, was attending a fashionable young ladies' school in Brussels, and Mary wrote to Charlotte while she and her brother John were visiting Martha. The letter, accompanied by a gift of a beautiful silk scarf and a pair of kid gloves, was full of vivid descriptions of art galleries and cathedrals and continental life in general. Charlotte wrote to Ellen in early August of the intoxicating effect Mary's letter had had on her: 'I hardly know what swelled to my throat as I read her letter – such a vehement impatience of restraint and steady work. Such a strong wish for wings ... such a thirst to see – to know – to learn – something internal seemed to expand boldly for a minute – I was tantalized with the consciousness of faculties unexercised – then all collapsed and I despaired.'[17]

At first Charlotte made no connection between her urgent, passionate 'wish for wings' and the school plan. In this same letter to Ellen, in fact, she said that the 'polar star' of their dream of establishing a school helped rescue her from the despondency into which the vision of Brussels in Mary's letter had plunged her. And their dream seemed within reach when Miss Wooler, who was on the verge of retirement, suggested that the Brontës take over her school at Dewsbury Moor. It was a generous offer and the most sensible course would have been to snap it up immediately. But Miss Wooler's school conjured up painful memories of failure: first Emily and then Anne and finally Charlotte had all broken down at Miss Wooler's. As Charlotte told Ellen, Dewsbury Moor was 'a poisoned place' to her; she 'burned to go somewhere else.'[18]

Mary Taylor, for her part, urged the Brontës to seek further education, particularly in French and perhaps Italian and German and music as well, in order to attract superior, wealthy pupils to their school. Admittedly, there was no way Charlotte and Emily could afford to study at Martha Taylor's school, the Château de Koekelberg, but Mary felt confident there must be a more modest seminary in Brussels where they could pursue advanced studies.

When Charlotte wrote home to Emily of her new plan to go to Belgium before starting their own school, Emily – who had not stirred from Haworth for three years – was naturally dismayed. In her own fantasies of their school, Emily pointedly omitted pupils and teaching, and now Charlotte wanted them to go abroad to become schoolgirls themselves again, schoolgirls in a strange land, amid strangers with a strange religion and language.

Emily argued that they should take up Miss Wooler's offer of Dewsbury Moor, and she also protested that it would be unfair to leave Anne behind at Thorp Green. Charlotte however, over-ruled Emily's objections. 'Grieve not over Dewsbury Moor,' she wrote home to her on 7 November. 'Anne seems omitted in the present plan,' Charlotte conceded, 'but if all goes right I trust she will derive her full share of benefit from it in the end. I exhort all to hope. I believe in my heart this is acting for the best; my only fear is lest others should doubt and be dismayed.'[19]

How could Emily, after the debacle of Roe Head and with sad memories of Law Hill, not doubt and be dismayed? And how could Charlotte contemplate dragging Emily off to Belgium, so far from home, when places as near as Halifax or Bradford were foreign lands to her? Every time Emily left home she became weak and ill. It was only at home that she could be, in her own words, 'stout and hearty'. Cast among strangers, she refused to eat. She also, as far as possible, refused to speak, refused to join any community beyond that of her sisters and brother, and even with them she had become increasingly remote. For much of the past three years Emily had lived alone in a house with two elderly, uncommunicative adults who made few demands on her time and energy and none on her imagination. At the age of twenty-three, she was as engrossed as ever in her childhood fantasy world of Gondal.

Charlotte perceived that Emily's life had gone beyond the limits of reclusiveness and eccentricity to a more dangerous region which might in the end render Emily irretrievable. Charlotte felt she must act now before Emily drifted even further afield, and she probably felt she had a better chance of regaining her in a radically alien environment devoid of all of Emily's familiar associations and props – a faraway place where it would be impossible to collapse and take a coach or a gig back home in one day, where one would be forced to 'stand it'. Charlotte must have realized that she was taking a great risk, but the prospect of not taking the risk – of losing Emily, of losing all hope for the future – was even more frightening.

During the autumn of 1841 letters flew back and forth between Rawdon and Haworth. One by one, Charlotte overcame Emily's objections: Dewsbury Moor wouldn't do; Anne was already settled at the Robinsons at Thorp Green and shouldn't be uprooted just yet, even though she intensely disliked her post. Tabby's health was on the mend, and she would be returning to the parsonage soon; in the meantime, the sexton's young daughter, Martha Brown, could take over most of Emily's chores.

In the end Emily relented, and Charlotte wrote to Aunt Branwell of their new plans. Without their aunt's financial assistance, they would be unable to go to Belgium. Charlotte's appeal to Aunt Branwell was, perhaps, the most carefully argued and diplomatic piece of writing she ever produced. Fully aware of her aunt's parsimonious ways, Charlotte based her arguments mainly on economic considerations. She told her aunt that in order to assure 'permanent success' for their school and raise it above the ordinary, run-of-the-mill young ladies' establishments, she and Emily must acquire educational 'superiority', especially in the form of 'accomplishments' such as music, drawing and, most of all, foreign languages. The bulk of Charlotte's letter, however, was devoted to money matters: it would cost them only £5 or less to travel to Brussels, and 'living is there little more than half as dear as it is in England, and the facilities for education are equal or superior to any other place in Europe.' Charlotte argued that 'if Emily could share' all the advantages of foreign study with her, these advantages 'would turn to vast account' when they opened their own school on 'a footing in the world' which they could never aspire to now if they took over Miss Wooler's school. Charlotte was also at pains to convince Aunt Branwell that if she underwrote their study in Belgium she would be making a sound financial investment. Touching the nerve she knew would provoke a response in her aunt, Charlotte wrote: 'you always like to use your money to the best advantage; you are not fond of making shabby purchases; when you do confer a favour, it is often done in style; and depend on it £50 or £100 thus laid out would be well employed.'[20]

Aunt Branwell was persuaded by Charlotte's letter and agreed to subsidize her two nieces' education in Belgium for six months – the amount of time Charlotte had stipulated. Charlotte, however, wrote privately to Emily that she hoped, even at this early date, to remain abroad for a full year. Either Aunt Branwell would be forthcoming for a second term, or Charlotte and Emily would be able to support themselves by giving lessons in English and music.

Once they had Aunt Branwell's financial backing and their father's consent to study abroad, it remained for them to find a suitable, economical school. For much of the autumn, Charlotte was taken up with a feverish correspondence with various friends and connections who might be able to recommend an appropriate establishment in Brussels.

As it turned out, the Nusseys indirectly knew of the British chaplain in Brussels, the Reverend Evan Jenkins, and suggested that Patrick Brontë apply to him for information concerning schools. At first the Reverend Jenkins, or rather Mrs Jenkins, who took the matter into her own capable hands, could recommend no French school which the Brontës could afford in Brussels, with the result that for a time it looked as if Emily and Charlotte would end up going to a school in France, at Lille, which the Haworth Baptist minister spoke highly of. But in late January Mrs Jenkins reported that she had found what seemed an excellent institution in Brussels, the Pensionnat Heger, *Maison d'Education Pour les Jeunes Demoiselles sous la direction de Madame Heger-Parent, Rue D'Isabelle*.

Charlotte returned home for good from the Whites on 24 December, and even though their destination remained undecided throughout the Christmas holidays and well into January,

Charlotte and Emily began industriously preparing for their departure. Charlotte wrote to Ellen how they had 'lots of chemises – night-gowns – pocket handkerchiefs and pockets to make – besides clothes to repair.'[21]

Once all their sewing was completed and the Pensionnat Heger decided upon, there were travel arrangements to plot out. Patrick Brontë, who at sixty-four had never been abroad, decided to accompany his daughters to Brussels, and while they were stitching night-gowns and handkerchiefs, their father compiled for himself a French phrasebook from Turenne's *New French Manual*. He copied out large extracts from it into a small, leather-bound notebook, on the first page of which he wrote, 'The following conversational terms, suited to a Traveller in France, or any part of the continent of Europe ... must be fully mastered and ready ... and kept ... There are first the French [phrases] – 2 – the right pronunciation – and lastly the English.' Nineteen pages of the notebook were carefully filled in by Patrick Brontë under such headings as 'Of the Mind', 'Of Food', 'Spices', 'Dessert and drink', 'Numerals', 'Days and Months', and 'French coins'.[22] It is not surprising that with his own dyspepsia and his daughters' erratic appetites, food loomed large in Patrick Brontë's little homemade French dictionary.

Just a week before their scheduled departure, Charlotte gave Emily the Book of Common Prayer, on the fly-leaf of which she inscribed: 'Emily Jane Brontë from her sister C. Brontë. Feb. 1sr 1842'. Apparently Emily did not already possess a prayer book, a fact not unrelated, perhaps, to her infrequent attendance at church. The gift of the Book of Common Prayer was in the nature of a covenant Charlotte wished to create between them – a promise that all would go well and be well for them in this world – in Brussels – as well as in the next.

On Tuesday, 8 February 1842, a chill, grey, frosty day, everyone rose early in the parsonage. Emily had packed her box the night before. She had probably scarcely slept at all and must have been too anxious to do more than perfunctorily touch her breakfast. The hired gig arrived at Church Lane as dawn was breaking. Aunt Branwell stood in the parsonage doorway, wrapped up in her heavy shawl, as they loaded the boxes into the gig. Then Emily and Charlotte, in their long woollen capes and black bonnets, entered, followed by their father in his equally dark clerical garb. They may have looked as if they were setting off for a funeral, but in fact they were bound for a new world, a new land, a new life.

The gig jolted off down the cobblestones of Main Street, and when they reached the bottom of the steep hill, Emily may not have had the heart to turn around and look back up at the clock tower of St Michael's and the grey stone parsonage above it on the edge of the barren, midwinter moors. The cart horse clopped along at a brisk pace; their train was scheduled to depart from Leeds at nine a.m. and arrive in London – where neither Emily nor Charlotte had ever set foot – at eight p.m. that evening.

· 8 ·

Brussels

London, 1842. Implacable February weather. Euston Square Station teeming with passengers arriving and departing, jostling one another, impatiently shouting for their boxes and trunks to be unloaded or wedged into already bursting train carriages. The high, vaulted arches of the station – suggesting a Gothic cathedral more than this terminus of a new technology – resounded with the tumult. The open entranceway let in the fog and din of hansom cabs and carriages outside. Gas lamps bathed the scene in a peculiar, lurid light, especially for the small band of Yorkshire travellers who alighted from the Leeds train shortly before ten at night, two hours late: Patrick Brontë, his two eldest daughters and Mary Taylor and her brother Joe who had joined the Brontës at Leeds and were to travel with them on to Brussels.

They threaded their way through the crowded, cold gloom of Euston Square and found a cab out on the street to convey them to the only inn which Patrick Brontë knew of – the Chapter Coffee House, where Branwell had stayed during his abortive Royal Academy adventure. Located on Paternoster Row, on the fringe of 'the City', the Chapter Coffee House was a small, unobtrusive, unremarkable establishment, once the convivial meeting place of such eighteenth-century men of letters as the poor, doomed boy poet Chatterton, Oliver Goldsmith, James Boswell and Dr Johnson. But by the time Patrick Brontë came to frequent it during his university days, the Chapter Coffee House had been reduced to the insignificant preserve of provincial clergymen visiting London on church business.

Emily and Charlotte glimpsed little of London on the way to the inn, and then they found themselves installed with Mary in a low-ceilinged room at the top of the house. It was only when they were settled in bed, exhausted but too excited to sleep, that they felt they had really arrived: 'a deep, low, mighty tone swung through the night', not once, nor twice, nor three times, but twelve echoing tollings altogether. It was midnight and Emily and Charlotte in their attic room 'lay in the shadow of St Paul's'. The next morning they were up with the dawn and, pulling back the curtains, saw by the early morning light, 'co-elevate almost with the clouds … [the] solemn, orbed mass, dark-blue and dim – THE DOME.' As soon as they had breakfasted, the Brontës and Taylors hastened to climb the great dome, and from its summit Emily and Charlotte gazed for the first time on the mighty spectacle of London below, 'with its river, and its bridges and its churches … antique Westminster and the green Temple Gardens with the sun upon them and a glad, blue sky.'[1]

They had three full days in London before the Ostend packet sailed to Belgium, and that first morning they gave themselves up to 'the heart of city life', following the Strand to Fleet Street, from where so much of what they knew of the world emanated in the newspapers they devoured in faraway Haworth. Haworth now seemed a life-time rather than twenty-four hours away as they made their way to Cornhill and the parks and squares of the West End and finally on to Pall Mall, St James's and Buckingham Palace.

After this first day of random roaming, Charlotte decided that for the remainder of their stay they must systematically lay siege to all the galleries and museums she had been dreaming of since childhood. Hours were spent at the Royal Academy, National Gallery, Royal Institute Galleries and all the treasures of the British Museum – especially the Elgin Marbles and the Egyptian Rooms. Charlotte organized these expeditions, but Emily, as always, had her own quixotic reactions and would wander off from the others to contemplate less well-known works or to look at celebrated masterpieces from a different vantage point in the galleries. In a museum, surrounded by mute, unresponsive works of art which nevertheless sounded one's depths of feeling and thought, Emily could be at ease, even at home. It was the crowds and noise and bewildering congestion of living, breathing, walking, pushing, carriage or cab riding humanity out on the streets which unnerved her.

But she left all this behind her when they boarded the Ostend packet at London Bridge wharf shortly before dawn on Saturday, 12 February. The fourteen-hour crossing was not a smooth one; by the time they reached Margate, Charlotte had discovered that her love of the sea was best indulged in on land. But while Charlotte succumbed to sea sickness and retreated to the cabin, Emily remained on deck, transfixed by the turbulent waters, undisturbed by the cold mist and dousings of spray when waves crashed against the ship's side. With her back to the deck, gazing directly before her, Emily saw Cowper's desolate sea and the perilous ocean of Coleridge's Ancient Mariner.

She was dismayed, however, by the flat, monochrome landscape they passed through on the 'diligence' or stage coach which conveyed them from Ostend to Brussels. For Charlotte, Belgium was the 'promised land'; she invested it with all her passionate dreams, desires and aspirations. Its physical appearance did not signify; it could have been as hot and barren as the Sahara or a frozen polar wasteland; 'nothing could look vapid to [her] ... all was beautiful, all was more than picturesque.'[2]

Looking out of the coach window during the day-long journey from Ostend to Brussels, Emily did not possess her sister's rose-hued vision. She saw the Belgian terrain for what it was: domesticated, tilled, flat, carved-up and cultivated. Every field, every fence post, every clod of earth bore the impress of man and the banishment of Nature: it was all 'bare, flat, and treeless ... slimy canals crept, like half-torpid green snakes, beside the road; and formal pollard willows edged level fields, tilled like kitchen garden beds.'[3] For Emily, the Belgian landscape seemed like a formal drawing room, cluttered with heavy, carved mahogany furniture, embroidered cushions, dark velvet curtains, every surface covered with crocheted antimacassars, china figurines, ivory fans and painted, gilt-framed miniatures. To live in Belgium would feel like being shut up indoors, confined to the house by illness or a blizzard, severed from the world of untilled moors and trees twisted with age and bowed by gales outdoors.

Towards evening they arrived at the main gate of Brussels, the Porte de Flandres. It was raining and cold, and they decided to spend the night in a hotel. The next morning Mary and Joe Taylor left for their sister Martha's school, the Château de Koekelberg, where Mary was to enroll as well, while Mr and Mrs Jenkins escorted the Brontës through the unfamiliar, twisting, narrow streets of Brussels to the Rue d'Isabelle and the Pensionnat Heger. The house dated back only to the beginning of the century, but the street itself, sunk some feet below the surrounding thoroughfares, so that one descended to it by a flight of stairs, was much older. It had been named after the Infanta Isabella when the Spanish governors of the Netherlands occupied Brussels. The design of the Heger Pensionnat differed from that of most English schools. The front of the house ran right alongside the edge of the Rue d'Isabelle without so much as a foot of garden and only a small ribbon of pavement for one or two pedestrians to take refuge from passing carts and carriages.

But once across the threshold all the noise and ceaseless movement of the city was shut out. The Pensionnat was a spacious, airy house, with marble-tiled floors and heavy double doors leading to large, well-lit school rooms, a refectory, an oratory and two drawing rooms. On the first floor were the Hegers' own domestic apartments and a long dormitory with twenty beds for the pupils who boarded at the school.

The Pensionnat was a self-contained, peaceful, efficiently run establishment which looked inward rather than out to the city life of the Rue d'Isabelle and beyond. For opposite the main entrance doors and across the large reception hall, where a portress embroidered or knitted in a small room, was another set of doors which opened out on to a beautiful garden, a garden so large that it might almost have been called a meadow or small wood set down in the midst of the city. Great pear and orange trees, grape arbours, lilacs and laburnums, rose bushes, and countless other trees and shrubs and flowers flourished here, many of them unfamiliar and exotic to Emily's and Charlotte's English eyes. Benches were strategically placed almost as if they, too, had taken root and sprung from the earth, and white cinder paths wove gracefully around trees, bushes and flowerbeds.

The Pensionnat garden – even on the chilly February day when the Brontës first saw it – was the inner sanctum of the school. Surrounded on all four sides by other houses, it was entirely cut off, like a fortress, from the din and dirt and noisy humanity of city life. It was a preserve of peace and beauty where students and teachers strolled, played games, talked, read, dozed and dreamt.

And yet there was something disturbing and discordant about this Eden. It all seemed so very natural and yet it was all so very artful. It was a product of horticultural ingenuity and calculation and required vigilant care and upkeep. And opposite to the doors which opened out on to the garden, on the further side of the garden, was a blank stone wall higher than the garden wall and incompletely covered with trees and creepers. This was the rear of the most prestigious boys' school in Brussels, the Athénée Royal. There was a narrow, shady walkway in between the Pensionnat garden wall and the Athénée Royal which could be observed from the top-floor windows of the boys' school, but this path was only accessible from the door which led to it in the Pensionnat garden wall. The 'demoiselles' of the Pensionnat were prohibited from entering this secluded avenue with its canopy of arching tree boughs, because if they had strolled there, they could have been observed by male eyes peeping out from the Athénée's top-floor windows. Hence the name given to the for-bidden walkway, the 'Allée Défendue'. But it was unlikely that any of the demoiselles would be tempted to loiter there, for legend had it that the ghost of a white-veiled, black-robed nun frequented the *allée* after nightfall. This spectre may have had its origin in the fact that the founder of the school had been an aunt of Madame Heger, a nun whose convent had been destroyed during the French Revolution and who had then settled in the Rue d'Isabelle and established her 'maison d'éducation' for young ladies, among whose early pupils was the displaced nun's own niece, Claire Zoë Parent.

Charlotte loved the Pensionnat and its garden at first sight, but Emily did not. For Emily all the carefully cultivated rose bushes and artfully pruned hedges in the world could not conceal the fact that the Pensionnat garden was – in addition to being a playground, open-air classroom and retreat – a prison. A prison within a prison. This, the first real journey of Emily's life, had carried her through the carved-up, manured, canal-fed fields of Belgium to the narrow, winding streets of Brussels, and then to the fortress of the Pensionnat Heger and finally to its internal 'place de détention', the garden: a real Palace of Instruction. There were no subterranean dungeons at the Pensionnat Heger, but its secure, maintained garden, high walls and the bolted door leading to the Allée Défendue all amounted to the same thing.

The portress of the school admitted the Brontës and Jenkinses and then hurried off to notify the headmistress, Madame Claire Zoë Heger, of the new arrivals. The Brontës knew very little about Madame Heger other than the fact that, unlike most English schoolmistresses, she was married. Her husband, Constantin Georges Romain Heger, was in fact a professor of French and mathematics at the neighbouring boys' school, and he also instructed his wife's pupils in rhetoric and French literature. Zoë Heger was a very handsome woman in her late thirties who, as the Brontës all took in at a glance, was eight months pregnant. Not only was Madame Heger beautiful, intelligent, poised, articulate and seemingly warm-hearted, she was also the first woman Emily and Charlotte had come into close contact with who possessed a sexual and maternal life. This was not Zoë Heger's first pregnancy; she already had three little girls upon whom she lavished care and attention and love as unstintingly as she did on her husband, while at the same time running a school of more than fifty pupils.

Zoë Heger exuded amplitude, ripeness and contentment as a wife, mother, teacher and headmistress. She actually taught very little – mainly catechism to the younger girls – but she ran her school meticulously, efficiently and, it seemed, effortlessly. Everything at the Pensionnat – the instruction, study periods, lessons, recreation periods, religious observance, food, clothing, sleeping quarters – was geared towards the students' comfort, health and happiness as much as to their intellectual development. But, like the garden, the pleasant atmosphere of the Pensionnat was not a natural phenomenon. The school was like a well-oiled machine, carefully kept in optimal working order just as the garden was ceaselessly weeded and pruned and manured. And the operator of this machine, who was familiar with every last cog and wheel in the running of it, was Madame Heger. With a careless air she glided about in velvet slippers so that the inmates were often unaware of her presence behind the door, outside the classroom, seated in a secluded bench in the garden. But she was aware of everything: no detail, no whispered confidence, no incoming or outgoing letters escaped her notice.

It would take Emily and Charlotte some time to fathom her depths, but Zoë Heger no doubt sized them up in a glance. In contrast to her other pupils – almost all of them Belgian, Catholic, well-to-do young girls of the upper and upper-middle classes – Emily and Charlotte must have appeared queer, even pathetic beings in their dark, unfashionable dresses. As they all stood in the large *carré* or entrance hall while the Jenkinses made the necessary introductions, Zoë Heger might have assessed these new additions to her school in much the same light as another Brontë acquaintance described them at about the same period: 'distant and distrait, large of nose, small of figure ... prominent of spectacles [referring to Charlotte] ; showing great intellectual development, but with eyes constantly cast down, very silent, painfully retiring.'[4]

On their day of arrival Charlotte and Emily may have seemed equally ill at ease, gauche and shy to Madame Heger and her pupils, but within a few days or weeks it became apparent that they differed sharply in their tolerance of and reaction to school life at the Pensionnat. Charlotte soon blossomed and throve like one of the rose bushes in the Pensionnat garden, while Emily became steadily more remote, inaccessible, silent and, in time, physically frail. Even in her own happiness, Charlotte couldn't ignore Emily's eccentric behaviour and imperviousness to influence, though once Charlotte saw that Emily wasn't going to collapse immediately, as she had at Roe Head, she did her best to minimize to herself and others the trial Emily was enduring day in and day out at the Hegers'.

Emily chafed, of course, under the school routine, however lax it might seem compared to that of a British seminary. It was not a Spartan regimen at the Pensionnat Heger. Lessons commenced at nine in the morning, following a hearty breakfast, and continued till noon. Late in the morning the girls sometimes glimpsed Madame through the classroom doors, still in her dressing gown and slippers, gliding past in the hall. After a well-cooked, ample dinner at mid-day, there were lessons for another two hours in the afternoon. In the evening, another study hour followed tea and a 'lecture pieuse' from which Emily and Charlotte, as Protestants, were exempted.

With this undemanding schedule there were plenty of free hours in the day. Yet, perversely, both Emily and Charlotte devoted almost all their spare time to extra lessons, additional reading, yet more study. But not, significantly, to their own writing, for virtually no poetry survives from their time in Brussels.

It wasn't until May, when the large, lush school garden was coming to life again after its winter-long suspension, that Charlotte wrote Ellen a full account of how she and Emily were getting on in Brussels:

> I was twenty-six years old a week or two since and at this ripe time of life I am a schoolgirl, a complete schoolgirl, and, on the whole, very happy in that capacity. It felt very strange at first to submit to authority instead of exercising it – to obey orders instead of giving them, but I like that state of things. I returned to it with the same avidity that a cow, that has long been kept on dry hay, returns to fresh grass. Don't laugh at my simile. It is natural in me to submit, and very unnatural to command. This is a large school, in which there are forty externes or day-pupils and twelve pensionnairs or boarders . . . There are three teachers in the school . . . No less than seven masters attend to teach different branches of education – French, Drawing, Music, Singing, Writing, Arithmetic and German. All in the house are Catholics, except ourselves, one other girl and the 'gouvernante' of Madame's children, an Englishwoman in rank something between a lady's maid and nursery governess . . . We are completely isolated in the midst of numbers, yet I think I am never unhappy; my present life is so congenial to my own nature compared with that of a governess. My time, constantly occupied, passes too rapidly.[5]

Soon Charlotte's greatest source of happiness at the Pensionnat, and also one of the most important reasons for Emily's discontent, were the French lessons they received from Madame's husband, Constantin Heger, a man, Charlotte described to Ellen, 'of power as to mind, but very choleric and irritable as to temperament; a little, black ugly being, with a face that varies in expression. Sometimes he borrows the lineaments of an insane tom-cat, sometimes those of a delirious hyena; occasionally, but very seldom, he discards these perilous attractions and assumes an air not above 100 degrees removed from mild and gentlemanlike.' Constantin Heger was a gifted teacher, quick to spot his pupils' talents and aware of how best to cultivate and nurture them. But he was also a taskmaster, inflexible, highly irritable and erratic. Not surprisingly, as Charlotte confided to Ellen, 'Emily and he don't draw well together at all.'[6]

Between Emily and Heger, in fact, a battle of wills was sustained during the whole of Emily's stay abroad. They clashed at the very first lesson over Heger's method of instruction. Instead of commencing with a thorough grounding in French grammar and vocabulary and working up to the complexities of composition, Heger adopted a new, unorthodox plan with the Brontës. He would read an extract from a celebrated French author and proceed to goad his pupils into analysing its merits and shortcomings. Then he would assign them a topic and require them to write an essay or *devoir* in a similar vein and style to the one they had dissected together. Of course, Heger had no idea that Emily and Charlotte had been writing poems and tales and essays from the time they could first hold a pen, nor did he know they had long since passed through the stage of imitative or derivative composition and found their own distinct voices. Charlotte acquiesced to Heger's method of teaching because she felt 'bound to obey him while she was his pupil'. But Emily protested: she 'said she saw no good to be derived from it; and that by adopting it, they should lose all originality of thought and expression.'[7]

And so the pattern was set for their sojourn in Brussels: Emily, as far as possible, rebelled while Charlotte almost too eagerly 'submitted' and 'obeyed'. With the *devoirs* Heger had his way, but the tension between him and Emily remained charged, despite her production of the required *devoirs*. Though Heger was fully aware that their mother had died while they were still small children, in an early assignment he asked Emily and Charlotte to compose a letter home to their 'chère Maman', informing her of their welfare and progress at school. Heger mercilessly corrected and annotated Emily's 'lettre' and severely condemned its lack of warmth and affection for her non-existent mother.

Emily's other essays, however, not only impressed but also unsettled Heger. Charlotte was true to both the spirit and letter of his assignments and dutifully produced uninspired imitations of the model essays Heger had read to them. Emily, however, abided by the set rules of the exercise while shocking her schoolmaster with the pessimistic and misanthropic content of the essays. In 'Le Chat' Emily praised cats because they are similar to humans – ungrateful, hypocritical and cruel – and concluded with the unsavoury image of a cat with a half-swallowed tail of a rat hanging from its mouth. She further castigated mankind in 'L'Amour Filial' for 'baseness', 'blindness' and 'infernal ingratitude'. In 'Le Papillon' and 'Le Palais de Mort' the diatribe continued. What we call 'civilization' is only intemperance and degradation; Nature is 'a vast machine constructed only to bring forth evil'.

Though marred by grammatical errors, for her command of French was inferior to Charlotte's, Emily's *devoirs* astounded Heger. He was impressed most of all by the daring and originality of mind they revealed, and years later he told Mrs Gaskell that Emily would have been 'a great navigator ... her strong imperious will would never have been daunted by opposition or difficulty, never have given way but with life.' Emily had, he said, 'a head for logic, and a capability of argument unusual in a man and rare indeed in a woman ... [but] impairing this gift was her stubborn tenacity of will which rendered her obtuse to all reasoning where her own wishes, or her own sense of right, was concerned.' Emily was also, according to Heger, 'egotistical and exacting', and exercised 'a kind of unconscious tyranny' over Charlotte.[8]

Emily's tyranny over Charlotte may not have been as unconscious as Heger thought. It is possible that Charlotte's eager submission to Heger and her fascination with him elicited not only Emily's scorn but also her jealousy. For as long as she could remember, Emily had been the most important person in Charlotte's life. Now she saw the ugly, dark, choleric Heger threatening to supplant her. Jealousy is often 'unconscious', but tyranny seldom is. One of the forms it took at the Pensionnat was that Emily defied Charlotte's 'maître' as far as she could short of a flat refusal to do what was asked of her. Emily also effectively cut off Charlotte from everyone else in the school with her anti-social behaviour.

In Brussels Emily was not merely aloof and silent, she was openly hostile to almost everything and everyone at the Pensionnat, and she acted as an insuperable barrier to Charlotte's participation in school life. Emily, herself, made only one friend at the Pensionnat, a much younger Belgian girl named Louise de Bassompierre, to whom Emily gave a signed drawing of a tree.[9] During lessons Emily made Charlotte sit with her in the furthest corner of the very last row of desks, as far removed as possible from the other pupils. Out in the garden, Emily clung to and leaned on her sister as they strolled the cinder paths – a strange, dependent posture considering that Emily was both taller and stronger than Charlotte. If anyone approached them and attempted to converse, Charlotte replied as briefly and swiftly as possible. Emily was scarcely ever heard to utter a syllable, except when some thoughtless girl rebuked her for her rudeness or criticized her strange-leg-of-mutton sleeves and lank skirts, and Emily lashed out with 'I wish to be as God made me.' Even in the long dormitory with its neat rows of iron bedsteads, Emily continued to monopolize Charlotte, for their beds were at the end of the long room and separated off from the others by a white curtain.

Emily isolated Charlotte at the Pensionnat and provoked conflict within Charlotte between her sense of loyalty to and love for Emily and her growing currents of warm feeling for Heger. But Emily could not clip her sister's wings entirely and prevent her from having contact with anyone else, especially with those outside school. They visited Mary and Martha Taylor at their school at Koekelberg on the outskirts of the city fairly regularly, and seemed to the Taylor sisters in every way their old selves. Mary confidently reported back to Ellen Nussey in England that 'Charlotte and Emily are well; not only in health but in mind and hope. They are quite content with their present position.'[10] On other outings, however, Emily successfully cast a pall of silent anti-sociability. When Mary and Martha took Charlotte and Emily to their cousins the Dixons for tea, Emily remained completely silent the whole evening, while Charlotte spoke, hesitantly and almost inaudibly, only when directly addressed.

Even worse, however, were the Sunday outings Emily and Charlotte made to the home of the Reverend Evan Jenkins, whose wife had placed them at the Pensionnat Heger. It was only during her stay in Brussels that Emily attended church regularly, possibly because it gave her the opportunity to escape from the school for a few hours. She and Charlotte attended the service at the Chapel Royal in the Place de Musée, the only Protestant place of worship in Brussels, where Mr Jenkins preached in English. After church they would return to the Pensionnat, eat the mid-day meal, and then await the arrival of the two Jenkins sons, John and Edward, who escorted them, in unbroken, strained silence, to their parents' home a good hour's walk away on the Chaussée d'Ixelles. Once they were settled in the Jenkinses' parlour, with tea and cakes laid out before them, matters did not improve. Mr and Mrs Jenkins would float innocuous, polite questions, or make benign observations on the weather, to little avail. 'Emily hardly ever uttered more than a monosyllable. Charlotte was sometimes excited sufficiently to speak eloquently and well – on certain subjects; but before her tongue was thus loosened, she had a habit of gradually wheeling round on her chair, so almost to conceal her face from the person to whom she was speaking.'[11] The cakes remained untouched; the tea grew tepid in their cups. The Jenkins sons soon protested against their tedious, time-consuming walks to and from the Pensionnat, and even their well-meaning and kind parents grew weary of the blank, silent mask Emily presented to them, and conversing with the side or back of Charlotte's head. In order to relieve them all of these painful occasions, in the end Mrs Jenkins ceased pressing her invitations on Emily and Charlotte.

In July, Madame Heger, the mother now of a baby boy named Prospère, born the previous March, proposed to Charlotte that she and Emily remain on for another half-year at the Pensionnat, but on a different footing. She suggested that Charlotte should take over the duties of an unsatisfactory English master Madame Heger was eager to dispose of, and that Emily, who was by this time studying piano under the finest teacher in Brussels, give instruction in music to the Pensionnat pupils. No salaries were offered, but in return for their services Charlotte and Emily would be allowed to continue their studies in French and German and also receive free accommodation and board. This arrangement was precisely what Charlotte had hoped for in order to extend their time abroad, and she probably didn't stop to ponder the astute economy of Madame Heger's proposal. Emily's reaction to it can be easily imagined. At the least, she must have felt dismayed and trapped. Yet reporting this new development of remaining on as teachers to Ellen Nussey, Charlotte wrote that 'Emily is making rapid progress in French, German, Music and Drawing – Monsieur and Madame Heger begin to recognize the valuable points of her character under her singularities.'[12] Emily was, however eccentrically and miserably, 'standing it' in Brussels. And in the end she agreed to stay on with Charlotte and endure the additional trial of having to teach as well as learn – to 'work like a horse', as Charlotte bluntly put it.

Inevitably, Emily's grudging acquiescence brought its own toll down on both Emily herself and Charlotte. In July, five English girls enrolled at the Pensionnat as day pupils. Their father, Dr Thomas Wheelwright, was a British doctor who had come to the Continent because of failing eyesight and financial embarrassment at home. (It was much easier, then, to live economically abroad than in England, and many families who had fallen on bad days went to Europe in an effort to recoup their losses or at least keep their heads above water.) Along with another English pupil, Maria Miller, the Wheelwright girls naturally tried to befriend Emily and Charlotte. Charlotte yearned to respond, but Emily held Charlotte fast in her possessive grip, and as far as possible prevented her from associating with the Wheelwrights by making herself unpleasant to them and undetachable from her sister. The eldest Wheelwright daughter, Laetitia, later explained their antipathy to Emily and how they wanted to invite Charlotte home for tea or to accompany them on excursions, but desisted because they knew Emily would veto all invitations, or, worse still, come along with Charlotte and ruin the occasion.

Of Emily, Laetitia later said, 'I simply disliked her from the first, her tallish, ungainly ill-dressed figure contrasting so strongly with Charlotte's small, neat, trim person ... always answering our jokes with "I wish to be as God made me." '[13] The Wheelwrights found Emily untidy, arrogant and rude, and were incensed at the way she seemed to bully Charlotte. And their dislike of her was exacerbated when Emily began to give piano lessons to the three youngest Wheelwright girls, Frances, Sarah and Julia. Emily insisted upon holding the lessons during the recreation period because she refused to give up any of her own study time to them. And so the three little girls had to remain indoors at the piano, submitting to Emily's exacting instruction, while their playmates ran about and played ball and picked flowers out in the garden.

What Emily had to bear in Brussels was every bit as painful and even dangerous as her sufferings had been seven years earlier at Roe Head. Charlotte, indeed, constantly feared that she would lose the great gamble she had taken by coercing Emily into coming abroad with her. It was only years later, in her biographical Preface to Emily's poems, that Charlotte at last described what happened to her sister at the Pensionnat Heger. Comparing Emily's time in Brussels to the trauma of Roe Head, Charlotte wrote: 'after the age of twenty, having meantime studied alone with diligence and perseverance, she went with me to an establishment on the Continent: the same suffering and conflict ensued ... Once more she seemed sinking, but this time she rallied through mere force of resolution: with inward remorse and shame she looked back to her former failure and resolved to conquer in this second ordeal. She did conquer: but the victory cost her dear. She was never happy till she carried her hard-won knowledge back to the remote English village, the old parsonage-house, and desolate Yorkshire hills.'[14]

Charlotte's retrospective account was compelling yet vague, but from her statement that in Brussels 'the same suffering and conflict ensued' which had plagued Emily and finally driven her from Roe Head on the verge of collapse, we can imagine what happened to her in Belgium. Once again Emily's 'health was broken', 'her white face, attenuated form and failing strength threatened rapid decline.' Laetitia Wheelwright described Emily as 'thin and sallow'; Louise de Bassompierre said she was 'very pale and thin'.[15] Emily couldn't or wouldn't eat; she grew weak and ill, was unable to concentrate or sleep properly. Yet in Belgium Emily's unhappiness and anger were not exclusively self-directed and self-inflicted. She projected them outwards as well and punished Charlotte and everyone else who came within her sphere with hostility and contempt.

The cast of mind and intelligence which Emily possessed were not malleable, not vulnerable or even amenable to outside influence and instruction. Emily could, with the aid of a few books, generate her own education; she entirely lacked Charlotte's need for external direction and approbation. Virtually everything Emily learned in her life – with the exception of needlework, at which she was never adept – was self-taught and acquired through solitary labour and inspiration at home – not at Cowan Bridge, Roe Head or Brussels. There was a kind of inviolate self-sufficiency about Emily in all things, including her intellectual development. She simply didn't require the outside stimulation, systematic instruction and praise that others need in order to learn. In fact, she suffered when exposed to any of these things, felt threatened, even violated. Hence her protests to Heger over his method of teaching French. In a late poem, Emily articulated her fierce independence of mind and heart:

> I'll walk where my own nature would be leading:
> It vexes me to choose another guide.[16]

Emily 'worked like a horse' at Brussels to prove a point – that she could stand it away from home, however miserably and at whatever cost. But she also studied relentlessly for the same reason that she restricted her life so severely and in so many small and large ways – by refusing to have anything to do with almost everyone she met and lived among in Belgium, by reducing the amount of food she would eat and probably her hours of sleep as well. Since she was exiled from what Charlotte described as her 'unrestricted and inartificial mode of life' at Haworth, Emily – at sea in a foreign and, to her, a wholly unattractive, hostile environment, far, far away from home – badly needed, once again, a sense that she had some sort of control over her life. And this fragile illusion of control she created by means of the driven, rigid and narrow existence she carved out for herself at the Pensionnat Heger: a life of denial and emptiness and self-deprivation.

Even when the long vacation began in mid-August, Emily and Charlotte remained bent over their books. The Hegers and their four small children went to the sea for a holiday, and all the boarding pupils returned to their homes. But Charlotte and Emily were not left entirely alone, because the five Wheelwright daughters spent the holiday at the Pensionnat while their parents made a trip up the Rhine. Given their aversion to Emily, the situation in the echoing halls and empty classrooms of the Pensionnat must have been awkward and unpleasant. While the Wheelwright girls kept their distance, Emily and Charlotte applied themselves to their German and French lessons. Their world remained confined to the Pensionnat Heger. The galleries, museums, cathedrals and boulevards of Brussels were still unexplored countries to them. The only holiday-like thing they allowed themselves was to read and write their lessons outdoors in the garden, under the expansive, drooping pear trees. At night, however, as they lay in the dark in their beds in the nearly empty long dormitory, Brussels was borne in to them through the windows opened to the warm evening breezes. They would hear the bells of Sainte Gudule striking the hours only two streets away and the music of band concerts held in the moonlight in the many large squares and parks in the city.

When the summer holiday ended, and the Hegers and their pupils returned, refreshed and ruddy-cheeked from their outdoor holidays, they found Charlotte much as they had left her and just as anxious and protective of Emily. Emily, herself, was, if possible, even more inaccessible and silent, and also strikingly pale and thin in contrast to the robust good health of all the returning students. The vacation had given her a partial reprieve, despite the presence of the Wheelwright daughters. But now with the reinstatement of the school routine and in the midst of all the boisterous Belgian pupils, Emily's reserves of physical strength and psychological stamina were depleted. Looking helplessly on at Emily's deterioration, Charlotte was torn over what to do.

As it turned out, she did not have to take any decisive action in order to save Emily. Events, a grim kind of Providence, overtook them instead. Just as all the vines and trees and flowers in the Pensionnat garden began to wither and autumn closed in with its blighting spell, death once again broke into Emily's and Charlotte's lives like a thief, robbing Charlotte of a foreseeable future while delivering Emily from an unendurable present.

In mid-September they received news from home that William Weightman – bonny Willie who had sent them valentines, lectured eloquently on the classics, assisted Patrick Brontë and his son in health and illness and succoured the poor and sick in the parish – had died on 6 September of cholera at the age of twenty-eight. It had been a miserable end following several weeks of incessant vomiting, dysentery, agonizing stomach cramps, fever and delirium. Patrick Brontë preached the funeral sermon on 2 October, rather understating his curate's gifts: 'His character wore well, the surest proof of real worth. He had, it is true, some peculiar advantages. Agreeable in person and manner, and constitutionally cheerful, his first introduction was prepossessing. But what he gained at first he did not lose afterwards.'[17]

Less than two weeks later Martha Taylor, Mary's younger sister at the Château de Koekelberg, also died of cholera after a similar harrowing period of acute illness.[18] Emily and Charlotte did not hear of Martha's condition until the day before she died. They rushed to their friends on 13 October only to learn that she had died in the night, at the age of twenty-three. She was buried in the Protestant Cemetery in Brussels and on Sunday, 30 October, Emily and Charlotte and Mary walked six miles to the cemetery to visit Martha's grave and leave some late autumn flowers on it. It was a gloomy, dark day, with storm clouds hovering low in the sky. As they walked back in the evening bolts of lightning irradiated the sky. On their return, they went to the Taylors' cousins, the Dixons' house, and spent the evening there, during which, Mary reported to Ellen Nussey, Emily uttered not a single word and Charlotte only one or two.

Death again seemed all around them – back at home where they were accustomed to its constant presence, and now it had followed them abroad as well and extinguished the youngest and liveliest of them all, Martha Taylor. But Martha wasn't the last. Just three days after their pilgrimage to her grave, Emily and Charlotte received news that Aunt Branwell was gravely ill. They immediately began to prepare to go home – conferring with the Hegers, packing their boxes and arranging their passages. But the next day, 3 November, they received another letter – this one with a thick black border around its edges – announcing that their aunt had died of 'internal obstruction' on 29 October, the day before they had visited Martha's grave. The exact cause of Aunt Branwell's death was unclear, but it was due to some sort of ailment of her digestive system – perhaps stomach or intestinal cancer. Its connection with food and eating would not have been lost on the Brontës, and her sufferings had been every bit as protracted and painful as those of Weightman and Martha Taylor. The funeral took place on 3 November, the day Charlotte and Emily had first had word of their aunt's illness. On Sunday, the 6th, they sailed home on the steam packet from Antwerp.

· 9 ·

Gondal Regained

When Emily and Charlotte finally reached Haworth on the evening of 8 November the parsonage seemed not only a house of death to them, but also a house of confusion, even chaos. Like an Egyptian pharoah, Aunt Branwell appeared to have taken her household gods of order, economy and punctuality to the grave with her. The family servant, Martha Brown, the sexton's young daughter, had merely been a domestic puppet in Aunt Branwell's hands, carrying out all the household chores under her close and exacting supervision. Now that Martha was spared the daily barrage of orders and commands, she scarcely knew how to manage. The household was like a ship without a captain or a rudder. Patrick Brontë, like other Victorian patriarchs, had never concerned himself with domestic matters and now wondered why his dinner tray did not appear precisely on the stroke of two in his study and why, when it did arrive, the joint was tough and the custard runny. The coal store dwindled; no preserves or pickles had been 'put up' while Aunt Branwell lay dying in her room upstairs. Dust accumulated in the unused dining room across from Patrick Brontë's study. A season of discontent and discomfort, as well as bereavement, pervaded the house, a season which struck Emily and Charlotte on their return even more forcefully than the bitter cold of the Yorkshire winter setting in.

Other developments, of which they'd been kept in ignorance while in Brussels, took them by surprise. Emily was dismayed to find out that during her absence Aunt Branwell had disposed of her pet geese and also her merlin hawk, Hero. The geese no doubt had long since found their way into someone's cooking pot – perhaps even into one at the parsonage – but Emily made every effort to recover Hero, scouring the countryside and asking those she met on the moors and at the farms she called at for news of the hawk, but to no avail.

Emily grieved for her lost pets, but she and Charlotte were dumbfounded by the presence of Branwell at home. Neither their father nor their aunt had written to them in Brussels of Branwell's latest disgrace. The previous March, just a month after they had gone to Belgium, Branwell had been dismissed from his well-paid job as clerk of the Luddenden Foot railway station on charges of gross negligence and mismanagement. The station's account books were hopelessly awry and copiously embellished with sketches, fragments of verse and caricatures. More seriously, £11 was missing from the till. Branwell's porter was the actual embezzler, but he had made off with the money while Branwell was at a nearby pub. Branwell's career as an obscure scion of the railway had failed as dismally as all his other endeavours. But this time failure was tainted by dishonesty and it was this which hardened Charlotte's heart against her brother and led in time to their complete estrangement. Not even the fact that Branwell had somehow pulled himself together and tenderly nursed both Willie Weightman and Aunt Branwell through their last illnesses could redeem him in Charlotte's eyes. In contrast, Emily's feelings for Branwell warmed the further he fell from grace. Emily's heart, usually so inaccessible and impenetrable, instinctively went out to the maimed, ill, dispossessed, poor, and all who had failed, whether unjustly or through their own fault like Branwell. Emily had, after all, rescued her hawk when his wings were so badly wounded that he could never fly again, and she named him, significantly, Hero.

Anne, too, was at home from her post as a governess at Thorp Green and so for the first time in nearly a year the entire family was reunited again at the parsonage. But each of them seemed cut off from the others in some way, absorbed by their own thoughts, concerns, hopes and sorrows. Anne was deeply unhappy with the Robinson family at Thorp Green, but she could not bring herself to complain to her sisters. Branwell was still smarting from his dismissal from Luddenden Foot and exhausted and grief-stricken by the illnesses and deaths of his close friend and aunt. Patrick Brontë also felt bereft and lost without his sister-in-law who had so conscientiously raised his children, run the household and read to him on many a long evening when the two were alone in the house. Now he was perplexed as to how to get the parsonage domestic machinery back in working order: fires laid in the grate, linen ironed, food procured from the village and transformed into meals served at predictable times. For her part, Charlotte was already yearning to go back to Brussels, and trying to calculate whether and when she might return.

Only Emily was at ease and contented during the early winter months of 1842 and in 1843. She was, at last, back home (and home for good, she vowed to herself, if not to the others). And home meant freedom, liberty for her 'chainless soul'. Emily, in fact, could look forward to more freedom than she had ever, perhaps, thought possible. With Aunt gone and Anne and Charlotte planning to return to Thorp Green and Brussels, Emily would be left alone at the parsonage with her father, for it was soon arranged that Branwell would make one more attempt to earn his own living by accompanying Anne back to Thorp Green to become the tutor of the Robinsons' son, Edmund. The exodus of her sisters and brother meant that the household would be left entirely in Emily's capable hands. She would be in complete control of her life and environment, in possession not merely of a room of her own, but a whole house to manage, cook, eat, sleep, live and, most of all, write in.

November and December passed quickly for Emily. Charlotte visited Ellen Nussey at Brookroyd for a week at the end of November. Anne went back to Thorp Green and most likely settled the matter of Branwell's employment before returning to Haworth again for the Christmas holidays. Emily meanwhile summoned Tabby back from her two-year exile at her sister's cottage in the village. This was one of Emily's first acts as the new mistress of the house. To her, Tabby was like one of the family, and now that there was no longer the impediment of Aunt Branwell to keep Tabby away, she returned to the parsonage and despite her infirmities helped out in the kitchen and with the lighter housework. Christmas itself passed quietly, as it always had in the parsonage, though Emily and Tabby must have prepared some special holiday treats like Christmas pudding, seed cake and treacle tarts. By early January, Charlotte reported to Ellen that on this holiday fare she had become 'as solid as a large dumpling.'[1]

Three days after Christmas, on 28 December, Aunt Branwell's will was 'proved' in the Prerogative Court at York in the presence of Patrick Brontë, who was one of the executors:

Depending on the Father, Son and Holy Ghost for peace here and glory and bliss forever hereafter, I leave this my last Will and Testament: Should I die at Haworth, I request that my remains may be deposited in the church in that place as near as convenient to the remains of my dear sister; I moreover will that all my just debts and funeral expenses be paid out of my property, and that my funeral shall be conducted in a moderate and decent manner. My Indian workbox I leave to my niece, Charlotte Brontë; my workbox with a china top I leave to my niece, Emily Jane Brontë, together with my ivory fan; my Japan dressing box I leave to my nephew, Patrick Branwell Brontë; to my niece Anne Brontë, I leave my watch with all that belongs to it; as also my eye-glass and its chain, my rings, silver spoons, books, clothes, etc., etc., I leave to be divided between my above-named three nieces, Charlotte Brontë, Emily Jane Brontë, and Anne Brontë, according as their father shall think proper. And I will that all the money that shall remain, including twenty-five pounds sterling, being the part of the proceeds of the sale of my goods which belong to me in consequence of my having advanced to my sister Kingston the sum of twenty-five pounds in lieu of her share of the proceeds of my goods aforesaid, and deposited in the bank of Bolitho Sons and Co., Esqrs., of Chiandower, near Penzance, after the aforesaid sums and articles shall have been paid and deducted, shall be put into some safe bank or lent on good landed security, and there left to accumulate for the sole benefit of my four nieces, Charlotte Brontë, Emily Jane Brontë, Anne Brontë, and Elizabeth Jane Kingston; and this sum or sums, and whatever other property I may have, shall be equally divided between them when the youngest of them then living shall have arrived at the age of twenty-one years. And should any one or more of these my four nieces die, her or their parts shall be equally divided amongst the survivors; and if but one is left, all shall go to that one: And should they all die before the age of twenty-one years, all their parts shall be given to my sister, Anne Kingston; and should she die before

that time specified, I will that all that was to have been hers shall
be equally divided between all the surviving children of my dear
brother and sisters. I appoint my brother-in-law, the Rev. P.
Brontë, A.B., now Incumbent of Haworth, Yorkshire, the Rev.
John Fennell, now Incumbent of Cross Stone, near Halifax; the
Rev. Theodore Dury, Rector of Keighley, Yorkshire; and Mr
George Taylor of Stanbury, in the chapelry of Haworth aforesaid,
my executors. Written by me, ELIZABETH BRANWELL, and
signed, sealed and delivered on the 30th of April, in the year of
our Lord, one thousand eight hundred and thirty-three[2]

The contents of Aunt Branwell's will came as a surprise to no
one. Branwell's exclusion from it, except for the strange bequest
of the Japan dressing box, reflected neither his aunt's feelings for
him nor his recent irresponsible behaviour. Aunt Branwell had
made out her will nine years earlier, in 1833, when Branwell's
prospects seemed golden and his opportunities to earn a comfortable living assured. But as a spinster herself, Aunt Branwell knew
all too well that the prospects and opportunities of her four nieces
(including Elizabeth Jane Kingston, the daughter of another
Branwell sister) were limited and bleak. Hence she divided her
total assets among them equally, leaving each a legacy of approxi-
mately £350.

During the Christmas holidays, Emily and Charlotte and
Anne discussed what to do with their new wealth; each was now
in possession of a sum nearly twice their father's annual income.
They agreed they should invest the money, but it was left to
the 'unworldly' Emily to decide where and how to do this.
Accordingly, Emily studied the financial pages of the newspapers
carefully and after closely following the fluctuations of various
commodities on the market, threw their lot in with the contemporary railway fever by buying shares for her sisters and
herself in the York and North Midland Railway Company. It
was a bold, if considered, gamble. Emily was taking a risk with
the railway shares, whose prices were soaring, but risk-taking
was in character for her. If Charlotte hadn't been in such a hurry
to return to Brussels, she and Emily might have argued over the
railway shares. But in the event, Charlotte and Anne handed
over their legacies to what they trusted was Emily's good judgement and hoped for the best. Emily was in control, not merely

of the house, but also of their finances. Her liberty now seemed complete.

Anne and Branwell were the first to leave in early January. Then Charlotte conferred with her father about returning to Brussels and showed – or rather read to him, for Patrick Brontë's eyesight was failing – a letter from Constantin Heger which Charlotte had brought home with her. Dated 5 November, the day before Emily and Charlotte left Belgium, Heger's letter contained warm praise for Emily's and Charlotte's progress at the Pensionnat, and urged their father to allow both or, failing that, at least one of them to return to Brussels to teach and continue their studies in French and German.

> You will no doubt learn with pleasure [Heger wrote] that your daughters have made very remarkable progress in all branches of teaching, and that this progress is entirely owing to their love of work and their perseverance ... In a year each of your daughters would have been quite prepared for any eventuality of the future; each of them while receiving instruction was at the same time acquiring the science of teaching. Miss Emily was learning the piano, receiving lessons from the best professor in Belgium, and she herself already had little pupils. She was losing whatever remained of ignorance, and also of what was worse – timidity. Miss Charlotte was beginning to give lessons in French and to acquire that assurance, that aplomb, so necessary to a teacher. Only another year and the work would have been completed and well completed. Then we should have been able ... to offer to your daughters, or at least to one of them, a position according to her taste and that pleasant independence so difficult for a young person to find.[3]

M. Heger's letter was both generous and encouraging, and Patrick Brontë was soon won over by Heger's proposal and Charlotte's strong desire to go back to Brussels, especially when Emily made it clear that she wanted to remain at home and manage the household. Furthermore, Charlotte was going to go back to the Pensionnat as a teacher rather than a pupil, albeit at the meagre salary of £16 per annum, minus ten francs a month for her German lessons and five francs for laundry.

Charlotte departed for Belgium on 27 January and initially all went well for her back in Brussels. Both Madame and Monsieur Heger welcomed her back 'with great kindness', as Charlotte wrote to Ellen. They urged her to take her meals with them and also to spend the evenings in their private sitting room. But only rarely did Charlotte take up these standing invitations, feeling she would be an intruder in their domestic midst, knowing, too, perhaps that seeing M. Heger surrounded by his happy family would cause her a nameless kind of pain. Soon what brought her the most pleasure were the private English lessons she began to give M. Heger and his brother-in-law, lessons during which Charlotte was 'maître' to her master. If Charlotte shrank from Madame, she relished the intimacy of her hours of instruction with M. Heger.

In the beginning of her second year in Belgium, Charlotte also enjoyed the social freedom which Emily's presence had severely curtailed the year before. Mary Taylor had gone to study at a new school in Germany after her sister's death, but there was still a pleasant circle of English friends to associate with in Brussels. Charlotte began to visit the Wheelwright family regularly at their home in the Rue Royale and became particularly close to Laetitia. She saw something, too, of the Taylor cousins, the Dixons. Mr and Mrs Jenkins renewed their weekly invitations to Sunday tea, and without Emily, these soon became enjoyable occasions. Charlotte also began to venture out into Brussels and visited galleries, museums, churches and parks.

Emily, too, was thriving back in Haworth with her father. She was in charge of her life again, and since she now had the power to shape her own existence, she no longer felt the need to control the size of her body. She cooked with Tabby in the kitchen and prepared delicacies for her father's fastidious appetite. She ate them as well and only failed to become 'solid as ... a dumpling' because of her rigorous hikes out on the moors.

But the clearest indication of Emily's wellbeing were the poems she wrote at the dining table or kitchen table during 1843 after the creative fast of all the months abroad. Almost half of this outpouring of verse was explicitly Gondal poetry, indicating that Emily had returned not only to Haworth, but to the home of her imagination as well. And yet perhaps the dominance of Gondal in her post-Brussels poetry disclosed more than return – something closer, in fact, to retreat.

Haworth was merely across the English Channel from Belgium. Gondal was on the other side of the world. While Charlotte was instructing a roomful of surly Belgian girls, and commanding their attention despite her low, hesitant voice and small stature, Emily, at the age of twenty-four, was dwelling in the fantastic, imaginative realm of her childhood. Scarcely a week after Charlotte left, Emily completed a long narrative poem entitled 'Written in Aspin Castle', swiftly followed on 24 February by 'On the Fall of Zalona'. Other Gondal poems were given cryptic titles which refer to one or more of its large cast of characters: 'To A.S.', 'E.G. to M.R.', 'Roderic Lesley' – suggesting that Emily was also producing now lost Gondal prose at the same time as the poems. The whole vast machinery of Gondal, in fact, appears to have been resurrected by Emily in the opening months of 1843, replete with wars, love affairs, imprisonment, betrayal and death.

Only one of Emily's poems written during this period seemed connected with or a reflection of her own experience, including the recent past in Brussels. Like so many of her personal lyrics, it was a night poem which opened with a celebration of the moon:

> How clear she shines! How quietly
> I lie beneath her silver light
> While Heaven and Earth are whispering me,
> 'Tomorrow wake, but dream tonight.'

She longed to escape from the 'Dark World' or 'Grim World',

> Where pleasure still will lead to wrong,
> And helpless Reason warn in vain
> And truth is weak and Treachery strong
> And joy the shortest path to Pain.

> And Peace the lethargy of grief
> And Hope, a phantom of the soul;
> And Life a labour void and brief
> And death, the despot of the whole![4]

'How clear she shines', with its harsh bitterness and despair, echoed the cynical, nihilistic essays Emily had produced for M.

Heger. Emily's education in Brussels had not been so much a matter of German, French and music lessons, but instead a growing conviction of the hollowness, deceit, injustice and meaninglessness that lay at the very heart of the 'world without'. Was it the conventionality and triviality of school life that had instructed her so, or the books – Voltaire and Goethe, perhaps – she had read, or was it her own morose ruminations, that had brought home this vision of the fundamental worthlessness of all human effort and endeavour? However she became infected with this dismal, paralysing vision, Emily refused to equate it with Byronic melancholy. Another poem of 1843 opens with 'Hope was but a timid friend' and closes with:

> Hope – whose whisper would have given
> Balm to all the frenzied pain –
> Stretched her wings and soared to heaven.
> Went – and ne'er returned again![5]

Yet life still had to go on in the 'world without' as well as the 'world within' of Gondal, and, alone at home with her father, Emily was responsible for its going on smoothly. Besides remaining in charge of the kitchen, she had to do all the heavier housework that Tabby was too old or rusty in the joints to handle. A village washerwoman did the laundry in the back kitchen, but Emily ironed everything – clothes, sheets and pillowcases, table linen and her father's yards-long cravats – herself. She became adept at combining these mundane chores with her studies. She kept up her French and German lessons while kneading the bread dough, waiting for the cakes to brown in the oven, ironing sheets or sweeping the stone-flagged entrance hall. While her hands were mechanically occupied, she could conjugate German verbs, mentally translate English poems she knew by heart into French, memorize vocabulary in both languages. All this she did by day, living on two planes, the domestic and the intellectual, simultaneously. Poetry was for the night, when the day's chores were completed and the splintered being who had performed them became one again. Then thought, emotion and action were fused as Emily wrote alone in the silent house.

Her life was almost too perfect now, and Emily felt guilty about her freedom and 'idleness' at home, as she wrote to Charlotte in

Brussels. To which Charlotte retorted: '*You* call yourself idle! absurd, absurd!'[6] And in truth it was absurd for Emily to feel herself lax and unoccupied at home. For on top of the housework, she had to tend to her father, who was by this time becoming increasingly restricted by his failing eyesight. Patrick Brontë was now confined to the house, for most of the day immured in his study, unable to write or read any of the books on his shelves. Fortunately he could still preach every Sunday, for he had long done so without the aid of a written text or even notes, standing at the pulpit, facing the congregation (a blurred mass of humanity to him now) and delivering an eloquent extempore sermon that precisely filled up the allotted time.

It was only on Sundays that Patrick Brontë got out and was active. Inevitably, depression enshrouded the rest of the week for him as he sat alone in his study. Emily did all she could to relieve her father from his morose solitude and immobility. She spent a good deal of the afternoons reading to him. After evening tea, she played the piano in his study, especially his favourites, Beethoven, Mozart and Haydn. It was sometimes difficult for the old man to accept his daughter's attentions; his pride or vanity was wounded just as surely as his eyes were afflicted. Nevertheless, a strong bond grew up between them during this period when they were at home alone together, a bond born of Patrick Brontë's increasing dependence on Emily, but one that was sustained by a very real and deep – if undemonstrative – affection.

It was at this time, too, that Patrick Brontë began to teach Emily how to shoot. He still insisted upon personally discharging his loaded pistol each morning, even at the risk of hitting one of his flock crossing the churchyard rather than the tower of St Michael and All Angels. But he would be helpless in the face of a more challenging or dangerous moving target, and so he decided that Emily must be taught how to handle his revolver. Emily's shooting lessons were observed and recorded by John Greenwood, the village stationer, who supplied the Brontës with their writing materials. Greenwood kept a diary, and in its pages he recorded what he saw and heard of the reclusive inhabitants of the parsonage, who clearly intrigued him. Emily, above all, fascinated Greenwood, and he confided to his diary how one day he encountered her on the verge of Haworth moor, just beyond the village. She was returning from one of her long walks, her cheeks flushed with exertion, her manner unusually open and free after the exhilaration of her hike. Emily returned Greenwood's greeting heartily and it seemed to him that her 'countenance was lit up with divine light'.

Given Greenwood's adoration of Emily, his account of her shooting lessons with her father was perhaps idealized:

Mr Brontë ... took a very great pleasure in shooting ... He had such unbounded confidence in his daughter Emily, knowing as he did, her unparalleled intrepidity and firmness, that he resolved to learn her to shoot too. They used to practice with pistols. Let her be ever so busy in her domestic duties, whether in the kitchen baking bread ... or at her ironing, or at her studies, raped [sic] in a world of her own creating – it mattered not; if he called upon her to take a lesson, she would put all down; his tender and affectionate 'Now my dear girl, let me see how well you can shoot today' was irresistable ... and her most winning and musical voice would be heard to ring through the house in response, 'Yes Papa' and away she would run with such a hearty good will taking the board to him and tripping ... to the bottom of the garden, putting it in its proper position, then returning to ... take the pistol which he had previously primed and loaded for her. 'Now my girl,' he would say, 'take time, be steady.' 'Yes Papa' she would say taking the weapon with as firm a hand and as steady an eye as any veteran of the camp and fire. Then she would run to fetch the board for him to see how she had succeeded. And she did get so proficient that she was rarely far from the mark. His 'how cleverly you have done, my dear girl,' was all she cared for ... She would return to him the pistol, saying 'load again Papa' and away she would go to the kitchen, roll another shelf-full of tea cakes, then wiping her hands, she would return again to the garden, and call out 'I'm ready again Papa,' and so they would go on until he thought she had had enough practice for that day. 'Oh,' he would exclaim, 'she is a brave and noble girl. She is my right hand.'[7]

John Greenwood was one of the few villagers who had direct contact with the Brontës, but even his knowledge was limited. Thus when Patrick Brontë's eyesight began to fail, very few knew of his affliction, and, like most people who have handicaps suddenly descend on them, Patrick Brontë did his best to conceal his condition. But his abandonment of his parish rounds and the way he cloistered himself in the parsonage all week aroused first comment and then rumour. People began to talk of how he groped his way down to the church pulpit each Sunday and took Emily's arm when he returned home after the service. And then there seemed to be a strange odour about him that people in the aisle pews scented as he passed. Could it be that their minister, formerly so upright and commanding, had taken to drink?

When the rumours of drunkenness finally reached the parsonage, as they were bound to do, Patrick Brontë was enraged. It was too much to bear on top of his own suffering over his eyesight, and in his distress he turned to John Greenwood, who may have been the one who informed him of the gossip circulating in the village. In a letter dated 4 October 1843, Patrick Brontë wrote to Greenwood: 'Since you and Mrs Greenwood called on me on a particular occasion, I have been particularly and more than ever guarded. Yet notwithstanding all I have done, they keep propagating false reports. I mean to single out one or two of these slanderers, and to prosecute them, as the law directs. I have lately been using a lotion for my eyes, which are very weak, and they have ascribed the smell of that to a smell of a more exceptionable character. These things are hard, but perhaps under Providence I may live to overcome them all.'[8]

During 1843 Emily and Charlotte wrote to each other as often as time and money allowed (postage between Haworth and Brussels was 1s. 6d., enough to make a dent in their pocket money). Emily's side of their correspondence is lost and so we can't know with certainty how much 'home news' she relayed to Charlotte. But it is unlikely that she dwelt on her father's encroaching blindness and depression, or even mentioned the humiliating rumours that he had taken to drink. Increasingly, as the months of late winter and early spring passed in Brussels, Charlotte needed Emily's bulletins of security back in Haworth.

By early March Charlotte began to perceive a change in the Hegers' treatment of her. She had found her English lessons with M. Heger so exhilarating and his praise for her teaching and encouragement of her studies in French and German so gratifying that Madame Heger had receded into the background of her field of vision. At the same time, however, Madame Heger's always eagle eye was trained with particular intensity on Charlotte. Not that Madame was the least bit jealous of the plain, timid English governess or doubted that her husband's attentions to her were motivated by anything other than benevolence tinged perhaps by pity. But the situation threatened to become uncomfortable and unpleasant. Charlotte, Madame saw with perfect clarity, was in love with her husband. Heger, for his part, was probably only aware that Charlotte admired, doted on and was awed by him – all very satisfying to his male vanity. Besides Charlotte herself, only Madame and very likely Emily – strange allies in their penetration of the situation – perceived what was developing and where it could lead. Above all, Madame Heger wanted to avert, at any price, an indecorous confrontation or scene. Nothing must mar the calm, even tenor of life at the Pensionnat. Even more, nothing must cast the faintest shadow on the domestic harmony and happiness of her family.

And so Claire Zoë Heger decided to 'deal' with Charlotte by using a strategy of benign neglect. The best way of nipping this potentially explosive problem in the bud was by frustrating and isolating Charlotte, subtly and discreetly, by slow, escalating degrees, so that M. Heger would scarcely notice that he was seeing less and less of the little *anglaise*. Accordingly, the invitations to join the Hegers in the evenings tapered off and then ceased altogether. So, too, did the high points of Charlotte's week – her English lessons with Heger. Madame, without a hint of reproach, merely pointed out to her husband that the English lessons took up precious time that might be better spent on his students or his children. Now, perhaps, Charlotte missed Emily's possessive 'tyranny', which had been easier to bear than this new isolation. And yet Charlotte considered her situation better than Mary Taylor's in her new school in Germany, because, as Charlotte told Ellen, Mary 'has nobody to be as good to her as M. Heger is to me; to lend her books, to converse with her sometimes.'[9]

The conversations and loans of books from Heger, however, became less and less frequent. As Charlotte wrote to Ellen in April, 'I never exchange a word with any other man than Monsieur Heger and seldom indeed with him.'[10] A month later she told Branwell: 'I rarely speak to Monsieur now.'[11] But it was only to Emily that Charlotte confided fully about the Hegers' neglect, of her estrangement from Monsieur and her suspicions of Madame. For Charlotte rightly held Madame responsible for her husband's aloofness, though it took her some time to comprehend Zoë Heger's motives. In late May Charlotte wrote to Emily: 'Of late days, M. and Mde Heger rarely speak to me ... You are not to suppose ... that I am under the influence of *warm* affection for Mde Heger. I am convinced that she does not like me – why, I can't tell, nor do I think she herself has any definite reason for the aversion ... M. Heger is wondrously influenced by Madame, and I should not wonder if he disapproves very much my unamiable want of sociability. He has already given me a brief lecture on universal "bienveillance," and perceiving that I don't improve in consequence I fancy he has taken to considering me as a person to be let alone – left to the errors of her ways; and consequently he has in a great measure withdrawn the light of his countenance, and I get on from day to day in a Robinson-Crusoe-like-condition – very lonely.'[12]

As the long summer vacation approached, Charlotte became increasingly apprehensive and distraught. Both the Wheelwrights and the Dixons had left Brussels. The Hegers and their pupils would all depart again for the holidays. As if Charlotte's cup weren't already bitter enough, when it came time to bid farewell to the Hegers, Charlotte realized that Madame Heger was pregnant again. The cosy family circle from which she felt banished was enlarging. By mid-August Charlotte was alone in the Pensionnat except for one other teacher, Mademoiselle Blanche, who, Charlotte wrote to Emily, was 'a regular spy of Madame Heger,' and of a 'character ... so false and so contemptible I can't force myself to associate with her.'[13]

Within days, even hours, of the departure of the Hegers and the students, Charlotte's breakdown became inevitable. She wrote of this soul-withering time in one of the most faithfully autobiographical passages in her novel *Villette*, when the heroine Lucy Snowe describes 'that vacation! Shall I ever forget it? ... My heart almost died within me; miserable longings strained its chords. How long were the September days! How silent, how lifeless! How vast and void seemed the desolate premises. How gloomy the forsaken garden – grey now with dust.' A desolate, barren landscape existed now within Charlotte as well as in the parched, hot garden of the Pensionnat. 'When I had ... to look on life as life must be looked on by such as me, I found it but a hopeless desert: tawny sands, with no green field, no palm trees, no well in view.'[14]

Charlotte wandered the classrooms and the garden of the Pensionnat; she found the key to the Allée Défendue and spent hours pacing its gloomy track back and forth, back and forth. She lost 'all power and inclination to swallow a meal'; 'sleep went quite away. I used to rise in the night, look round for her, beseech her earnestly to return.' The empty, desolate Pensionnat became an insupportable prison. Weak as she was for want of food and sleep, Charlotte began to leave the Rue d'Isabelle each morning to walk the streets and suburbs and surrounding countryside of Brussels all day, yearning for distraction or at least exhaustion which would enable her to sleep at night.

Utterly alone in Brussels, Charlotte was poised 'to pitch head-long down an abyss'. And in her extremity she sought out and desperately confided or 'confessed' the anguish which was over-whelming her to the nearest thing to a psychiatrist at that time – a Roman Catholic priest. Charlotte, in fact, made a double confession: to the priest and to Emily, to whom she gave a detailed account of what she had done.

Writing to Emily on 2 September, Charlotte explained how 'I should inevitably fall into the gulf of low spirits if I stayed always by myself here without a human being to speak to, so I go out and traverse the Boulevards and streets ... sometimes for hours ... Yesterday I went on a pilgrimage to the cemetery, and far beyond it on to a hill where there was nothing but fields as far as the horizon. When I came back it was evening; but I had such a repugnance to return to the house, which contained nothing that I cared for, I still kept threading the streets in the neighbourhood of the Rue d'Isabelle and avoiding it.'

Passing the Cathedral of Sainte Gudule several blocks from the Pensionnat, Charlotte paused to listen to the familiar tolling bells of the evening *salut*. And then, propelled by a force which seemed to come from outside herself, which bore no connection with conscious thought or impulse, Charlotte entered the cathedral for the first time. It was dusk; myriads of candles illuminated the altar; a soothing, incense-laden hush pervaded the church. Charlotte had developed a great antipathy towards Roman Catholicism during her time in Brussels and heartily condemned what she called the 'humbug', and 'mummeries' and 'idiotic idolatry' of 'Papistry'. And yet here, in Sainte Gudule, for the first time in weeks she felt some measure of peace and relief. She stayed for vespers and prayed her own Protestant prayers, but, as she wrote to Emily, 'still I could not leave the church or force myself to go home – to school I mean.'

Instead Charlotte watched several people at the confessionals, and longed for the solace and absolution they received by kneeling and murmuring their secret fears and guilts to the priest on the other side of the confessional grating. She felt as if her heart would burst if she did not do the same, and so, after the last penitent left, Charlotte walked down the aisle and knelt in the niche of the confessional. The wooden door inside the grating opened and she could dimly see the profile of the priest as he bent his ear towards her. But at this critical moment, Charlotte was mute; she didn't know the fixed formula with which one began confession and after some moments of strained silence, she finally was able to get out the words that she was a Protestant, only to have the priest reply that she could not, in that case, 'jouir du bonheur de la confesse'. But as she wrote to Emily, 'I was determined to confess … I actually did confess – a real confession.' The priest acquiesced in the end because, as he told her, he hoped that her confession might be the first step of her return to 'the true church'. Charlotte ended her letter to Emily by asking her not to tell their father of what she had done, and reassuring her that she was not 'going to turn Catholic' or ever enter the church or see the priest again.[15]

The great mystery of Charlotte's account of her confession to the priest in Sainte Gudule was what she actually said to the priest. Did she not tell Emily what she had whispered through the grating because Emily already knew? And if so, was this shared knowledge that Charlotte was in love with a married man and so wracked with guilt that she was driven to confess her illicit love?

Charlotte did have what a Catholic priest would have judged a sin or crime in her heart, but whether she disclosed it in the box-like confessional in Sainte Gudule on 1 September 1843 we shall never know. That her 'real confession' did her scant good and yielded little solace, however, we can see from her letters and actions in the weeks and months following it. The real poignancy of the situation lay in the fact that it was not a moral or religious crisis that Charlotte was suffering, but an emotional or psychological one. And Emily with her highly unorthodox vision of love – of its destructive, obsessive passion and existence outside of marriage – would have instinctively grasped this.

By the time Charlotte left Sainte Gudule it was dark. She hastened back to the Pensionnat and was relieved to find that she was too late for dinner with Mademoiselle Blanche. She wasn't hungry anyway, and so she went directly to bed in the long empty dormitory. The row of white curtained beds looked like tombs in the darkness. Charlotte lay awake listening through the long night to the bells of Sainte Gudule as they struck the hours.

Several weeks after Charlotte's confession, the Hegers – Madame far advanced now in her pregnancy – and students returned to embark on the new academic year. The Hegers soon proved, if possible, more aloof than ever, and slowly it dawned on Charlotte what lay behind this coolness and distance. She wrote to Ellen of Madame Heger's total indifference to her on weekends and holidays, when all the other pupils went out visiting or to enjoy themselves in the city. Charlotte remained behind, wandering 'from room to room' until 'the silence and loneliness of all the house' weighed down her 'spirits like lead ... I fancy I begin to perceive the reason of this mighty distance and reserve', she wrote to Ellen; 'it sometimes makes me laugh, and at other times nearly cry.'[16] Charlotte had finally realized that Madame was doing her utmost to separate her from her husband. But Charlotte's perception of Madame's motives was probably not entirely accurate beyond this. She no doubt suspected Madame was jealous of Monsieur's attentions to her – the loan and gifts of books, the intimate English and French lessons, the praise he bestowed on Charlotte for her progress in her studies and her teaching. But Zoë Heger was perturbed by none of these things. What disturbed her was Charlotte's behaviour and the consequences to all of them if her infatuation with M. Heger went unchecked. The only way to control it in the short run was to keep the two of them apart. But beyond this strategy was her plan to make Charlotte so miserable at school that she would resign and go back to England.

As early as 1 October, Charlotte was already considering this course of action herself and broached it in a letter to Emily written on a dismal Sunday morning when, once again, she was left on her own while all the other inmates of the house were 'at their idolatrous "messe"'. The letter was permeated with Charlotte's gnawing homesickness as she imagined all the goings-on at the parsonage: 'I should like uncommonly to be in the dining room at home, or in the kitchen, or in the back kitchen. I should like ... to be cutting up hash', with Emily 'standing by, watching that I put enough flour, and not too much pepper, and above all, that I save the best pieces of the leg of mutton for Tiger and Keeper, the first of which personages would be jumping about the dish and carving knife, and the latter standing like a devouring flame on the kitchen floor. To complete the picture, Tabby blowing the fire in order to boil the potatoes to a sort of vegetable glue. How divine are these recollections to me at this moment.' She closed her letter to Emily with 'Write to me again soon. Tell me whether papa really wants me very much to come home and whether you do likewise.'[17] Charlotte yearned, in fact, for a summons from home. 'Otherwise,' as Emily wrote in a note to Ellen Nussey, Charlotte 'may vegetate [in Brussels] till the age of Methuselah for mere lack of courage to face the voyage.'[18] Mary Taylor as well as Emily urged Charlotte to leave, and only a week or so after the letter to Emily, Charlotte did in fact muster the courage to give notice to Madame Heger, who, of course, promptly accepted the resignation with, one imagines, a great sigh of relief. But according to Charlotte, when Madame conveyed the information to her husband 'Monsieur Heger ... sent for me ... and pronounced with vehemence his decision that I should not leave.'[19]

Charlotte gave in to her 'maître' immediately. Yet nothing changed. She remained as isolated and lonely and homesick as ever. Only a day or two after Monsieur's 'vehement' directive that Charlotte should remain at the Pensionnat, Charlotte scrawled on the fly-leaf of her *General Atlas of Modern Geography*:

Brussels, Saturday morning. Oct. 14th 1843. First Class. I am
very cold – there is no Fire – I wish I were at home with Papa –
Branwell – Emily – Anne & Tabby – I am tired of being among
foreigners – it is a dreary life – especially as there is only one
person in this house worthy of being liked – also another who
seems a rosy sugar plum but I know her to be coloured chalk.[20]

It was Heger, of course, who was the only worthy human
being in the house. Madame, blooming in late pregnancy, looked
'good enough to eat' but was in reality like an artificial sweet –
the kind displayed in confectionery shop windows to attract
customers, which if tasted turn out to be made of coloured chalk:
dry, bitter and completely inedible.

Not even Queen Victoria's visit to Brussels that autumn could
alleviate Charlotte's depression, staunch monarchist though she
was. Emily, however, was eager, as always, for news of the Queen
and so Charlotte dutifully but unenthusiastically reported the
advent of the royal family, describing the Queen in particularly
in a very prosaic way: 'You ask about Queen Victoria's visit to
Brussels. I saw her for an instant flashing through the Rue Royale
in a carriage and six, surrounded by soldiers ... She looked a
little stout, vivacious lady, very plainly dressed, not much dignity
or pretension about her.'[21]

On 15 November Madame Heger gave birth to her fifth child,
a little girl who was named Victorine. The baby's very name, as
well as her arrival, must have galled Charlotte, for by this time
she felt herself cruelly persecuted by Madame. In Charlotte's
first novel, *The Professor*, set in Brussels (but not published until
after Charlotte's death), Zoë Heger was exposed as the calculating and heartless Mademoiselle Zoraïde Reuter. The plain
little governess heroine, Frances Henri, triumphs over her cruel
headmistress, marries the professor, and their first-born son is
named Victor. Belatedly Charlotte thus redressed her wounds.

In late November of 1843, however, Charlotte felt herself
entirely defeated. Once again she gave notice and this time there
was no dispute over the matter. Monsieur's 'vehemence' had
evaporated; perhaps Charlotte had misinterpreted, exaggerated
or even largely imagined it in the first place. Heger's personality,
after all, was a histrionic one. On 19 December Charlotte

informed Emily that she intended to be home by 2 January. 'Low spirits have afflicted me much lately,' she wrote, 'but I hope all will be well when I get home.'[22]

Madame Heger orchestrated Charlotte's departure with all the kindness and generosity she had withheld from her for many a long month. On the eve of her leaving, Charlotte was invited once again into the private family sitting room. M. Heger gave her a diploma testifying to her qualifications, which he affixed with the seal of the Athénée Royal. (There were, of course, at this time no official or standardized certificates, diplomas or degrees granted to women when they completed their education.) The Hegers also presented Charlotte with a parting gift of an anthology of French poetry, *Les Fleurs de la Poésie Française*, which Charlotte inscribed the next day with, 'Given to me by Monsieur Heger on the 1st of January 1844, the morning I left Brussels.'

New Year's Day 1844. A day for resolutions, commitments, hopes and dreams. For Charlotte it was a bitter-sweet day, tasting of both exile and homecoming. Madame Heger, despite her six-week-old baby, Victorine, and the cold, winter weather, accompanied Charlotte all the way to Ostend to the packet, which would sail the next day. The generous gesture of a benevolent headmistress; the final dismissal by a jealous wife? Whichever may have been the case, Madame Heger was safely seeing Charlotte off to England, and also firmly escorting her out of their lives – she hoped – for good.

· IO ·

Comfortable and Undesponding

Emily, of course, warmly welcomed Charlotte on her return from Brussels. It was almost a year since they had last seen each other. But very soon it became clear that estrangement rather than reunion was the dominant note of Charlotte's homecoming.

While Emily sat writing at the dining room table, Charlotte sewed on those January evenings after Patrick Brontë went to bed, or she turned over the pages of the volume of poetry Heger had given to her. When they followed their father upstairs at midnight or later, they parted for the night, for after Charlotte's return she and Emily began, for the first time in their lives while under the same roof, to sleep apart. Emily remained in the tiny, unheated 'children's study' where twelve and fifteen years earlier she and Charlotte had lain awake together fabricating their secret 'bed plays', while Charlotte took over Aunt Branwell's much larger room, with a fireplace, and slept in the same bed her mother and aunt had both died in. Perhaps they discussed these new sleeping arrangements; more likely, Charlotte simply moved into Aunt Branwell's room. Emily couldn't be seduced away from her narrow cell. She had no need of the large room and mahogany bed and fireplace. Indeed, the room had been unused since their aunt's death. But what Emily did require was mental space and privacy, the freedom to lie awake and write, if she wished, far into the night.

Emily wanted to preserve the *status quo* she had carefully created during Charlotte's absence, while Charlotte required activity, something – *anything* – to deliver her from her obsessive thoughts of Heger. Now that her education was completed, as attested by the seal-embossed diploma given to her by her 'maître', she knew she must resurrect their long-cherished, long-nourished dream of establishing their own school. On one of those January nights Charlotte raised the issue, and Emily, who had been anticipating Charlotte's revival of the school plan, was prepared for the confrontation. Charlotte might do as she pleased, but Emily no longer harboured any illusions about a 'pleasant and flourishing seminary' such as she had sketched in her 1841 birthday note. She told Charlotte that she would not under any condition teach in their prospective school; she refused even to give instruction in music or German, neither of which Charlotte could teach.

But Emily did not refuse all assistance or participation. While declining any direct contact with students, she was nevertheless willing to take upon herself all the housekeeping and cooking at the school. She would never again stand before a class of pupils and unveil the complexities of German grammar, but she was willing to wash and iron the girls' frocks, sheets and pillowcases, and spend the greater part of every morning preparing their mid-day dinner, and the afternoon baking bread and biscuits for evening tea.

Charlotte, of course, was dismayed by Emily's narrow, self-appointed role in the as yet chimerical school. Was Emily – the most gifted and intelligent of the three of them – to be relegated to the most menial tasks, tasks which could easily be performed by a servant from the village? But it was useless to protest, or to try to argue that the duties Emily consented to take on were beneath her. A compromise of sorts was reached, however unsatisfactory to both. Yet this did not remove the major obstacle to establishing the school: Patrick Brontë's failing eyesight and the dependence and low spirits it had reduced him to. It was now unthinkable for Charlotte and Emily and Anne to leave their father at home alone and establish a school at Burlington or anywhere else.

Finally, after several months of indecision, uncertainty and deepening depression, Charlotte settled on a severely modified version of their original conception of the Misses Brontë's Establishment. Instead of setting up a boarding academy in some pleasant location on the coast or near the urban centres of York or Leeds, Charlotte realized that the only way she could salvage her dream was by opening up a very small school for a handful of pupils at the parsonage itself after making necessary repairs and renovations to the house. Emily didn't encourage this new plan, but she also didn't frustrate it. Her life, in fact, would not be substantially altered by it: she would continue to be occupied with housework and cooking during the day – albeit on a larger, more demanding scale – and after her sister's young pupils went to bed, at about the same hour as Patrick Brontë, Emily could write in the dining room while her sisters prepared lessons or corrected exercise books.

During the early spring and summer months of 1844 Charlotte did everything she could to make their school a reality. She enlisted Ellen's aid in her attempts to recruit pupils. She wrote to Miss Wooler, her former employers, acquaintances, acquaintances of acquaintances, even going so far, on at least one occasion, as to enclose her Athénée Royal diploma as evidence of her credentials (requesting, of course, that it be returned by the next post). She deferred embarking on renovations to the house, but she did go ahead and have prospectuses printed, modelled closely on that of the Pensionnat Heger:

THE MISSES BRONTE'S ESTABLISHMENT

FOR

THE BOARD AND EDUCATION

OF A LIMITED NUMBER OF

YOUNG LADIES,

THE PARSONAGE, HAWORTH

NEAR BRADFORD

TERMS	£	S.	D.
Board and Education, including Writing, Arithmetic, History, Grammar, Geography and Needle Work, per Annum	35	0	0
French ⎫ German ⎬ each per quarter Latin ⎭	1	1	0
Music ⎫ Drawing ⎭ each per quarter	1	1	0
Use of Piano Forte, per quarter	0	5	0
Washing, per quarter	0	15	0

Each young Lady to be provided with One Pair of Sheets, Pillow
Cases, Four Towels, a Dessert and Tea-spoon
A Quarter's Notice, or a Quarter's Board, is required previous to the
Removal of a Pupil.[1]

However energetic were Charlotte's efforts to bring the Misses
Brontë's Establishment into being, they could not consume all
her time. She wrote to Ellen that 'Emily and I walk out a good
deal on the moors, to the great damage of our shoes, but I hope
to the benefit of our health', and in another letter, 'Emily and I
have set to shirt-making', presumably for Branwell, who needed
to keep up appearances at the Robinsons', 'and have stuck to it
pretty closely.'[2] But these reports of shared walks and sewing
were misleading. Emily refused to discuss the school until it
actually came into being and she was called upon to perform her
own limited role in it, so all Charlotte's plans and ideas were
brooded upon by her alone.

In March Charlotte visited Ellen at Brookroyd for three weeks,
and in May both she and Ellen went to stay at Hunsworth with
Mary Taylor, recently returned from Germany. Then in July
Ellen came for a lengthy visit to the parsonage. With Ellen and
Mary, Charlotte could give free rein to her hopes for the school;
they provided the enthusiasm and encouragement which Emily
withheld. And yet to neither of her close friends could Charlotte
disclose the heartache over Heger or the painful distance which
was growing up between herself and Emily. Returning from
Ellen's in late March, she went out of her way to tell Ellen how
'Emily is much obliged to you for the flower seeds' that Ellen
had sent home with Charlotte, and that Emily wished 'to know
if the Sicilian pea and crimson corn-flower are hardy flowers or
if they are delicate and should be sown in warm and sheltered
situations.' A postscript also brought Emily into the picture:
'Our poor little cat has been ill two days, and is just dead . . .
Emily *is* sorry.'[3] Other than this Charlotte had little to report.

Emily was, in fact, devoting herself more seriously and single-
mindedly than ever before to her writing. She, too, was experi-
encing a kind of crisis of vocation. She made her own gesture of
commitment in February of 1844 when she sat down and took

stock of all her poems to date – destroying some, revising others, and producing new ones at an unprecedented rate. She then began transcribing what she decided was her 'canon', covering the past eight years, into two separate manuscript booklets, one devoted to Gondal productions and headed 'Emily Jane Brontë. Transcribed February 1844 / GONDAL POEMS', and the other to non-Gondal verse and inscribed simply with 'E.J.B. Transcribed February 1844'.

Many of Emily's most arresting poems date from this period, and the division between the Gondal and non-Gondal ones, despite the two separate booklets, was muted by their shared recurrent themes of rebellion, isolation, estrangement and liberation. Some, indeed, could be read as coded statements of Emily's rejection of Charlotte's exertions towards establishing 'their' school. In the evenings, seated across from Charlotte at the dining room table, Emily addressed poems to 'My Comforter', or 'Imagination' or 'God of Visions' – to her muse, in fact. She wrote, too, of her 'resentful mood', and 'savage heart' and of her 'sullen ... peevish woe'. She scorned 'Stern Reason' and sought to explain

> Why I have persevered to shun
> The common paths that others run;
> And on a strange road journeyed on
> Heedless alike of Wealth and Power –
> Of Glory's Wreath and Pleasure's flower.[4]

Much of Emily's poetry written in 1844 dwelt on the irreconcilable claims of the 'real' world and the realm of 'Imagination', to which she steadfastly gave her allegiance. These poems had a defensive, bold tone and invoked abstractions like 'Truth', 'Reason', 'Fancy' and 'Liberty' to explain and justify Emily's rejection of Charlotte's 'world without'. But to reject the 'real' world meant also to some extent to reject Charlotte herself, and not even Emily's self-sufficiency and dreamy solitude wished for such renunciation. Hence the sad, elegiac mood which pervaded the 1844 poems. One which was transcribed in the 'E.J.B.' booklet reflected Emily's own sense of loss and how much she, as well as Charlotte, suffered as they strayed further and further apart during the spring and summer after Charlotte's return from Brussels:

> We used to love on winter nights
> To wander through the snow.
> Can we not woo back old delights? ...
> So closer would my feelings twine,
> Because they have no stay in thine.
> Nay, call me not; it may not be;
> Is human love so true?
> Can friendship's flower droop on for years
> And then revive anew?
> No; though the soil be wet with tears,
> How fair soe'er it grew;
> The vital sap once perished
> Will never flow again ...
> Time parts the hearts of men.[5]

Emily's absorption in her poetry was a continual reproach to Charlotte, reminding her of her own creative drought. But just as she had formally renounced the 'world below' in her 'Farewell to Angria', Charlotte reiterated her renunciation of imaginative writing in her first surviving letter to M. Heger. She told both Heger and later Mrs Gaskell that the reason why she had ceased writing poems and stories during this period was that she feared for her own eyesight as well as her father's. To Heger, she wrote: 'Formerly I passed whole days and weeks and months in writing, not wholly without result, for Southey and Coleridge – two of our best authors, to whom I sent certain manuscripts – were good enough to express their approval; but now my sight is too weak to write. Were I to write much I should become blind. This weakness of sight is a terrible hindrance to me ... The career of letters is closed to me – only that of teaching is open. It does not offer the same attractions; never mind, I shall enter it.'[6]

But if Charlotte was really in danger of going blind, how was she able to write letter after letter concerning the school or contemplate being a schoolmistress and spending most of her hours poring over books, preparing lessons and marking students' exercises? The truth was that Charlotte's eyesight was much as it had always been – near-sighted and weak, but no more incapacitating than when she had spent 'whole days and weeks and months' writing of Angria. Emily's continued immersion in Gondal, her prolific output of prose as well as poetry, stung Charlotte to the quick. She too longed to be writing something other than supplicating letters and prospectuses. But she had said farewell to all that, and, to account for her own creative aridity, exaggerated her poor eyesight.

By October, Charlotte begun to lose hope of the Misses Brontë's Establishment ever becoming a reality. Despite all her efforts, all her letters, the handsome prospectuses, and the encouragement and aid of friends, not one pupil had materialized. Emily now felt rescued and delivered, but she could not exult in her freedom as she watched all of Charlotte's hope and energy ebb out of her during the autumn months of 1844. Deprived of her only outlet for exertion, her only distraction from remembrance and longing, her only way of collaborating once again with Emily towards a shared goal (however peripheral and limited Emily's share), Charlotte felt more than ever before in her life helpless, useless, incapacitated. Her gnawing sense of powerlessness led to an obsession with control. When chaos threatens from within, it becomes essential to make the external environment as orderly, methodical, constricted and limited as possible. An open drawer jars and must be closed; chairs which have strayed from desks and tables must be pushed back into place. Locks must be checked and rechecked, and virtually everything in the nineteenth-century home was under lock and key.

Emily was untidy; she left drawers open, pushed away chairs in order to sit on the hearthrug, forgot her sewing on the sofa, left her messy lap desk open on the dining room table. The kitchen was always in a disorganized state, with the floured bread board and vegetable peelings and meat scraps intended for Keeper and unwashed crockery and pots and pans littered about as the stew simmered on the coal stove and the bread baked in the oven. Incongruously, a book or two peeped from behind a stack of dishes; fragments of pencilled paper were put out of harm's way on the window sill.

Increasingly, Charlotte found it difficult to eat Emily's meals; she was too overwrought from furtively putting things to right, back where they belonged, from worrying over scores of trivial details that she had scarcely ever noticed before. And then there was the truth, a felt but inchoate, largely unconscious truth, that Charlotte did not want to take food from Emily, did not want to be fed by her. Hadn't Charlotte herself always been the stronger, older, more practical one, protecting her younger, frail, eccentric, reclusive sister? Now it was Emily who was large and strong. Charlotte could not consume the food Emily cooked for her, could not eat or write at the dining room table.

The worst time of day for Charlotte was late morning, when Emily was noisily preparing dinner in the kitchen. As noon approached Charlotte became taut with anxiety, every nerve strained for one sound – the postman's bell. For an hour that felt like eternity, life seemed to hang in the balance. As she later described this ordeal in *Villette*:

> My hour of torment was the post-hour. Unfortunately I knew it too well, and tried as vainly as assiduously to cheat myself of that knowledge; dreading the rack of expectation, and the sick collapse of disappointment which daily preceded and followed upon that well-recognized ring. I suppose animals kept in cages, and so scantily fed as to be always upon the verge of famine await their food as I awaited a letter ... the letter ... would not come and it was all of sweetness in life I had to look for.[7]

The only food Charlotte needed was not anything prepared by Emily just across the hallway, but nourishment in the form of a few words hastily scrawled on a small sheet of notepaper by Constantin Heger across the channel in Belgium. And this meagre fare, day in and day out, was denied her.

Charlotte wrote to Heger at least six times between the spring of 1844, when she was full of news about the school plan, and the closing winter months of 1845, when it seemed to her that she had nothing left to live for other than the very dim hope of a letter from him. In the beginning Heger did, sometimes, answer her – brief notes which are now lost – but soon he became alarmed by Charlotte's ardour and exorbitant need. He instructed her to write only on impersonal matters which had nothing to do with him: her father's health, the activities of her sisters and brother, the status of the Misses Brontë's Establishment. Then he prohibited her from writing more often than once every six months. And in the end, Heger did what nine out of ten men in his position probably would have done. Without informing Charlotte of his intention, of his 'solution' to this small but annoying problem of her importunate letters, he ceased replying to them altogether.

Four of Charlotte's letters have survived; not that Heger attached any importance to them, but because his alert and clever wife did. Madame Heger noted the arrival of each, recognizing the familiar handwriting even when the letter bore no English stamp. (Charlotte became distrustful of the post which brought her nothing from Belgium, and asked one of the Taylors or Dixons or Wheelwrights to carry her letters to Brussels and hand-deliver them to the Pensionnat.) A day or two after the arrival of a letter, Zoë Heger would stealthily retrieve it from her husband's wastebasket, uncrumple and smooth it out and carefully stitch or glue together the ragged fragments. What passed through her mind as she did this only confirmed her earlier suspicions and her conviction that she was well rid of the little *anglaise*. Yet Zoë Heger was also a woman, and the only other woman who could comprehend the depth of feeling which her husband aroused in Charlotte.

At first Charlotte wrote to Heger of the school plan, of Emily and her father, of her visits to her friends, but by the new year of 1845, almost exactly a year after Charlotte had left Brussels, the principal theme of her letters to Heger was Heger himself and Charlotte's anguish over being separated from him. On 8 January she violated his instructions regarding the frequency and subject of her correspondence and recklessly confessed, 'Day and night I find neither rest nor peace. If I sleep I am disturbed by tormenting dreams in which I see you always severe, always grave, always incensed against me.' The entire letter is a *cri de coeur*, full of the entangled and strangulating cords of reproach, need, anger, supplication, love and hunger. Hunger most of all: 'Monsieur, the poor have not need of much to sustain them – they ask only for the crumbs that fall from the rich man's table. But if they are refused the crumbs they die of hunger.'[8] For eight months, Charlotte had suffered 'torments' of starvation on Heger's account; he should know, *must* know, of her state.

Without having the courage to reread what she had written, Charlotte hastily dispatched the letter.

Heger himself probably did not reread it either before tearing it up and tossing it into the wastebasket. He did not reply; nor did he answer when Charlotte wrote again in May. She then abided by the six-month rule, vainly hoping, no doubt, that her self-control might merit a note from him. Nothing arrived from Belgium at the parsonage.

Charlotte's final letter, dated 18 November 1845, was, if possible, even more desperate than the earlier ones. In it she told Heger how his 'last letter was stay and prop to me – nourishment to me for half a year. Now I need another.' She had done everything in her power to forget him, even going so far as to deny herself 'absolutely the pleasure of speaking about you – even to Emily.' So Charlotte had not endured her 'torments' in complete solitude. Sometimes over dinner, in the hour of 'sick collapse', the distance between herself and Emily had dissolved and they were united, however momentarily, again, and Charlotte unburdened something of her grief to her sister. Emily now saw before her what she had only read and dreamt and written of – a love so passionate and strong and exclusive that it annihilated all else and reduced its victim to an abject, pleading shadow of herself.

These mid-day breakdowns at the dining table brought no relief, no catharsis. And with the paranoia of the wretched and depressed, Charlotte afterwards felt guilty over inflicting her pain on Emily. Hence she resolved to stop speaking of Heger. The dinner hour passed in silence. Charlotte closed her last letter to her 'maître' with a stark account of the effect his refusal to write had had on her. When Charlotte allowed herself to believe that he would never write again, 'then fever claims me – I lose appetite and sleep – I pine away'.[9]

Heger kept this final letter longer than the previous ones. Not that he cared or was touched by it in any way, not even by the veiled threat of its closing lines, which insisted that the very survival, not merely the wellbeing, of another human being depended on whether or not he replied. No, Heger kept Charlotte's letter for a few days folded up in his waistcoat pocket because, after glancing through it, he scribbled the name and address of a Brussels shoemaker in the margin. When this cobbler had repaired his boots, Heger discarded Charlotte's letter as he had all the others, and soon after his wife, unnoticed, fished it out of the wastebasket and preserved it, along with its predecessors, in a locked box in a locked drawer in her dressing room.

Charlotte's anguish over Heger went on for a period of nearly two years. In a letter to Miss Wooler she spoke of 'the tyranny of Hypochondria' with its 'insufferable moments and the heavy gloom of many long hours – besides the preternatural horror which seemed to clothe existence and Nature and ... made life a continual waking nightmare [in which] ... the morbid nerves can know neither peace nor enjoyment – whatever touches pierces them – sensation is for them all suffering. A weary burden nervous patients consequently become to those about them – they know this and it infuses new gall – corrosive in its extreme acritude, into their bitter cup.'[10]

Woodenly, mechanically, one day followed the next in a monotonous procession. For Emily, the predictability of their circumscribed life was reassuring and liberating. But Charlotte felt 'as if we were all buried here'. She wrote to Ellen: 'I can hardly tell you how time gets on ... at Haworth – There is no event whatever to mark its progress – one day resembles another – and all have heavy, lifeless physiognomies – Sunday, baking day and Saturday are the only ones that bear the slightest distinctive mark – meantime Life wears away – I shall soon be 30 – and I have done nothing yet.'[11]

With the abandonment of the school plan, Charlotte and Emily had to face their precarious financial situation once again, especially considering the fact that their father was now sixty-eight and virtually blind. Charlotte felt it would be irresponsible and heartless of her to seek a teaching position in a school or a private family, and Emily made it clear that she would never again leave home on any account, for any employment. They discussed taking out life annuities, and Charlotte wrote to Miss Wooler for advice and information. Miss Wooler referred them to a reputable firm, but when they made further enquiries they decided the interest was too high for them to take out annuities for the present. This meant that they only had their railway investments to fall back on. Charlotte was beginning to have anxieties over the fluctuating price of shares, but Emily, who, Charlotte told Miss Wooler, 'had made herself mistress of the necessary degree of knowledge for conducting the matter, by dint of carefully reading every paragraph and every advertisement in the newspapers that related to rail-roads', convinced Charlotte their investment was not in immediate danger, and that they should not sell out.[12]

In May 1845 Patrick Brontë acquired a new curate, a twenty-nine-year old Irishman named Arthur Bell Nicholls. Nicholls' advent ensured that Patrick Brontë would not be relieved of his position because of his failing sight. Charlotte and Emily thus welcomed Nicholls' appointment for their father's sake. Of the man himself, though, they were not the least bit curious. However respectable and conscientious he seemed, in their eyes he belonged to the 'self-seeking, vain, empty' race of Anglican curates among whom Willie Weightman had been such an anomaly. 'A cold, far-away sort of civility' was the only terms on which they consented to meet Mr Nicholls.

In June, Anne returned from Thorp Green and announced that she would not be returning after the summer holidays. She gave no specific reason for her abrupt resignation after four years with the Robinson family. Charlotte and Emily could read her unhappiness, strain and fatigue in the circles round her soft grey eyes and the pallor of her flawless complexion. They didn't press for an explanation. Instead, they all made plans for a summer holiday. Emily and Anne decided to make an excursion on their own to York and Charlotte to visit Ellen at her brother Henry's parsonage at Hathersage. Charlotte's erstwhile suitor had finally secured a bride and was off with her on their honeymoon while Ellen remained at Hathersage in order to prepare the house for the return of the newly-weds.

Emily wrote an account of the York excursion in her July 1845 diary note: 'Anne and I went [on] our first long journey by ourselves together, leaving home on the 30th of June, Monday, sleeping at York, returning to Keighley Tuesday evening, sleeping there and walking home on Wednesday morning. Though the weather was broken we enjoyed ourselves very much, except during a few hours at Bradford. And during our excursion we were, Ronald Macalgin, Henry Angora, Juliet Angusteena,

Rosabella Esmaldan, Ella and Julian Egremont, Catharine Navarre, and Cordelia Fitzaphnold, escaping from the palaces of instruction to join the Royalists who are hard driven at present by the victorious Republicans.'[13]

Not so much as a sentence, phrase or word was expended by Emily on the awesome beauty of York Minster or the views of the city they enjoyed while walking the circuit of its ancient, encompassing walls. York – the greatest and most beautiful city in the North of England with all its monuments, landmarks, warren of twisting, cobblestoned streets and, above all, its magnificent cathedral – was insubstantial and insignificant to Emily juxtaposed next to Gondal, which she and Anne apparently 'played at' the whole time they were gone. Emily took a holiday of the imagination rather than an outing to York during the three days she and Anne were away from home.

On 3 July, the day after their return, Charlotte went to visit Ellen at Hathersage. She originally intended to stay only ten days, but both Emily and Ellen felt the change of scene would help to alleviate her demoralized condition and urged her to stay longer. Hence Emily wrote to Ellen on the 11th: 'if you have set your heart on Charlotte staying another week, she has our united consent. I, for one, will take everything easy on Sunday. I am glad she is enjoying herself; let her make the most of the next seven days to return stout and hearty. Love to her and you from Anne and myself – and tell her all are well at home.'[14]

Less than a week after Emily wrote this reassuring bulletin to Ellen and Charlotte, however, all had become suddenly and disastrously unwell back at Haworth, and what Charlotte returned to at the end of the month was a house of confusion, chaos and disgrace rather than the eventless existence she had fled when she left on her holiday. On 17 July Branwell returned from the Robinsons at Thorp Green, and swiftly on his heels followed a threatening letter of dismissal from his employer, the Reverend Edmund Robinson, who wrote that he had 'discovered [Branwell's] ... proceedings, which he characterised as bad beyond expression and charging him on pain of exposure to break off instantly and forever all communication with every member of his family.'[15]

Emily, Charlotte and their father were shocked by Branwell's summary dismissal. But Anne had apparently been waiting for the storm, in all its furore, to break. In her diary note written only a few days after Branwell's return from Thorp Green, she wrote that she had 'just escaped from' her 'wretched' employment there, and she cryptically referred to 'some very unpleasant and undreamt-of experience of human nature' she had been forced to witness while at the Robinsons'.[16]

Since neither Mr Robinson nor Anne specified the nature of Branwell's 'proceedings', they must have been too disgraceful to speak of openly. Yet Branwell himself did not attempt to mystify his father and sisters. He told them, roughly, what he wrote to his old railway friend from Luddenden Foot, Francis Grundy: that he had been carrying on an adulterous affair with Mrs Lydia Robinson, the mother of his pupil. 'This lady', Branwell wrote to Grundy, '(though her husband detested me) showed me a degree of kindness which ... ripened into declarations of more than ordinary feeling. My admiration of her mental and personal attractions, my knowledge of her unselfish sincerity, her sweet temper ... although she is seventeen years my senior, all combined to an attachment on my part, and led to reciprocations which I had little looked for. During nearly three years I had daily troubled pleasure soon chastised by fear.'[17]

Such was Branwell's lurid tale. Anne, who had been with him at Thorp Green, did not contradict it, and none of the others seem to have doubted it. When Mrs Gaskell published her account of the 'Robinson affair' in her biography of Charlotte, Patrick Brontë was particularly impressed by the portrayal of his son's 'diabolical seducer', and Mrs Robinson herself threatened a libel suit. With hindsight, however, there is some reason to question Branwell's sensational story of what happened at Thorp Green. Lydia Robinson was a well-connected, wealthy, forty-three-year-old society matron. If she had grown weary of her husband (who was also forty-three, and not the aged invalid Branwell described) and decided to have a liaison, it is unlikely that she would have chosen her son's insignificant, twenty-six-year-old, carrot-haired, bespectacled tutor as a lover. But if she had, and Mr Robinson had discovered the dalliance, it is even more unlikely that he would have threatened Branwell with 'exposure' when his own wife as well as Branwell would be exposed as an adulterer. In his threatening dismissal letter, Mr Robinson ordered Branwell to sever ties 'with every member of his family', not just with his wife, 'on pain of exposure'. If Branwell had made 'improper advances' to his pupil, young Edmund Robinson, rather than Mrs Robinson, Branwell alone would be tainted and irrecoverably harmed should Mr Robinson go ahead and make his behaviour public. Branwell, indeed, would shrink from anyone, and most of all his family, knowing that he had homosexual inclinations and desires.

Furthermore, if Branwell explained to one and all – as he in fact did explain to virtually everyone he encountered in the next three years – that he had had an affair with a married woman almost old enough to be his mother, he would, in effect, publicly expose his 'proceedings' himself. And this self-exposure garnered him far more pity than condemnation. Mrs Gaskell, always a trustworthy barometer of the times, believed Branwell's tale and was even more eloquent than usual in castigating his 'traducer': 'the man became the victim; the man's life was blighted, and crushed out of him by suffering, and guilt entailed by guilt; the man's family were stung by keenest shame', while 'the wretched woman ... survives ... [and] passes about in the gay circles of London ... vivacious, well-dressed, flourishing.'[18] It was far better to be thought of as a 'guilty accomplice' in adultery, to use Mrs Gaskell's phrase, than a homosexual who had preyed upon and tried to deprave an innocent boy. Young Edmund Robinson's moral development as well as his intellectual education had been entrusted to Branwell. To attempt to exploit the boy sexually would indeed have been a serious offence.

Mrs Gaskell said 'The story must be told.'[19] Yet the truth of the matter will never be known; only a handful of those involved – Branwell, Mrs Robinson, young Edmund and possibly Anne – ever knew it. But what is more important even than the truth is, indeed, the 'story' and the fact that Emily and Charlotte and Patrick Brontë never questioned the veracity of Branwell's account.

The immediate aftermath of the 'Robinson affair' was that Branwell lost all self-control. As Charlotte wrote to Ellen, after receiving Mr Robinson's letter, Branwell 'thought of nothing but stunning and drowning his distress of mind' with laudanum and drink. 'So long as he remains at home, I scarce dare hope for peace in the house. We must all, I fear, prepare for a season of distress and disquietude.'[20] In order to fortify themselves for this season, Branwell was sent away in the custody of the sexton, John Brown, for what was hoped would be a restorative visit to Liverpool and Wales.

It was during this interlude, while Branwell was away, that Emily and Anne wrote their third set of diary papers on 31 July, the day after Emily's birthday, which had inadvertently slipped past unnoticed in the midst of all the turmoil Branwell had set loose in the house. Emily wrote as if out of the eye of a hurricane, with both detachment and complacency, of family affairs over the past four years:

> This morning Anne and I opened the papers we wrote four years since, on my twenty-third birthday. This paper we intend, if all be well, to open on my thirtieth – three years hence, in 1848. Since the 1841 paper the following events have taken place. Our school scheme has been abandoned, and instead Charlotte and I went to Brussels on the 8th of February 1842.
>
> Branwell left his place at Luddenden Foot. C. and I returned from Brussels, November 8th, 1842 in consequence of aunt's death.
>
> Branwell went to Thorp Green, where Anne still continued, January 1843.
>
> Charlotte returned to Brussels the same month, and after staying a year came back again on New Year's Day 1844.
>
> Anne left her situation at Thorp Green of her own accord, June 1845.

After laconically enumerating the movements of the family members (including Aunt's from this world to the next at the end of the second paragraph), Emily went on to the York excursion, or rather the Gondal developments which transpired in the course of it, and then continued:

> The Gondals still flourish as bright as ever. I am at present writing a work on the First Wars. Anne has been writing some articles on this, and a book by Henry Sophona. We intend sticking firm by the rascals as long as they delight us which I am glad to say they do at present. I should have mentioned that last summer the school scheme was revived in full vigour. We had prospectuses

printed, despatched letters to all acquaintances imparting our plans, and did our little all; but it was found no go. Now I don't desire a school at all, and none of us have any great longing for it. We have cash enough for our present wants, with a prospect of accumulation. We are all in decent health, only that papa has a complaint in his eyes, and with the exception of B., who, I hope, will be better and do better hereafter. I am quite contented for myself: not as idle as formerly, altogether as hearty and having learnt to make the most of the present and long for the future with[out] the fidgetiness that I cannot do all I wish; seldom or never troubled with nothing to do, and merely desiring that everybody should be as comfortable as myself and as undesponding, and then we should have a very tolerable world of it.

Emily also noted the return of Tabby, and the state of the parsonage pet population: 'We have got Flossy [Anne's spaniel] , got and lost Tiger [a cat], lost the hawk Hero, which, with the geese, was given away, and is doubtless dead ... Keeper and Flossy are well, also the canary acquired four years since.' And then she closed with:

We are now all at home, and likely to be there some time. Branwell went to Liverpool on Tuesday to stay a week. Tabby has just been teasing me to turn as formerly to 'Pillupotate.' Anne and I should have picked the black currants if it had been fine and sunshiney. I must hurry off now to my turning and ironing. I have plenty of work on hand, and writing, and am altogether full of business. With best wishes for the whole house till 1848, July 30th, and as much longer as may be.[21]

In the midst of illness, blindness, depression and profound uncertainty over the future, Emily was 'hearty', 'contented', 'comfortable', 'undesponding', 'writing' and 'full of business'. Aunt's death was overshadowed by Hero's; her father's eye 'complaint' and Branwell's condition pale in the light of the Gondals flourishing 'as bright as ever'. Emily, in fact, was writing some of her finest poems about them in 1845: 'Cold in the Earth' (the Gondal title is 'R. Alcona to J. Brenzaida'), 'Death That Struck When I Was Most Confiding', 'How Beautiful the Earth is Still' and 'Julian M. and A. G. Rochelle'. Secure in her own private domain, much occupied with housework and immersed in her writing, Emily was flourishing as luminously as the creatures of her imagination, and her only desire was that the rest of the family should be as comfortable and undesponding, 'and then we should have a very tolerable world of it'.

Anne's corresponding diary note dwelt on much that was unpleasant in addition to her 'undreamt-of' experiences at Thorp Green. Branwell, she reported, had suffered 'much tribulation and ill health' and been sent off with John Brown to Liverpool. The school scheme had failed; none of them had a situation. Anne herself had made scant progress on any front: a grey print silk frock she was sewing, her novel 'Passages in the Life of an Individual' (later retitled *Agnes Grey*), her resolve to wake up earlier in the morning, or the Gondal Chronicles. The Gondals, she bluntly said in contradiction to Emily, were 'at present in a sad state' and 'in general ... not in first-rate playing condition'. Nor were their creators and creators' family. Anne looked ahead to 1848 with trepidation and wondered 'what changes shall we have seen and known [then]; and shall we be much changed ourselves? I hope not, for the worse at least. I for my part cannot well be flatter or older in mind than I am now.'[22]

Branwell returned to the parsonage in early August in much the same state. On 4 August he wrote to his Bradford friend, the sculptor Joseph Leyland, 'I returned yesterday from a week's journey to Liverpool and North Wales, but I found during my absence that wherever I went a certain woman robed in black and calling herself 'MISERY' walked by my side, and leant on my arm as affectionately as if she were my legal wife.'[23] Throughout the months to come, Branwell proclaimed that this dark female shade haunted him.

Meanwhile he did a great deal more than haunt his sisters and father. He exercised remarkable ingenuity in acquiring, borrowing and cadging sufficient money to spend his nights at the Black Bull and his days in bed, dosing himself with laudanum. His moods and behaviour vacillated wildly between megalomania and depressed stupor. During moments of sobriety (when he could not finagle a penny even out of John Brown or persuade the village chemist to give him a bit more credit), Branwell lugubriously lamented his fate. He reduced life in the parsonage to a frightening and often squalid affair. Charlotte minced no words in her letters to Ellen, telling her that Branwell

'will never be fit for much ... his bad habits seem deeply rooted
... It is only absolute want of means that acts as any check to
him.'[24] Though there was a chance of securing another railway
position, Branwell refused to seek another job of any sort. He
told his family that he was too ill to work, and also that he was
writing a novel. Given Branwell's condition, Charlotte could not
invite Ellen to Haworth and subject her to their ordeal of living
under the same roof with him. In September she wrote to Ellen:
'I neither intend to go and see you soon, nor to ask you to come
and see us. Branwell makes no effort to seek a situation, and
while he is at home I will invite no one to come and share
our discomfort.'[25] A month later she reiterated: 'Branwell still
remains at home, and while *he* is here – *you* shall not come. I am
more confirmed in that resolution the more I see of him.'[26]

Branwell, in effect, was holding them all hostage at home. His
behaviour was so unpredictable that not even close friends were
asked to visit. And if intimate, sympathetic people like Ellen
(whose own brother George had gone mad and eventually had
to be committed to an asylum) could not come, then there was
no longer any question of soliciting a 'limited number of young
ladies' to take up residence at the Misses Brontë's Establishment
at Haworth. Branwell's breakdown was the death knell of the
school plan. It had failed already, but with his collapse the dream
of four long years had vanished altogether.

Emily, busy with writing and home affairs (she kept on
cooking, turning and ironing without regard to Branwell's state),
could now heave a sigh of relief, secure in the knowledge that
the house would not be stretched to the breaking point with
pupils. Emily, in fact, coped with Branwell better than anyone
else could. Physically she was able to deal with him when he
became uncontrollable, or when he pounded on the front door
late at night, coming home from the Black Bull long after everyone except Emily had gone to bed. Emily stayed up waiting for
Branwell, reading or writing in the dining room. She unbarred
the door and guided or hauled him up the stairs to bed. Emotionally, too, Emily was able to tolerate Branwell's histrionic pos-
turing and lamentations, and to empathize with the genuine
pain they concealed. It didn't matter where this pain came
from – a thwarted love affair, secret sexual desires, or simply

the unbearable realization that one was an unredeemed and irretrievable failure. The pain was real. Why else did Branwell have to 'drown' and 'stun' it day and night?

Emily pitied Branwell, but Charlotte was enraged at him for turning the household into a living hell, for weakly fleeing from all the opportunities she had been denied, for destroying the school scheme once and for all, and, finally, for succumbing (as Charlotte thought) to the very same temptation that had been tormenting her for almost two years – the sinful temptation of loving and desiring an older, married person. Branwell, Charlotte believed, had indulged and still indulged in this criminal alliance. He was wallowing in his illicit passion, feeding and tending it as if it were a delicate, hothouse bloom, while Charlotte had done everything in her power to subsist without the crumbs of Constantin Heger's regard.

Charlotte believed that Branwell had done what it had nearly cost her her sanity and physical health *not* to do. But this shared source of their misery could not be expressed, perhaps not even consciously acknowledged by Charlotte. Hence the animosity and disgust which Branwell aroused in her baffled the rest of the family, especially Emily, who was doing her best to help him. Legend holds that Charlotte did not speak to Branwell for the next two years, until the crisis of his last illness. Such a long, unrelenting silence is unlikely; there must have been moments when Charlotte broke down and pity overcame hostility within her. But it was true that her relationship with Branwell – her old ally in Angria, the brother who had walked forty miles in one day to visit her at Roe Head, Branwell, for whom she had first gone out as a governess so that she could contribute to his education at the Royal Academy in London – was permanently and irrevocably damaged.

What was plain to Charlotte, almost from the moment Branwell was dismissed from Thorp Green in July, was that after this last disgrace, he would never recover and would instead proceed to ruin their lives. And this, indeed, was what seemed to happen in the autumn months of 1845. What were Charlotte and Emily and Anne to do? There appeared to be no way out of the claustrophobic, dark, hopeless corner into which their father's blindness and brother's collapse had driven them. They couldn't leave home to work or live or merely breathe freely, nor could they allow anyone or anything – a ray of sunlight, a fresh harvest breeze scented with chestnuts and ripe apples – in. Emily lived much of the time in Gondal, in her head, and among the inmates of the parsonage now she suffered the least.

It was Charlotte who spent long afternoons sitting unoccupied in the dining room, staring like one hypnotized into the fire, as if she saw all the ashes of their dreams, plans and hopes in the flames. Everything they had desired, dreamt of and worked hard for had come to naught. This was the Hour of Lead, and with a stiffened heart Charlotte mechanically enumerated all their losses: the school scheme, her father's sight, Branwell. But it is in such leaden hours that hope may unexpectedly revive and become most exorbitant and reckless. Six months or a year or two earlier Charlotte would never have believed Emily capable of pointing the way out of their house of blindness and despair, but this, in fact, was precisely what Emily unwittingly did when she carelessly left her untidy lap desk open on the dining room table one afternoon in October 1845.

· 11 ·

Ellis Bell

The poems Charlotte discovered in Emily's lap desk were the stuff dreams were made of and they acted on Charlotte's imagination like an elixir. But it was no easy task persuading Emily that her verse should be published. The idea of professional authorship had been repugnant to her as far back as December 1836 when Charlotte and Branwell had sent off specimens of their writing to Southey and Wordsworth and *Blackwood's Magazine*. But under the 'veiled' pseudonym of Ellis Bell – the first name of Emily's Irish grandmother, Ellis Brunty, grafted on to the middle name of Patrick Brontë's Irish curate, Arthur Bell Nicholls – Emily eventually consented to Charlotte's dream that they attempt to establish themselves as writers.

Emily's concession over the poems and what it cost her were not repeated, however, in other matters. In a letter to Miss Wooler, Charlotte confided that she and Emily had quarrelled over the 'Railway Panic' that was sweeping the country in the early months of 1846 and threatening the fortunes of small investors such as the Brontë sisters. Emily had managed their financial affairs since their aunt's death and taken great pains in investing their legacies in the York and North Midland line. Now faced with the 'panic', Charlotte, as she told Miss Wooler, was 'most anxious ... to sell our shares ere it be too late – and to secure the proceeds in some safer, if for the present, less profitable investment.' But Emily refused to sell out. Either she had complete confidence in her financial astuteness or she was determined that having acquiesced over the poems she would not yield again to Charlotte. As Charlotte rather defensively wrote to Miss Wooler, 'if [Emily] ... be not quite so tractable or open to conviction as I could wish I must remember perfection is not the lot of humanity, and as long as we can regard those we love, and to whom we are closely allied, with profound and never-shaken esteem, it is a small thing that they should vex us occasionally by what appears to us, unreasonable and headstrong notions.'[1] Charlotte could only hope that if they lost their meagre fortunes in the Railway Panic, they might regain them with their poetry and other writing as well.

For Charlotte's discovery of Emily's poems seemed to unbar the way to the whole realm of professional writing, a realm Charlotte had not dared hope to enter since Robert Southey had told her that 'literature cannot be the business of a woman's life and it ought not to be.' In their present situation, literature was the *only* business they could attempt to practise. Their careers as governesses and teachers were suspended, if not over. Housework and sewing and cooking and reading to their father occupied only so many hours a day. Patrick Brontë went to bed at nine, after evening prayers, by which time Branwell was ensconced at the Black Bull and well on his way to inebriation. Then, relieved of their daily chores and released for a while from the demands of their father and brother, Charlotte, Emily and Anne drew their chairs together round the dining room table and wrote communally and openly for the first time since the secession of Gondal from Angria more than ten years before.

The first product of these nightly sessions for Emily was one of her finest and most defiant poems, 'No Coward Soul', written in January 1846. It contained Emily's unequivocal repudiation of orthodox religion – 'vain are the thousand creeds / That move men's hearts ... / Worthless as withered weeds' – and her celebration of her own individual faith which she affirmed armed her against fear and doubt and made a mockery of death. 'No Coward Soul', in fact, marked the culmination of many of the ideas and preoccupations and beliefs that had coloured Emily's verse for over a decade – it was a kind of coda, even, of her poetic career. At the same time, its tone and diction possessed a new clarity and assurance that align it more closely with *Wuthering Heights* than the poetry which preceded it. 'No Coward Soul' is the next to the last surviving poem from Emily's pen; it was a bridge of sorts between the nearly two hundred poems she had written since 1836 and the novel she would soon embark on.

Meanwhile Anne continued to work on the novel she had begun while still with the Robinsons at Thorp Green. She and Charlotte and Emily were aware of the fact that Branwell, too, was writing a novel in fits and starts during his intermittent periods of lucidity and control. This was a laboured, Byronic attempt entitled *And the Weary are at Rest*, a thinly veiled account of his purported affair with Lydia Robinson. It was probably Branwell, in fact, who made his sisters realize that fiction was likely to be more lucrative than poetry. As Branwell explained in a letter to his friend Joseph Leyland, 'I knew that in the present state of the publishing and reading world a Novel is the most saleable article, so that where ten pounds would be offered for a work the production of which would require the utmost stretch of a man's intellect – two hundred pounds would be a refused offer for three volumes whose composition would require the smoking of a cigar and the humming of a tune.'[2] Branwell no doubt counted upon his lurid tale of adultery and heartbreak to fetch him a tidy sum as well as literary notoriety, but at just about the time that Emily and Charlotte were beginning novels of their own Branwell discovered that bringing *And the Weary are at Rest* to a close would require considerably more effort than smoking a cigar and humming a tune. It was never completed. But *Wuthering Heights* and *The Professor* were finished, along with Anne's retitled Thorp Green novel, *Agnes Grey*. Not that Branwell was ever aware of his sisters' novel writing. They wrote almost exclusively at night when he was out of the house and did not tell him about their books even after they had been published. No doubt they kept silent to spare him yet another reminder of his own failure.

During those cold winter nights of 1846, writing together once again in the dining room, Charlotte and Anne, at least, strained to redress some of the grievances and heartaches they had endured in the years since the heyday of Glass Town and the Young Men. In true Glass Town fashion, Anne made William Weightman 'alive again' in *Agnes Grey* in the character of Edward Weston, a curate like Weightman. She then married him off in the final chapter to her autobiographical heroine, Agnes, rewarding Agnes with a husband and children and delivering her at the same time from the soul-destroying servitude of govern-essing.

Charlotte, too, found poetic justice and emotional balm in writing *The Professor*. Set in Brussels, the novel followed the fortunes of the professor of its title, William Crimsworth, and charted the growth of his love for a timid, oppressed, orphaned governess named Frances Henri. They too married in the final chapter, but before being united, they escaped and triumphed over the devious machinations of the headmistress, Zoraïde Reuter, whose very name revealed that she was modelled on Zoë Heger.

Wuthering Heights, however, was not a soothing wish-fulfilment tale. Nor was there any reason why it should have been, for Emily was the one member of the family who was not profoundly unhappy at this time. Yet in its own way, *Wuthering Heights*, like *Agnes Grey* and *The Professor*, accurately reflected the period and state of mind out of which it was born. It certainly portrayed the chaos which had descended on the household when Branwell, under the influence of gin and laudanum, like Hindley Earnshaw, turned the parsonage into an 'infernal house' with his violent outbursts and drunken ravings. It would have been impossible for Emily to render Hindley's alcoholic degradation and Heath-cliff's ranting misery without the protracted spectacle of Branwell's breakdown before her eyes day in and day out.

Yet *Wuthering Heights* was not principally a saga of Byronic usurpation and revenge, but rather one of transcendent, death-defying love. In Catherine Earnshaw and Heathcliff, Emily created mythic figures in the grip of a titanic passion. They are driven, tormented, violent lovers, and there are no wedding bells for them in the final chapter. In fact, as in Gondal, love in *Wuthering Heights* is unconnected with marriage. Catherine marries Edgar Linton, and Heathcliff weds Edgar's sister Isabella, but these marriages have no impact on Catherine and Heathcliff's passionate love. Nor does death; Catherine dies in the middle of the novel in childbirth (perhaps giving birth to Heathcliff's rather than Edgar's child), but Heathcliff is relent-lessly haunted by her until eighteen years later he too finally rests by her side under the long grass on the edge of the church-yard. Before he dies, Heathcliff makes a ghoulish arrangement with the sexton to knock out the adjoining sides of his own and Catherine's coffins so that in death they might finally achieve the consummation of their love – a perfect and irrevocable union – which had tormented and eluded them when they were alive.

Catherine and Heathcliff are chainless souls: no social or religious or moral laws constrain them. Their love is like some immutable force of nature – a hurricane or an earthquake – that can't be questioned or resisted or escaped. And it is as a love story that *Wuthering Heights* has variously shocked, baffled, haunted and awed readers since it was first published. But it is also a book profoundly concerned with food and hunger and starvation. The story is largely set in kitchens – Emily's own particular domain at the parsonage – not on the heather-covered moors between Wuthering Heights and Thrushcross Grange. The kitchen at the Heights is a room of warmth and comfort, with a roaring fire and the kettle on the hob, but the kitchen is also the stage or arena where the most passionate and violent scenes of the novel take place. Catherine declares 'I *am* Heathcliff' to Nelly Dean in the kitchen at the Heights. Edgar Linton confronts and assaults Heathcliff in the kitchen at Thrushcross Grange. Hareton is confined to the kitchen at the Heights after a shooting accident, and it is in the midst of the ceaseless cooking of meals that the love between him and young Catherine comes into being, nourished by books and primrose-studded porridge.

Emily, in fact, made porridge or gruel the staple food in *Wuthering Heights*. It is, of course, prisoners' and invalids' fare, and Catherine plays both roles in the novel after she marries Edgar and becomes the lady of Thrushcross Grange. She feels incarcerated in her husband's fine home and undergoes recurrent bouts of 'brain fever' when her will is checked or her desires are thwarted, and each time she falls ill she refuses to eat. Like Emily at Roe Head and in Brussels, Catherine starves herself as an act of rebellion and despair. Wayward, selfish and passionate, she repeatedly refuses food when others refuse to allow her to have her own way. And at the end of the novel Heathcliff too goes on a hunger strike. He dies as much of starvation as from the torment of being separated from Catherine.

In *Wuthering Heights* Emily combined her two overriding preoccupations with words and food and disclosed their close connection. Writing and fasting are two available responses to conditions of helplessness and powerlessness. Both provide the illusion of mastery and control. And yet there is a crucial difference between the two: writing is essentially an act of rebellion by which one says: 'I don't like the world as I find it and so will create a better one for myself.' But refusing to eat is an act of despair and defeat. The body is punished because the environment it inhabits cannot be changed.

By early April Charlotte and Emily and Anne were far enough along on their novels for Charlotte to write to Aylott and Jones that 'C., E. and A. Bell are now preparing for the Press a work of fiction, consisting of three distinct and unconnected tales which may be published either together as a work of 3 vols of the ordinary novel size or separately as single vols as shall be deemed most advisable.' Charlotte enquired whether Aylott and Jones 'would be disposed to undertake' these new works from the Bells' pens, but she also stated that they were not willing 'to publish these tales on their own account'.[3] They had already paid £31 10s. for the *Poems* to be printed, an expenditure they could justify as the price necessary to bring their names before the reading public. But the novels, they hoped, would earn them an income, not further deplete their meagre financial resources. Aylott and Jones promptly informed Charlotte, however, that they were not 'disposed' to publish the Bells' novels on any terms whatsoever, and, for a while at least, Charlotte was baffled over what to do with their manuscripts which were fast nearing completion.

The *Poems* of Currer, Ellis and Acton Bell were published at the end of May 1846. What should have been an occasion of celebration – the launching of the Bells into print – was soon swept aside by domestic cataclysm. Branwell's erstwhile employer, Edmund Robinson, died on 26 May. Branwell was jubilant at the tidings from Thorp Green, or pretended jubilation so that he could add yet another chapter to the fiction of his affair with Lydia Robinson. For by this time Branwell had abandoned *And the Weary are at Rest* and was living out, rather than writing down, the tale he wanted to tell. Unlike his sisters' stories, there were to be no wedding bells in Branwell's final chapter, though he had confidently told his friends Leyland and

Francis Grundy that Lydia Robinson wanted nothing more than to unite her fortune and life with his own as soon as she was free to do so. Now that her husband was dead, there was no impediment to their union. Hence one had to be manufactured, either by Lydia herself if indeed she had been Branwell's mistress, or by Branwell if the affair had been his own fabrication.

All we have are the bald events recorded by Mrs Gaskell, who heard them from first-hand observers, including Charlotte and Patrick Brontë and the barmaid at the Black Bull. Either Lydia Robinson or Branwell invented a codicil to Edmund Robinson's will which stipulated that Mrs Robinson would forfeit all claims to her late husband's fortune if she had any further communication with Branwell. The Robinson coachman was dispatched to Haworth to convey this information, and when he arrived at the Black Bull, he sent for Branwell. Branwell 'came down to the little inn and was shut up with the man for some time. Then the groom came out, paid his bill, mounted his horse, and was off. Branwell remained in the room alone. More than an hour elapsed before sign or sound was heard; then those outside heard a noise like the bleating of a calf, and, on opening the door, he was found in a kind of fit, succeeding to the stupor of grief which he had fallen into on hearing that he was forbidden by his paramour ever to see her again, as if she did, she would forfeit her fortune.'[4]

On 17 June Charlotte wrote to Ellen that

the death of Mr Robinson ... served Branwell for a pretext to throw all about him into hubbub and confusion with his emotions, etc. etc. Shortly after came news from all hands that Mr Robinson had altered his will before he died and effectually prevented all chance of a marriage between his widow and Branwell by stipulating that she should not have a shilling if she ever ventured to reopen any communication with him. Of course, he then became intolerable. To Papa he allows rest neither day nor night, and he is continually screwing money out of him, sometimes threatening that he will kill himself if it is withheld from him. He says Mrs Robinson is now insane; that her mind is a complete wreck owing to remorse for her conduct towards Mr Robinson (whose end it appears was hastened by distress of mind) and grief for having lost him.[5]

Such were the conditions under which Charlotte and Emily and Anne completed their novels during the long, sunny days of June, days so long in fact that it was often still light when they settled down at the dining room table to write after their father went to bed. At the end of *The Professor* Charlotte wrote the date, 17 June 1846. *Wuthering Heights* and *Agnes Grey* were also finished by this time, and on 24 June Charlotte boldly sent them off to the London publisher Henry Colburn, who may have been recommended to her by Aylott and Jones after their refusal to consider the novels. On 4 July, the very same day that Charlotte sent Colburn the manuscripts, their *Poems* were favourably reviewed in the *Critic* and *Athenaeum*. The *Critic* praised the Bells' 'wholesome, refreshing, vigorous poetry' and the 'original thoughts' it expressed. 'It is long since we have enjoyed a volume of such genuine poetry as this', the unidentified reviewer enthused; the Bells' volume, he continued, 'has come like a ray of sunshine, gladdening the eye with present glory and the heart with promise of bright hours in store.' The *Athenaeum* was more temperate in its praise and also distinguished the relative merits of the three poets to Emily's benefit. Ellis Bell was deemed to possess 'a fine quaint spirit ... which may have things to speak that men will be glad to hear – and an evident power of wing that may reach heights not here attempted.'[6] Aglow with this appreciative response to the *Poems*, Charlotte and perhaps Anne and even the cautious Emily as well looked ahead to the possibility of a successful and also solvent future.

Meanwhile, however, the present had to be endured. Charlotte escaped it temporarily by paying a visit to Ellen Nussey, and so relieved was she to be out of touch with her brother's wildly erratic behaviour and her father's deep despondency that she wrote home asking for an extension of her leave. This Emily immediately granted as she had done before when Charlotte asked to stay on longer than originally planned at the Nusseys'. Emily now wrote to Ellen: 'Papa, of course, misses Charlotte and will be glad to have her back. Anne and I ditto; but as she goes from home so seldom you may keep her a day or two longer ... that is if she still be with you when you get this permission.'[7] It is significant that it was Emily who apparently had the power to decide Charlotte's movements and also that Emily did not mind Charlotte enjoying herself in Birstall while Branwell made life so uncomfortable in Haworth.

Just how uncomfortable Charlotte realized almost as soon as she got back. She wrote to Ellen saying: 'I went into the room where Branwell was to speak to him about an hour after I got home. It was very forced work to address him – I might have spared myself the trouble as he took no notice and made no reply – he was stupefied. My fears were not vain. Emily tells me that he got a sovereign from Papa while I have been away under pretence of paying a pressing debt. He went immediately and changed it at a public house and has employed it as was to be expected ... [Emily] concluded her account with saying he was a hopeless being – it is too true. In his present state it is scarcely possible to stay in the room where he is. What the future has in store I do not know.'[8]

After Mr Robinson's death, Branwell's periods of drugged and drunken stupefaction decreased while his violent rages intensified. Emily and her father were the only members of the family who were large and strong enough to restrain him when he became uncontrollable, but Patrick Brontë's blindness made it impossible for him to help Emily when Branwell held a pistol to his temple and threatened to blow his brains out or slashed at the empty air before him with a carving knife and vowed to cut his own throat.

Patrick Brontë's descent into total blindness coincided with his son's downfall, which may have been fortunate, for it spared the old man from literally seeing the wreck Branwell had become. But by the summer of 1846 it was obvious that Emily could no longer cope with Branwell on her own. Her father would have to emerge from his world of darkness, and to this end Emily and Charlotte travelled to Manchester in early August to consult an eye doctor. Apart from the excursion to York, it was the first time Emily had left home since she had returned from Brussels three and a half years earlier. The trip could have brought her little pleasure, but she and Charlotte were able to consult an eminent oculist, William James Wilson, at the Manchester Institution for Curing the Diseases of the Eye. Dr Wilson was optimistic that an operation to remove Patrick Brontë's cataracts would restore his vision, but he could not tell whether the cataracts were sufficiently 'ripe' for surgery without an examination. It was therefore arranged that Charlotte would return to Manchester with her father later in the month.

On 19 August Patrick Brontë and Charlotte travelled to Manchester and took lodgings in a boarding house at 83 Mount Pleasant near Boundary Street and Oxford Road. The very next day Patrick Brontë was seen by Dr Wilson, who said that his eyes were ready for the cataract surgery and scheduled the operation for the 25th. Wilson also told them they would have to remain in Manchester for at least a month-long recuperation, and Charlotte was very concerned about how Emily and Anne would manage during her long absence. 'I wonder how poor Emily and Anne will get on at home with Branwell', she wrote to Ellen on the 21st; 'they too will have their troubles.'[9]

The operation – a fifteen-minute ordeal without anaesthetic – took place as planned. At her father's request, Charlotte was present and she was greatly moved by his 'extraordinary patience and firmness'. Dr Wilson pronounced the surgery a success and they returned to their lodgings immediately after it was over with instructions that Patrick Brontë was to keep his eyes bandaged, remain in bed in his darkened room, and speak and be spoken to as little as possible.

After seeing to their dinner and making sure her father was comfortably settled in bed, Charlotte turned to the post and found unwelcome news in a letter from home. Emily wrote to say that Henry Colburn had turned down their novels. Silently and solitarily, in the unfamiliar rented rooms, Charlotte turned this rejection over in her mind. She was determined that they should submit the manuscripts to another publisher and probably dashed off a note to this effect to Emily. Charlotte, in fact, had never been entirely sanguine about Colburn and had already drawn up a list of other prospective publishers. She urged Emily now to send off *The Professor*, *Wuthering Heights* and *Agnes Grey* to the next firm on her list. Yet it would be a month or longer before they could expect another verdict, and in the meantime four weeks of silent days in the darkened Manchester rooms punctuated only by meals and occasional letters from Ellen and more bulletins from Emily in Haworth loomed ahead. Cut off from the long, bright summer days outdoors, Charlotte sat down to write at the table in her room the day after her father's operation. Slowly her lonely, uneasy, unfamiliar predicament receded from her consciousness while another vivid, imaginary situation took sway of her. Several paragraphs into her narrative, she decided that the name of the poor, victimized child she was writing about should be Jane Eyre. By the time she and her father returned to Haworth late in September she was deep into her second novel.

They found Emily, Anne and Branwell as well as could be expected, which is to say apparently no worse than when they had left them a month earlier. Perhaps the very first night she was back Charlotte read the opening chapters of *Jane Eyre* to her sisters. An argument ensued. Emily and Anne protested that Jane was not beautiful and therefore not interesting, to which Charlotte responded with considerable warmth: 'I will show you a heroine as plain and as small as myself, who shall be as interesting as any of yours.'[10] Charlotte had thrown down her gauntlet, and it is significant that she conceived of Jane Eyre as deficient in size as well as beauty. For her whole life, Charlotte was intensely self-conscious about her physical smallness. It was all right for Emily to be 'lean' because she was tall. Emily's drive to be slender was imbued with yearnings to be pure and spare, light and agile and free. Her body possessed the angularity and grace of a wild deer's. Charlotte's, in contrast, was like a child's; indeed, she was so small even when full-grown that she had to wear children's chemises and underwear.

The later summer days gave way to cooler, showery autumnal ones, and the heather began to wither out on the moors. Patrick Brontë's vision was now fully restored, 'a continual subject of gratitude', as Charlotte wrote to Miss Wooler. '*Now* to see him walk about independently – read, write, etc. is indeed a joyful change.'[11] But there was soon more than enough reason to feel anxiety again. One evening when Patrick Brontë was out, Anne found Branwell sprawled unconscious across his bed with the bed curtains on fire. He had apparently been reading in bed, under the influence of drink or opium, and knocked over the candle before sinking into unconsciousness. Anne tried to rouse him with screams, but only succeeded in alarming the rest of the household. Emily reached Branwell's room first, took one look at the burning bed, seized her brother, dragged him into the corner of the room, tore the blazing bedding from the bed and then rushed downstairs for a pail of water to douse the fire. All was over in a matter of minutes. The flames were extinguished and Emily carried Branwell into her own room and put him to bed. Aware of her father's terror of fires, she warned her sisters not to tell him what had happened.[12]

The lingering stench of smoke and singed bedclothes, however, could not be concealed from Patrick Brontë when he returned home. Now that he could see again, he decided that henceforward Branwell should sleep with him in the master bedroom overlooking the graveyard. Dreadful, usually sleepless nights they had together. According to Mrs Gaskell, Branwell 'would declare that either he or his father would be dead before morning. The trembling sisters, sick with fright ... often listened for the report of a pistol in the dead of the night ... In the mornings young Brontë would saunter out, saying with a drunkard's incontinence of speech "The poor old man and I have had a terrible night of it; he does his best – the poor old man! But it's all over with me ... it's *her* fault, *her* fault."'[13]

The worst winter in living memory descended upon them in the closing months of 1846. Charlotte wrote to Ellen in December: 'I hope you are not frozen up in Northamptonshire. The cold here is dreadful. I do not remember such a series of North-Pole-Days. England might really have taken a slide up into the Arctic Zone. The sky looks like ice. The earth is frozen, the wind is as keen as a two-edged blade. I cannot keep myself warm.'[14] They all had bad colds from the severe weather and Anne's asthma flared up while Charlotte was plagued by an old enemy, toothaches, which made eating painful and sleep elusive and fitful.

Even if all their trails and paths on the moors hadn't been frozen over and effaced by snow, they wouldn't have ventured from the house. It was too cold and they were too ill even to go into the village and purchase writing paper from the stationer, John Greenwood. But in December a most unwelcome, rare visitor did make his way over the snowbound roads from York to the parsonage. A sheriff's officer came in search of Branwell, and ordered him to settle his drinking debts or return with the officer to the county prison at York. Of course Patrick Brontë had to pay his son's drinking bills, and not for the first time either.

The first four or five months of 1847 were virtually eventless except for yet more severe weather and illness in the family. In January, Patrick Brontë was bedridden with a bad attack of influenza and catarrh, and he sank back into the old depression which had enveloped him before his sight was restored. On Valentine's Day, Charlotte wrote to Ellen that 'the excessively cold weather' had taken away her appetite and brought on more toothaches, with the consequence, she said, that 'I look almost old enough to be your mother – grey – sunk and withered.'[15] There was no sign of spring and renewed health in early April when Charlotte reported to Ellen 'we are all in the full enjoyment of colds; much blowing of noses is heard, and much making of gruel goes on in the house.'[16]

Yet throughout these months of cold weather and illness Emily and Charlotte and Anne were all hard at work on their second novels. They continued to write together in the evenings round the dining room table and to read and discuss their manuscripts out loud. This sense of community – of the underlying inter-connection binding their books together – was also reflected by the way in which *Wuthering Heights* profoundly influenced both *Jane Eyre* and Anne's *The Tenant of Wildfell Hall*. Charlotte and Anne, in fact, were the first of the stunned and awed readers of Emily's novel, and each in her second book strongly reacted to what Emily had accomplished.

Hence the paramount importance of food in *Jane Eyre*, and also the recurrence of Emily's themes of starvation and fasting. Throughout the novel Jane is passionately hungry. But instead of refusing to eat like Catherine and Heathcliff, she is consistently denied food – literal, emotional and intellectual sustenance – by others: her aunt, Mrs Reed, Mr Brocklehurst and his reign of hunger at Lowood School, and the heartless people who refuse to help her when she flees from Rochester and Thornfield. As she moves from one place to another, Jane actively seeks nourishment, especially bread, the prisoners' and invalids' fare comparable to the porridge in *Wuthering Heights* and the gruel Charlotte herself was consuming to ward off illness during the winter months when she was writing *Jane Eyre*. Like Catherine Earnshaw, Jane rebels, but her rebellion takes the form of a relentless quest for food from a society which cruelly withholds it. Her strength of will seeks the opposite goal of Catherine and Heathcliff. In contrast to their suicidal fasting, Jane *will* be fed; she *will* survive; she *will* grow up, love and marry; she *will* become large and whole.

Perhaps even more consciously than Charlotte, Anne conceived *The Tenant of Wildfell Hall* as an 'answer' to *Wuthering Heights*. The resemblances between the two books are unmistakable. They are dominated by the two similarly named houses, Wildfell Hall and Wuthering Heights. Anne's characters Hargrave, Huntingdon and Hattersley echo Emily's trio of Hindley, Hareton and Heathcliff. Structurally both novels are narrated by two characters in the story, one male and one female. The opening male-narrated chapters create a mystery; the central female-narrated ones reach into the past and gradually unravel and resolve the mysteries; and the concluding chapters return to the present and the framing male narratives.

Technically Anne was greatly indebted to Emily, but morally she was at complete odds with her. She imposed a highly Christian, didactic vision on Emily's themes of marital infidelity, drunkenness and violence. In relating the story of Helen Huntingdon's disastrous marriage to her husband Arthur, Anne, perhaps, was imagining what might have happened had Catherine married Heathcliff and lived to tell the tale. Unlike Catherine Earnshaw, however, Helen has a second chance. At the end of the novel Huntingdon dies of an illness brought about by his dissipated life. In the best Victorian fashion, Helen nurses her reprobate husband through his last illness, and then after his death she marries the Edgar Linton-like Gilbert Markham.

While Emily was working on her second novel, then, Charlotte and Anne were preoccupied with reacting to her first. What they made of her sequel to *Wuthering Heights* is unrecorded. In fact, not a trace remains of Emily's second book. The only reason we know that she commenced and made considerable progress on it is because she kept a letter from the publisher T. C. Newby in which he said,

I am much obliged by your kind note and shall have great pleasure in making arrangements for your next novel. I would not hurry its completion for I think you are quite right not to let it go before the world until well satisfied with it, for much depends on your next work. If it be an improvement on your first, you will have established yourself.[17]

During the spring of 1847, while Emily and Charlotte and Anne were hard at work on their second novels, their first were still making the rounds of publishers in London. Time after time *Wuthering Heights*, *The Professor* and *Agnes Grey* were rejected, often with a curt note that made no mention of the merits or flaws of the novels and merely dismissed them as 'unsuitable' for publication. Charlotte added new publishers to her established list and each time the manuscripts were returned to Haworth she drew a line through the name and address of the rejecting firm and then wrote to the next one below it and forwarded the packages under the same cover. This economy meant that each publisher to whom the novels were submitted saw before even opening the parcel how many times and by which publishers the manuscripts had already been turned down.

The *Poems* of Currer, Ellis and Acton Bell were also faring poorly. After the notices in the *Critic* and *Athenaeum* had appeared there was only one subsequent review, in the *Dublin University Magazine*, which commended the 'Cowperian amiability and sweetness' of the Bells' verse and pronounced it not 'unfragrant to our critical nostrils'.[18] In June, more than a year had passed since the publication of the *Poems*; there was no denying now that their first literary venture had been a failure. In a last bid for some sort of recognition Charlotte sent copies of the *Poems* to Wordsworth, Tennyson, Lockhart and De Quincey, accompanied by the same letter to each:

Sir,
My relatives, Ellis and Acton Bell, and myself, heedless of the warnings of various respectable publishers, have committed the rash act of printing a volume of poems.

The consequences predicted have, of course, overtaken us: our book is found to be a drug; no man needs it or heeds it. In the space of a year our publisher has disposed but of two copies, and by what painful efforts he succeeded in getting rid of these two, himself only knows. Before transferring the edition to the trunk-makers, we have decided distributing as presents a few copies of what we cannot sell. We beg to offer you one in acknowledgement of the pleasure and profit we have often and long derived from your works.

> I am, Sir, yours very respectfully.   Currer Bell[19]

Not surprisingly, none of the recipients of Charlotte's gift even acknowledged receiving it. Almost two years had now passed since Charlotte had discovered Emily's poetry manuscript note-book, and all they had to show for their efforts was a tall pile of unsold copies of their poems.

And yet there was at least one thing to be grateful for as one glorious, balmy summer day succeeded the next. 'Branwell is quieter now', Charlotte wrote Ellen, 'and for good reason; he has got to the end of a considerable sum of money of which he became possessed in the spring and consequently is obliged to restrict himself in some degree.' Branwell's improvement meant that at last Charlotte could invite Ellen to visit them again. She warned Ellen, however, that she 'must expect to find [Branwell] ... weaker in mind and the complete rake in appearance. I have no apprehension of his being at all uncivil to you; on the contrary, he will be as smooth as oil.'[20]

Ellen came to Haworth in July. It had been months since Charlotte, Emily and Anne had spoken to anyone outside the family, and Ellen must have been shocked at their inbred and old-fashioned ways. Their odd clothes and shrinking manner were more striking than ever. Ellen cajoled them into a shopping expedition to Bradford to purchase cloth for new dresses. Char-lotte and Anne stuck to dark-coloured silks, but Emily surprised everyone by choosing a white stuff patterned with lilac thunder and lightning. By this time Emily was not so much beautiful as striking in a negligent, gypsy-like way. She was tall and very slender. Her clothes and appearance were idiosyncratic; she favoured ample, freely hanging skirts and wore her long brown hair loosely fastened up behind with a Spanish comb.[21]

Of course none of the Brontës breathed a word about their poems or novels to Ellen during her stay, but Ellen had her suspicions. There was a flurry of suppressed commotion one day after the postman's bell and Ellen overheard fragments of conversation without grasping completely what had in fact happened. In the midst of her visit, the London publisher Thomas Cautley Newby had written to say that he was pleased to accept *Wuthering Heights* and *Agnes Grey* for publication but not *The Professor*. The terms he offered Ellis and Acton Bell were, however, far from generous. They were to pay him £50 for an edition of 300 copies of the novels; when 250 were sold he promised to refund their £50. This amounted to only a slight improvement over the arrangement with Aylott and Jones for the *Poems*. But after a brief consultation, Emily and Anne decided to accept Newby's 'offer'. Charlotte, meanwhile, sent *The Professor* off on its own to the next publisher on her list, Smith, Elder & Co.

Ellen was aware that something was afoot and perhaps saw a parcel being wrapped and letters dashed off. One day when they were walking out on the moors, she indirectly challenged them all when 'a sudden change and light came into the sky'. 'Look,' said Charlotte, and pointed to three suns shining clearly overhead. They stood a little while silently gazing at the beautiful parhelion, that rare solar phenomenon which occurs when 'mock suns' are reflected through the prism of the sun's halo. Charlotte and Ellen and Anne stood together gazing at the vision of the rainbow-hued triple suns. Emily too looked up from where she was standing apart on a higher knoll of heather. Ellen seized her chance and said the parhelion was a portent of her friends' fortunes as writers. '"That is you," she declared, "You are the three suns."' Charlotte flushed with embarrassment and began denying Ellen's 'nonsense', but, according to Ellen, Emily seemed greatly pleased with the parhelion and smiled as if in accord with Ellen's reading of its significance.[22]

In August, soon after Ellen's departure, Charlotte received word from Smith, Elder that they too declined to publish *The Professor*. But they had been impressed by the manuscript and indicated that 'a work in three volumes would meet with careful attention.'[23] By this time *Jane Eyre* was nearly finished, and on 24 August Charlotte sent off the completed manuscript. William Smith Williams, the editor who had liked *The Professor*, read *Jane Eyre* immediately and passed it on to the director of the firm, a young man named George Smith who had recently taken over control of the business upon the death of his father. Smith took the manuscript home with him and began reading it on a Sunday morning. He cancelled an appointment for noon in order to continue reading, took luncheon on a tray in his study, rushed through dinner to return to the manuscript, and finished it before going to bed. The next day he wrote Charlotte a warm letter of acceptance which reached her less than a week after she had sent off the manuscript.

In the meantime Newby had begun sending Emily and Anne the first proof sheets of *Wuthering Heights* and *Agnes Grey*. In September, Charlotte visited Ellen in Birstall, taking the proofs of *Jane Eyre* along with her, and she read them seated across from Ellen in the family sitting room. Ellen must have felt that her parhelion portent was vindicated, but she had learned to keep silent on the topic of the Brontës' writing, and made no enquiry about the proofs. Charlotte returned to Haworth at the end of the month laden with gifts from Ellen: a screen for her father, a cap for Tabby, a collar and a basket of apples for Emily, crab cheese for Anne, and, to Charlotte's indignation, a jar of preserves for herself which Ellen had secretly slipped into her box.

Jane Eyre was published on 16 October and created an immediate sensation. Thackeray wrote to George Smith saying that he had 'lost (or won if you like) a whole day in reading it at the busiest period with the printers I know wailing for copy.'[24] George Henry Lewes was similarly mesmerized and wrote to Smith that he planned to review the book and wished to be put into direct contact with Currer Bell. Reviews, in fact, filled the London papers and magazines. Readers had to join a long waiting list at the subscription libraries, and bookshops sold out of copies so quickly that a second edition was almost immediately in preparation.

Smith, Elder had a best-seller on its hands, a fact which was not lost on the hitherto desultory Newby. Though *Wuthering Heights* and *Agnes Grey* had been accepted more than a month before *Jane Eyre*, by October no date for publication had been set, even though Emily and Anne had carefully corrected and returned the proofs by the end of August. Newby was only stirred into action by the overnight success of *Jane Eyre*. He hoped

Wuthering Heights and *Agnes Grey* would do as well, and he deliberately created confusion over the identity of Ellis and Acton
Bell, clearly hoping they would be mistaken as one and the same
as Currer, the author of *Jane Eyre*. There was already a good
deal of speculation over Currer Bell – especially over whether
'he' was a man or woman – and Newby's publication of *Wuthering
Heights* and *Agnes Grey* in mid-December added fuel to the controversy. The books themselves, however, were not prepossessing.
Newby had been so eager to capitalize on the *Jane Eyre* fever
raging in literary London that he couldn't be bothered to heed
Emily's and Anne's corrected proofs, and the typesetters carelessly introduced a number of additional errors in their haste to
get the books out. As Charlotte wrote to William Smith Williams,
'the books are not well got up – they abound in errors ... the
orthography and punctuation ... are mortifying to a degree.'[25]

Up in Haworth, as the winter of 1847 set in, the old cramped,
starved life of the past several years continued at the same time
as the Bells' novels became the talk of London. And Emily
and Charlotte and Anne kept up the fiction of their eventless,
monotonous existence both within and outside the family.
Neither their father nor their brother knew there were three
published novelists in the house. Currer Bell continued to black-
lead the stove, make beds and scorch the linen; Ellis reigned in
the midst of crockery and pots and pans in the kitchen; Acton
sat in the dining room with a lap full of mending. In letters to
Ellen, they had nothing to report other than the uninteresting
news – Anne observed that it was really 'no news at all' – that
the curate Arthur Bell Nicholls had gone on holiday to his
family home in Ireland. Charlotte mentioned in passing that 'the
parishioners express a desire that he should not trouble himself
to re-cross the channel.'[26] Other than the movements of the
uninteresting and unadmired Mr Nicholls they pretended to
have only the autumn weather to write of. Anne wrote to Ellen
that the east wind had abated and with it the coughs and colds
it always seemed to bring in its wake. She and Charlotte were
glad of the reprieve, but Emily was indifferent – as Emily so often
was – because she considered it 'a very uninteresting wind'.[27]

It wasn't the east wind which blew around and through
Haworth Parsonage in the early winter months of 1847, but the

much more forceful and 'interesting' winds of change. A gale of literary acclaim and protest was gathering down in London, and it was only a matter of time before Ellis Bell and his 'brothers' Currer and Acton would be exposed to its onslaught.

· I 2 ·

The Shattered Prison

What Emily and Charlotte dreaded most in the lull between the acceptance of *Wuthering Heights* and *Jane Eyre* and their publication was not so much bad reviews as none at all. Like Keats, like all writers, they feared their names – or rather Ellis and Currer Bell's – would be writ in water, that their novels would share the fate of their poems and sink without a trace. But the reviews and notices which in October and November and December began to arrive at the parsonage with the postman's bell – in that hitherto dreaded hour just before dinner – soon assured them that neglect and obscurity were no longer to be their portion. On the contrary, recognition and controversy invaded their lives, neatly sealed in the white parcels of clippings which William Smith Williams posted at frequent intervals to Haworth.

The one word which was used over and over again in the early reviews of *Wuthering Heights* and *Jane Eyre* was 'power'. However prudish, parochial and uncomprehending the reviewers were, none could remain immune to the underlying emotional force of the novels. It took their breaths away. The critic in the popular *Douglas Jerrold's Weekly Magazine* wrote uneasily of *Wuthering Heights*: 'There seems to be a great power in the book, but it is a purposeless power which we feel a great desire to see turned to a better account ... In *Wuthering Heights* the reader is shocked, disgusted, almost sickened by details of cruelty, inhumanity and the most diabolical hate and vengeance and anon come passages of powerful testimony to the supreme power of love.' The *Era* proclaimed of *Jane Eyre* 'for power of thought and expression we do not know its rival among modern productions', and the *Atlas* agreed that it 'was one of the most powerful domestic romances which has been published for many years'. The sheer energy of *Wuthering Heights* and *Jane Eyre* mesmerized reviewers, but many of them had qualms about the books' 'vigour' and 'passion'. They felt uncomfortable with the unbridled emotions Emily and Charlotte had evoked in their tales. Passion judged morally, especially in the pages of magazines like *The Christian Remembrancer* or the *Church of England Quarterly*, was deemed 'coarseness', especially of authors who were believed to be women.

The sex of both Ellis and Currer Bell was almost as important to their early reviewers as the power of their stories. Indeed, a double critical standard clearly operated in the reactions to the novels. Power exercised by a male writer was one thing – usually permissible and even admired; in the hands of a woman, however, it could easily trespass the boundaries of good taste and become 'coarse', or, even worse, 'brutal', 'depraved' and 'vulgar'. Such were some of the epithets heaped on *Wuthering Heights*. If many readers had scruples about the power displayed in *Jane Eyre*, they were often aghast at what they found in *Wuthering Heights*. The *Atlas* summed up the moral dilemma the novel seemed to provoke: 'There are evidences in every chapter of a sort of rugged power – an unconscious strength – which the possessor seems never to think of turning to the best advantage. The general effect is inexpressibly painful ... A more natural, unnatural story we do not remember.' The reviewer in the *Britannia* was similarly torn between awe and censure: 'it is difficult to pronounce any decisive judgement on a work in which there is so much rude ability displayed yet in which there is so much to blame.' Of course, there were readers who fixed solely on what they considered blameable in *Wuthering Heights*, finding it 'wild, confused, disjointed and improbable' and condemning its 'brutality', 'cruel and semi-savage love', 'moral taint' and 'vulgar depravity and unnatural horrors'. The reviewer in the *New Monthly* said it should have been entitled '*Withering* Heights', and the critic in *Graham's Magazine* wondered 'how a human being could have attempted such a book as the present without committing suicide before he had finished a dozen chapters.' But more thoughtful, intelligent readers were, as one of them wrote, 'perplexed to pronounce an opinion on it or to hazard a conjecture on the future of the author. As yet it belongs to the future to decide whether he will remain a rough hewer of marble or become a great and noble sculptor.'[1]

Living as they did in complete isolation from what Charlotte in a letter to William Smith Williams called 'the great world' of London, she and Emily had never anticipated such a vociferous response to their books. After a lifetime of insignificance they suddenly had repeated tidings that they loomed large in the London literary scene. An undreamt-of abundance of critical attention was lavished upon their novels of hunger and fasting and starvation. Even the critics seem to have been infected by Emily's and Charlotte's preoccupation with food and hunger. One reviewer wrote of *Wuthering Heights* that it was 'eagerly caught by a famished public ... There is an old saying that those who eat toasted cheese at night will dream of Lucifer. The author of *Wuthering Heights* had evidently eaten toasted cheese.'[2]

Emily carefully put away the five longest and most ambivalent reviews of *Wuthering Heights* in her lap desk. It must have given her great satisfaction to have startled and perplexed what passed for the most discerning critical intelligence in London. But while Emily hoarded and read and reread her notices without comment, Charlotte was moved to protest against the charges of coarseness and immorality levelled at them. By the end of December, scarcely two months after *Jane Eyre* was published, it went into a second edition, and Charlotte seized the opportunity to write a preface defending herself against accusations of 'godlessness' and 'perniciousness' and other moral failings. In her preface Charlotte arraigned her 'timorous' and 'carping' detractors and reminded them of 'certain simple truths': 'conventionality is not morality. Self-righteousness is not religion. To attack the first is not to assail the last.'

These distinctions were important and not over-subtle, but they went unheeded because of the even greater controversy created by the closing paragraphs of Charlotte's preface. She had decided to dedicate the second edition of *Jane Eyre* to Thackeray, who had by this time replaced the Duke of Wellington in her pantheon of human gods to worship. She considered Thackeray the greatest living writer, and precisely the kind of moralist she herself sought to emulate. The dedication to

Thackeray, in fact, was not unconnected with Charlotte's insistence on her own moral principles in *Jane Eyre*. For Charlotte, Thackeray was 'the first social regenerator of the day ... the very master of that working corps who would restore to rectitude the warped system of things.'[3] But all Charlotte's ethical intentions in the preface were lost on the reading public, who instead saw a very different connection between Currer Bell and her esteemed Thackeray, a connection of which Charlotte herself was wholly ignorant.

The unfortunate truth was that Thackeray's domestic life was a shambles and not so very different from Rochester's plight in *Jane Eyre*. Thackeray's wife, like Rochester's, had gone insane and been committed to an asylum, leaving her urbane, charming and still legally bound husband in a social and emotional limbo. Furthermore, Thackeray's best-selling novel *Vanity Fair* was coming out in serial form during the winter months of 1847 and 1848, and after the second edition of *Jane Eyre* appeared, it was rumoured that Currer Bell was none other than the infatuated governess of Thackeray's children, and the real-life model of Becky Sharpe. Early in the new year Thackeray wrote to Charlotte, or rather Currer Bell, via Smith, Elder and gallantly thanked her for her tribute; but he also felt obliged to inform her of the uncanny coincidence respecting his own and Rochester's situations. Charlotte, of course, was mortified by her blunder and nearly heartsick over the pain and embarrassment she felt it must have caused Thackeray. Her attempt to silence her critics and quell controversy had only stirred up yet more speculation and rumour.

By January, *Jane Eyre* had found its way to Haworth, and Charlotte wrote to William Smith Williams saying that she had seen an elderly clergyman reading it, who instantly recognized Cowan Bridge School and William Carus Wilson in her portrayal of Lowood and Mr Brocklehurst. It was only at this juncture, when their fame had almost reached their own doorstep, that Charlotte and Emily decided to tell their father about their novels. *Jane Eyre* had received the greatest number of favourable reviews and had already earned Charlotte some money, so they agreed she should give Patrick Brontë a copy of it to read. Mrs Gaskell had the story straight from Charlotte, and told how Charlotte knocked on her father's study door one afternoon with a copy of *Jane Eyre* in one hand and clippings of several reviews (both favourable and unfavourable) in the other. Patrick Brontë told her to enter. After an awkward silence, Charlotte abruptly announced:

'Papa, I've been writing a book.'
'Have you, my dear?'
'Yes, and I want you to read it.'
'I'm afraid it will try my eyes too much.'
'But it is not in manuscript: it is printed.'
'My dear! You've never thought of the expense it will be! It will almost sure to be a loss; for how can you get a book sold? No one knows you or your name.'
'But, papa, I don't think it will be a loss; no more will you if you will just let me read you a review or two, and tell you more about it.'

Charlotte sat down and 'read some of the reviews to her father; and then giving him the copy of *Jane Eyre* that she intended for him, she left him to read it. When he came into tea he said, "Girls, do you know Charlotte has been writing a book, and it is much better than likely?"'[4]

It was probably only after this positive, if laconic, verdict on *Jane Eyre* that Patrick Brontë was given *Wuthering Heights* and *Agnes Grey* to read as well. Branwell remained in ignorance of his sisters' writing, past and present, for in the early months of 1848 Emily and Anne continued to work on their second books. Charlotte thought for a while of taking up *The Professor* again and revising it, but after some discouragement from Smith, Elder she abandoned the idea and began to contemplate ideas for a new novel. Both *Wuthering Heights* and *Jane Eyre* in the meantime were selling well. On 15 February, Newby wrote to Emily about her next book, and two days later Charlotte received £100 from Smith, Elder, the profits from the recent sales of the second edition of *Jane Eyre*. Newby, however, had still not refunded a single penny of the £50 which Emily and Anne had invested in the publication of their novels. Both George Smith and William Smith Williams had read *Wuthering Heights* and *Agnes Grey* with great interest and told Charlotte they would be eager to publish

Ellis and Acton Bell's next books, but Emily and Anne refused to switch publishers despite Newby's irresponsible treatment of them. The identities of the Bell brothers were becoming too blurred as it was, and Emily no doubt stuck with Newby too for the same reason she had been recalcitrant over the railway shares: she had a need to preserve her independence apart from Charlotte.

As spring approached, the prevailing mood at the parsonage – excluding Branwell, of course – was one of wary hope. Wary because Charlotte, Emily and Anne had been thwarted and rejected too often and for too long a time to give themselves up wholly to the dreams of fame and fortune that the publication of their novels inspired. And then, too, it wasn't unadulterated success which arrived in postal instalments in Haworth; the Bells were misunderstood as often as they were praised. Nevertheless, hope was no longer the 'timid friend' of Emily's poem. Their protracted 'letter to the world', a letter which had begun long ago with the Young Men, the secret 'bed plays', Angria and Gondal, the letter which had been sent vainly to Southey, Wordsworth, Coleridge and De Quincey, which had been distilled into the unregarded *Poems* and then again into *Jane Eyre*, *Wuthering Heights* and *Agnes Grey*, had finally been received, and, what is even more important, read. They had written books which stood on shelves all over England alongside Milton, Bunyan, Scott and Byron – not in terms of greatness (so they thought), but as physical objects: bound sheaves of printed paper with gilt letters along the spine. In lives which were at once so constrained and uncertain – because of Branwell's deterioration and their father's age and ill health – their writing was their only passport and their only resource. And it bore indelible traces of the passion, hunger and desire out of which it was born. Well might Matthew Arnold later speak of the 'hunger, rebellion and rage' of Charlotte's novels. Such ingredients make a potent recipe for writing fiction, and as summer approached, Emily continued to work on her second novel, Anne was in the last stages of *The Tenant of Wildfell Hall*, and Charlotte had embarked on her next book, *Shirley*.

The only other person besides their father whom they let share in their secret of writing and publishing their novels was Mary

Taylor, now far away in Wellington, New Zealand, where she had emigrated with her brother and was thriving as a general merchant with her own store. Long ago, Mary had been privy to the existence of 'the world below' of Angria and had likened its furtive activity to 'growing potatoes in a cellar'. Despite Mary's scepticism and common sense, Charlotte and Emily and Anne knew she would be able to appreciate their novels and applaud their relative success, for Mary had long been prodding all three of them to be more resourceful and economically self-sufficient. Ellen, who of course was much closer to home and Mary Taylor's opposite in every way, was still kept in the dark. But ever since the parhelion episode, she had had suspicions about her friends' writing and she now obliquely – and to Charlotte very annoyingly – inserted them into her letters to Haworth. While not denying the substance of Ellen's hints, Charlotte replied waspishly: 'I have given *no one* a right either to affirm or hint, in the most distant manner that I am "publishing" – (humbug!) whoever has said it . . . is no friend of mine . . . though twenty books were ascribed to me, I should own none. I scout the idea utterly.'[5]

Despite her caustic rejoinders to Ellen, Charlotte was not entirely averse to 'owning up' to being a writer. What reined her in was Emily's insistence that they remain anonymous. Emily wanted no commerce – or at least no direct contact – with the appreciative or dismayed readers of the Bells' novels. It was actually Emily's rather than Charlotte's own view of things that Charlotte expressed when she wrote to Ellen that 'the most profound obscurity is infinitely preferable to vulgar notoriety; and that notoriety I neither seek nor will have.'[6] The terms upon which Emily had agreed to the publication of her poems and novel were the unnegotiable ones that they appear under a pseudonym. That Charlotte had agreed to this anonymity with some reluctance is apparent in her letters to William Smith Williams. Soon after the success of *Jane Eyre* was assured, Williams urged Charlotte – or Currer Bell, for neither he nor George Smith had yet penetrated the Bells' pseudonyms – to visit London to observe the literary milieu which was endlessly making conjectures about *Jane Eyre* and *Wuthering Heights*. But Emily automatically vetoed any such course of action. Hence Charlotte wrote to Williams in February: 'I should much – very much – like to take that quiet view of the "great world" you allude to, but I have as yet won no right to give myself such a treat: it must be for some future day – when, I don't know. Ellis ... would soon turn aside from the spectacle in disgust. I do not think he admits it as his creed that "the proper study of mankind is man" – at least not the artificial man of cities.'[7]

The 'future day' when Charlotte would be able to come to London and divulge her identity to her publishers suddenly came to pass in July, shortly after Newby brought out Anne's *The Tenant of Wildfell Hall*. Ever since the publication of *Jane Eyre* and *Wuthering Heights*, Newby had done his best to delude the reading public into thinking that Ellis or Acton or both were one and the same as the best-selling Currer Bell. Charlotte had tried to defy Newby's mischief-making when a third edition of *Jane Eyre* came out in April by appending a 'note' in which she stated 'my claim to the title of novelist rests on this one work alone; if, therefore, the authorship of other works of fiction has been attributed to me, an honour is awarded where it is not merited: and consequently, denied where it is justly due. This explanation will serve to rectify mistakes which may already have been made, and to prevent future errors.'

Charlotte was overconfident that her caveat would clear up the muddle deliberately created by Newby, who continued to advertise Emily's and Anne's novels as 'by the author of *Jane Eyre*'. But Newby went too far when he sold *The Tenant of Wildfell Hall* to the American firm of Harper Brothers as the new novel by Currer Bell. Smith, Elder had already promised Charlotte's next novel to Harpers and they were mystified when they received word from the American publishers that they had already acquired *The Tenant of Wildfell Hall* from Newby. Charlotte was deeply embarrassed as well as chagrined when Smith, Elder wrote to her for clarification. On the same day that she received their letter, 7 July, she impulsively decided that she and Anne must go to London at once in order to explain the true situation to Smith, Elder and then confront Newby with his chicanery.

Before Charlotte's resolution could subside and before, too, Emily could argue her into staying home and writing – if she must – carefully worded letters to both Smith, Elder and Newby, Charlotte was packing a box for herself and Anne and calculating how much time they had to get to Leeds for the night train to London. Emily not only refused to accompany Charlotte and Anne, she almost certainly did everything in her power to persuade them not to go. But for Charlotte it was as if the letter from Smith, Elder had released the opening of a trap that had long enclosed them all. She and Anne set off directly after tea – an unpleasant, silent meal with Emily – walked to Keighley through a driving rainstorm which thoroughly soaked them, got to Leeds in the nick of time, and, in Charlotte's words, 'whirled up by the night train to London with the view of proving our separate identity to Smith and Elder, and confronting Newby with his *lie*.'[8]

Charlotte wrote a detailed account of their adventure – so different in every way from Emily and Anne's excursion to York three years earlier – in a long letter to Mary Taylor in which she described both the keen excitement of their three-day visit and the heavy psychological and physical toll it exacted. She wrote to Mary:

> We arrived at the Chapter Coffee House (our old place ... we did not know where else to go) about eight o'clock in the morning. We washed ourselves, had some breakfast, sat a few minutes, and then set off in queer inward excitement to 65 Cornhill [the premises of Smith, Elder]. Neither Mr Smith nor Mr Williams knew we were coming – they had never seen us – they did not know whether we were men or women, but had always written to us as men.
>
> We found 65 to be a large bookseller's shop, in a street almost as bustling as the Strand. We went in, walked up to the counter. There were a great many young men and lads here and there; I said to the first I could accost: 'May I see Mr Smith?' He hesitated, looked a little surprised. We sat down and waited a while, looking at some books on the counter, publications of theirs well known to us, of many of which they had sent us copies as presents. At last we were shown up to Mr Smith. 'Is it Mr Smith,' I said, looking up through my spectacles at a tall young man. 'It is.' I then put his own letter into his hand directed to Currer Bell. He looked at it and then at me again. 'Where did you get this?' he said. I laughed at his perplexity – a recognition took place. I gave

my real name: Miss Brontë. We were in a small room – ceiled with a great skylight – and there explanations were rapidly gone into; Mr Newby being anathematised, I fear, with undue vehemence. Mr Smith hurried out and returned quickly with one whom he introduced as Mr Williams, a pale, mild, stooping man of fifty ... Another recognition and a long nervous shaking of hands. Then followed talk-talk-talk; Mr Williams being silent, Mr Smith loquacious.[9]

George Smith was astonished at the unprepossessing appearance of Charlotte and Anne: 'two rather quaintly dressed little ladies, pale-faced and anxious-looking.'[10] He could scarcely believe that these small, retiring, plain women in their old-fashioned dark frocks were the famous Currer and Acton Bell who had caused such a furore with their books. But he quickly gained control of his amazement, and began to make plans for the entertainment of the two celebrated authors: the Miss Brontës must come to stay with the Smiths in Bayswater, Thackeray would be summoned to dinner and G. H. Lewes and Dickens to tea. They must go to the theatre and opera and see the latest exhibitions.

But Charlotte and Anne firmly if somewhat reluctantly refused all plans for their lionization. They had come to London solely to see Mr Smith and Mr Newby and wanted no one else to know of their identity. In fact, while in London they wished to be known only by the incognito of the 'Miss Browns'. They also insisted on keeping their lodgings at the Chapter Coffee House, but they did say that they would be pleased to receive Mrs Smith and her daughters there in the evening. Fortunately, George Smith had the intelligence and good breeding to recognize that it would be futile to try to overcome Charlotte and Anne's reserve; they were like curious but very timid animals plucked out of their natural environment and set down in an alien one which both dazzled and frightened them.

In her letter to Mary Taylor, Charlotte described the aftermath of this dramatic introduction to her publisher:

We returned to our inn and I paid for the excitement of the interview by a thundering headache and harassing sickness. Towards evening, as I got no better and expected the Smiths to call, I took a strong dose of sal-volatile. It roused me a little; still, I was in grievous bodily case when they were announced. They came in, two elegant young ladies, in full dress, prepared for the opera – Mr Smith himself in evening costume, white gloves, etc. We had by no means understood that it was settled we were to go to the opera and were not ready. Moreover, we had no fine, elegant dresses with us, or in the world. However, on brief rumination I thought it would be wise to make no objections – I put my headache in my pocket, we attired ourselves in the plain, high-made country garments we possessed and went with them to their carriage where we found Mr Williams. They must have thought us queer, quizzical-looking beings, especially me with my spectacles. I smiled inwardly at the contrast, which must have been apparent, between me and Mr Smith as I walked with him up the crimson-carpeted staircase of the Opera House and stood amongst a brilliant throng at the boxdoor, which was not yet open. Fine ladies and gentlemen glanced at us with a slight, graceful superciliousness quite warranted by the circumstances. Still, I felt pleasantly excited in spite of headache and sickness and conscious clownishness, and I saw Anne was calm and gentle, which she always is.

The performance was Rossini's opera of the 'Barber of Seville,' very brilliant, though I fancy there are things I should like better. We got home after one o'clock; we had never been in bed the night before, and had been in constant excitement for twenty-four hours. You may imagine we were tired.

The next day, Sunday, Mr Williams came early and took us to church. He was so quiet, but so sincere in his attentions, one could not but have a most friendly leaning towards him. He has a nervous hesitation in speech, and a difficulty finding appropriate language in which to express himself, which throws him into the background in conversation; but I had been his correspondent and therefore knew with what intelligence he could write, so that I was not in danger of undervaluing him. In the afternoon Mr Smith came in his carriage with his mother, to take us to his house to dine. Mr Smith's residence is Bayswater, six miles from Cornhill; the rooms, the drawing-room especially, looked splendid to us. There was no company – only his mother, his two grown up sisters, and his brother, a lad of twelve or thirteen, and a little sister, the youngest of the family, very like himself. They are all dark-eyed, dark-haired, and have clear, pale faces. The mother is a portly, handsome woman of her age, and all the children more or less well-looking – one of the daughters decidedly pretty. We had a fine dinner, which neither Anne nor I had the appetite to eat, and were glad when it was over. I always feel under an awkward constraint at table. Dining out would be hideous to me.

Mr Smith made himself very pleasant. He is a *practical* man. I wish Mr Williams were more so, but he is altogether of the contemplative, theorising order. Mr Williams has too many abstractions.

On Monday we went to the Exhibition of the Royal Academy and the National Gallery, dined again at Mr Smith's, then went home with Mr Williams to tea and saw his comparatively humble but neat residence and his fine family of eight children. A daughter of Leigh Hunt's was there. She sang some little Italian airs which she had picked up among the peasantry in Tuscany in a manner that charmed me.

On Tuesday morning we left London laden with books which Mr Smith had given us, and got safely home. A more jaded wretch than I looked when I returned it would be difficult to conceive. I was thin when I went, but meagre indeed when I returned; my face looked grey and very old, with strange, deep lines in it; my eyes stared unnaturally. I was weak and yet restless. In a while, however, the bad effects of excitement went off and I regained my normal condition. We saw Mr Newby, but of him more another time.[11]

Charlotte's letter to Mary Taylor describing the whirlwind visit to London was intriguing both for what it said and left unsaid. Important things were omitted: the confrontation with Newby, the disclosure of a third sister, Emily or Ellis Bell, the selection of Tennyson's new feminist poem, 'The Princess', as a gift to take home to Emily. And seemingly insignificant details were carefully noted: Williams' stoop and speech impediment, Mrs Smith's portliness, Charlotte's 'awkward constraint at table', her headaches, loss of appetite and weight. She returned to Haworth, in fact, a nervous wreck: 'meagre indeed', shaky and weak, unnaturally pale and exhausted but unable to rest.

Soon Charlotte had a great deal more cause to be uneasy and anxious when she described the interview with George Smith and Williams to Emily. At first, Emily was eager to hear every detail of the London adventure despite her initial opposition to it. For, as Charlotte explained to Williams, 'Emily would never go into any sort of society herself, and whenever I went I could on my return communicate to her a pleasure ... by giving the distinct, faithful impression of each scene I had witnessed. When pressed to go, she would sometimes say, "What is the use? Charlotte will bring it home to me."'[12] Apparently there had been some sort of agreement made, or understood, before Charlotte and Anne went to London that they would divulge only their own identities. The Newby and Smith, Elder quarrel, after all, concerned Acton and Currer Bell alone; there was no need to drag Emily into it. But Charlotte did just this when she explained to George Smith and Williams that there were actually three of them writing from under the cover of the Bell pseudonym. Emily was enraged at what she felt was Charlotte's betrayal of her. Soon after returning to Haworth, Charlotte wrote to Williams of Emily's anger at the revelation, and she also warned him to ignore it in all future correspondence: 'Permit me to caution you not to speak of my sisters when you write to me. I mean, do not use the word in the plural. Ellis Bell will not endure to be alluded to under any other appellation than the *nom de plume*. I committed a grand error in betraying his identity to you and Mr Smith. It was inadvertent – the words "we are three sisters" escaped me before I was aware. I regretted the avowal the moment I had made it; I regret it bitterly now, for I find it is against every feeling and intention of Ellis Bell.'[13]

And yet Emily's wrath did not deter Charlotte from pushing forward with more plans for the Bells' literary careers. In September she wrote to George Smith proposing that Smith, Elder reissue the *Poems* now that Currer, Ellis and Acton Bell were no longer the unknown quantity they had been when the little volume of verse first came out two years earlier. Smith immediately agreed to the proposal and began negotiations to buy up the unsold copies. In the meantime *The Tenant of Wildfell Hall* was receiving a great deal of critical attention in the newspapers and magazines, and Charlotte and Emily were hard at work on their new novels.

As autumn approached and the days grew shorter and darker and colder, Emily and Charlotte and Anne continued to write at the dining room table every evening. Letters from Cornhill kept them abreast of their growing reputation; and the *Poems* were scheduled to be reissued in October. Their lives had been utterly transformed in the space of just twelve months.

Yet everything in their domestic existence – the monotony of sewing and cleaning and cooking – remained unchanged, including Branwell's condition. There was no more talk of his seeking a job. He continued to sleep for the better part of the day, to go out to the Black Bull in the evening, and then come home and terrify his father and sisters late into the night with his drunken ravings and fits. He was often hard pressed for the means to buy drink and laudanum, and borrowed money from whatever quarter he could; and when all his resources were exhausted, he ran up large debts at numerous pubs in the area. In June, Branwell had received a letter from Thomas Nicholson, the landlord of the Old Cock in Halifax, threatening him with arrest and imprisonment unless his drinking bills were speedily paid. Branwell wrote to his friend Leyland that he'd sent the sexton John Brown with ten shillings to placate Nicholson until Branwell had received more cash from Lydia Robinson's physician, Dr Crosby. Branwell maintained that his alleged former mistress aided him financially, using Dr Crosby as her courier. It is more likely, however, that it was Patrick Brontë who again bailed out his son and saved him from going to jail.

This close call and the continuing threat of imprisonment – one Mrs Sugden of the Talbot Inn was also dunning Branwell for money owed her – did not in the least restrain him. If anything, he became even more desperate and dependent on drink and opium. One Sunday morning, when the rest of the family was at church, he scrawled a hasty, furtive note to John Brown:

> Dear John. I shall be very much obliged to you if [you] can contrive to get me Five pence worth of Gin in a proper measure. Should it be speedily got, I could perhaps take it from you or Billy at the lane top, or, what would be quite as well, sent out for, to you. I anxiously ask the favour because I know the good it will do me. *Puntualy* [*sic*] at Half-past Nine in the morning you will be paid the 5d out of a shilling given me then.
>
> Yours. P.B.B.[14]

Drink and opium, and the urgent subterfuges to get money to

buy them, now governed Branwell's life. No one could have disputed what he wrote to Leyland: 'I shall never be able to realize the sanguine hopes of my friends, for . . . I am a thoroughly *old man* – mentally and bodily.'[15] Branwell subsisted now almost entirely on gin and laudanum. He was so emaciated that his clothes hung on him. The village children taunted him as he made his way to the chemist for opium or the Black Bull for a pint and asked if he was wearing his father's coat, it was so large for him.

Francis Grundy, Branwell's old friend from the Luddenden Foot railway days, visited Branwell in September and was shocked by his appearance and behaviour. They met at the Black Bull (Branwell's drinking friends were never received at the parsonage). Branwell was so altered that at first Grundy could scarcely believe that the bizarre apparition who stumbled down from the parsonage was indeed the same person as his mercurial, gifted friend from Luddenden Foot. The door to the Black Bull 'opened cautiously, and a head appeared. It was a mass of red, unkempt, uncut hair, wildly floating round a great gaunt forehead; the cheeks yellow and hollow, the mouth fallen, the thin white lips not trembling but shaking, the sunken eyes, once small, now glaring.' Grundy drew Branwell into the warm room, plied him with hot brandy and even got him to eat 'some dinner, a thing which he said he had not done for long.' Before parting, Branwell drew a knife from his coat and told Grundy how he thought it was the devil himself who had summoned him to the Black Bull on such a cold, wet night. Branwell explained he had planned to assault him with the knife, but was brought to his senses by the sound of Grundy's familiar voice.[16]

On 22 September, Branwell dragged himself into the village as usual. By this time the shopkeepers, weavers, chemist, postmaster and publicans were all accustomed to the spectacle of the parson's son lurching his way down Main Street and so they scarcely noticed his erratic, unsteady progress. But William Brown, the sexton's brother, came upon Branwell in Church Street, struggling to make his way home up the gradual incline of the cobblestones, gasping and panting at the slight exertion. Branwell willingly accepted William's offer of a strong shoulder to lean on, and together they haltingly made their way back to the parsonage, where Branwell went to bed immediately and the doctor was summoned.

There was nothing to be done. Drink and drugs, irregular eating, and a chronic lung complaint had all contrived to shatter Branwell's constitution, and it was too late now to repair the damage even if he could be persuaded or forced to abstain. The next day, however, Branwell didn't touch any stimulants, and actually managed to keep some food down. Even more dramatic was the psychological calm which descended on him. There was no more raving about his paramour, no more threats of suicide or execrations at 'the old man', his father, who had in the past interposed himself between his son and the barrel of a pistol that Branwell had variously pointed at his own temple or his father's. Instead, Branwell's 'demeanour, his language, his sentiments were all singularly altered and softened.' The 'calm of better feelings' and 'a return of natural affection' held sway in the sickroom which had in the past been the scene of so many verbal and physical skirmishes.[17]

Though neither the doctor nor the family knew it – for Branwell had collapsed in this way more than once or twice in the past – Branwell must have realized that time was closing in on him. Instead of histrionic declarations of ruin and imminent death, he now spoke and responded to his family with affection and understanding and remorse. His mind was unclouded; his feelings were focused and uncontaminated, not so much for want of drugs or drink but because death was so real now and so close.

Branwell remained in bed the day following his collapse, and the next morning, Sunday, 24 September, while Charlotte and Emily and Anne walked across the graveyard to church with their father, John Brown came to sit with Branwell upstairs in Patrick Brontë's bedroom overlooking the churchyard. Suddenly Branwell's calm of the previous day deserted him. He seized his friend's hand and half cried out: 'In all my past life I have done nothing either great or good. Oh John, I am dying!' The sexton immediately called back the family. While Emily and Charlotte and Anne helplessly watched their brother struggle for his life, 'perfectly conscious till the last agony came on', Patrick Brontë took his son in his arms and prayed aloud until Branwell was past hearing. 'The awe and trouble of the death scene – the first'

Emily, Charlotte and Anne 'had ever witnessed' – was soon over, just as Branwell's life had so quickly run its course from the promise of youth to the bitterness, exhaustion and defeat of premature old age.[18] After his father had closed Branwell's eyes for the last time, John Brown slipped out to toll the passing bell of St Michael's. The following Thursday Branwell was laid to rest under the stone floor of the church alongside his mother and Maria and Elizabeth.

The immediate aftermath of death is what Charlotte called 'a marble calm' in a letter to William Smith Williams the day after Branwell's funeral. Awe, stillness and numbness predominate over pain: the heart and mind are like heavy stones within. But all too soon anguish wells up and overwhelms the leaden calm of loss. Charlotte wrote to Williams how her father 'naturally thought more of his *only* son than of his daughters ... and he cried out for his loss like David for that of Absalom – my son! my son – and refused at first to be comforted.'[19] Charlotte, too, soon broke down just when her father needed her most. She wrote to Ellen a week later how 'it was my fate to sink at the crisis, when I should have collected my strength. Headache and sickness came on first ... I could not gain my appetite. Then internal pain attacked me. I became at once much reduced – it was impossible to eat a morsel – at last bilious fever declared itself.'[20] She wrote to Williams, too, how 'weak and reduced' she had become, 'especially as I am obliged to observe a very low spare diet.'[21] Branwell had been emaciated by the time he died, and now Charlotte, who had been 'meagre' after her visit to London in July, was becoming yet thinner and weaker.

After a week confined to bed, Charlotte rallied sufficiently to get up and help with the daily chores. No one was writing now, nor had been since Branwell's death. It took all their energy just to get through each day and to sustain their aged father in his misery. Anne's asthma attacks became more frequent and severe. Emily, who bore the brunt of the housework and continued to do all the cooking, had caught a cold sitting in the chill, damp church during Branwell's funeral and then walking home across the saturated churchyard in her thin shoes. By the end of October, Charlotte was very worried about her. She wrote to Ellen on the 29th that 'Emily's cold and cough are very obstinate

... She looks very, very thin and pale. Her reserved nature occasions me great uneasiness of mind. It is useless to question her; you get no answers. It is still more useless to recommend remedies; they are never adopted.'[22]

Four days later Charlotte wrote in much the same vein to Williams: 'I would fain hope that Emily is a little better this evening, but it is difficult to ascertain this. She is a real stoic in illness; she neither seeks nor will accept sympathy. To put any questions, to offer any aid, is to annoy; she will not yield a step before pain and sickness.' By this time Emily was refusing both to eat and, as far as possible, to speak. She seemed to be closing down, in retreat from life, 'yearning in desire' for death like her heroines Augusta Geraldine Almeda and Catherine Earnshaw. But at the same time Emily behaved as if nothing were amiss, and as if she were not in the least unwell. Charlotte told Ellen and Williams how she insisted upon performing all her usual 'avocations ... you must look on and see her do what she is unfit to do.'[23] 'From the trembling hand, the unnerved limbs, the faded eyes, the same service was exacted as they had rendered in health.'[24] The only chore Emily did relinquish was exercising the dogs outdoors, which the curate, Arthur Bell Nicholls, now took it upon himself to perform.

During those short, cold, dark winter days, despite her silence, Emily was still communicating with Charlotte. They were locked, in fact, in their last power struggle. Only Charlotte's side of the conflict was written down, but Emily's refusal to eat or speak, to see a doctor, or even acknowledge that she was ill disclosed her own side of things. She sought to be free of Charlotte's domination and demands, and to control her own fate – even if this meant dying to do so – rather than submit to her sister or, in Emily's words, some 'poisoning doctor'. Charlotte could not passively sit by and watch Emily recede from her life. As Emily became even more inaccessible behind her fortification of silence and fasting, and as she daily grew more and more frail and insubstantial, Charlotte's fear and anxiety and sense of helplessness all escalated. Finally, in complete opposition to Emily's wishes, Charlotte summoned the doctor, Dr Wheelhouse. But when he arrived at the parsonage, Emily would not let him examine her or even see her. Charlotte and Anne gave him as detailed an account as they could of her symptoms, and he prescribed some medicine, but Emily refused to take it.

The *Poems* came out in October under Smith, Elder's imprint, and now that Currer, Ellis and Acton Bell were known for their novels, their verse at last received a considerable number of reviews in diverse magazines and newspapers, such as the *Spectator*, *Standard of Freedom*, the *Morning Herald*, and the *Revue des Deux Mondes*. And the novels themselves continued to attract attention, especially in America, where they had been published in the autumn by Harper Brothers. Williams sent Charlotte a long article on them in the *North American Review*, and she wrote a poignant account of how the review was received by the Bell brothers up in Haworth: 'What a bad set the Bells must be! What appalling books they write! To-day, as Emily appeared a little easier, I thought the "Review" would amuse her, so I read it aloud to her and Anne. As I sat between them at our quiet but now somewhat melancholy fireside, I studied the two ferocious authors. Ellis, the "man of uncommon talents, but dogged, brutal and morose," sat leaning back in his easy-chair, drawing his impeded breath as best he could, and looking, alas! piteously pale and wasted; it is not his wont to laugh, but he smiled half-amused and half in scorn as he listened. Acton was sewing, no emotion ever stirs him to loquacity, so he only smiled too, dropping at the same time a single word of calm amazement to hear his character so darkly portrayed. I wonder what the reviewer would have thought of his own sagacity could he have beheld the pair as I did.'[25]

In November Charlotte received another £100 from the sales of the third edition of *Jane Eyre*. But now at last when financial security was within their reach, Emily's severe illness made it seem irrelevant. George Smith was eager to recruit Ellis Bell as one of his authors and sent some books for her to read. Charlotte had to reply that Emily was 'at present too ill to occupy herself with writing, or indeed with anything', but she could report that Emily was pleased with the books, which would 'be a source of interest for her when her cough and fever will permit her to take interest in anything.'[26]

By this time the family legacy of tuberculosis – the same dread disease which had killed Maria and Elizabeth and in the end

Branwell as well – had ravaged Emily's lungs. She now coughed incessantly, often bringing up thick lumps of phlegm, gasping and panting at the slightest exertion. Even at rest, sitting in her easy chair (she refused to stay even a day in bed), her breathing was rapid, shallow and laboured. But tuberculosis was not the primary cause of Emily's hasty and seemingly irreversible physical deterioration. Consumption had long been latent in the constitutions of all the Brontës. Patrick Brontë's voluminous cravat had swathed his neck for more than thirty years, ever since his children could remember, warding off tuberculosis. It wasn't cravats or shawls which could keep it at bay, but rather a minimal level of health and nourishment. When Emily, who had always been a poor eater while performing as an accomplished cook, reduced her food consumption even more in the autumn of 1848, she was exposing herself to all the tubercular bacilli which inhabited the cold, damp parsonage no less than its remaining four human occupants.

Emily had also been the one family member who had had the closest physical, as well as emotional, contact with Branwell, hauling him upstairs to bed, changing his clothes, bringing him meals and helping him eat. He almost certainly had infected her, and after his death she fell victim to all the tell-tale consumptive symptoms as Charlotte described them in a letter to Williams: 'slow inflammation of the lungs, tight cough, difficulty of breathing, pain in the chest, and fever.'[27] Of course, Emily grieved bitterly for Branwell as well, and losing him poisoned her will to live. Deeply depressed, she sank rapidly in the weeks following his death.

Or rather, she sank *physically*, for her willpower and resolve not to eat, not to speak, and not to see a doctor were all strengthened day by day. As Charlotte later recalled, 'Never in all her life had she lingered over any task that lay before her, and she did not linger now ... She made haste to leave us. Yet while physically she perished, mentally she grew stronger than we had yet known her. Day by day when I saw with what a front she met suffering, I looked on her with an anguish of wonder and love.'[28] Emily was not only pitted in a battle of wills against Charlotte. There was also a civil war of mind against body waged within her, 'a conflict', as Charlotte described it, between 'the strangely strong spirit and the fragile frame ... relentless conflict – once seen, never to be forgotten.'[29] Emily's body craved food, rest, warmth, cough wafers and soothing tonics (the only palliatives at that time for 'galloping consumption'), but her mind refused to relinquish control to her body and denied all its pains and needs. Like Catherine Earnshaw, she longed to escape the 'shattered prison' of her body and to be 'incomparably beyond and above' Charlotte and the others she would soon leave behind.

Charlotte's position remained exquisitely painful, for it was unendurable to stand by and watch Emily grow weaker and frailer and thinner without attempting to interfere. But Emily would brook no interference, and so Charlotte turned increasingly to Williams for counsel and support. Williams urged homoeopathy and wrote to Charlotte at length about this new, controversial mode of medical treatment. Charlotte soon reported the failure of this approach, and Emily's resistance to any advice or help. 'I put your most friendly letter into Emily's hands as soon as I had myself perused it, taking care, however, not to say a word in favour of homoeopathy – that would not have answered. It is best usually to leave her to form her own judgment and *especially* not to advocate the side you wish her to favour; if you do, she is sure to lean in the opposite direction and ten to one will argue herself into non-compliance. Hitherto, she has refused medicine, rejected medical advice; no reasoning, no entreaty, has availed to induce her to see a physician. After reading your letter, she said "Mr Williams' intention was kind and good, but he was under a delusion. Homoeopathy was only another form of quackery."'[30]

On 23 November Charlotte reported to Ellen that Emily was '*very* ill', and that in 'this state she resolutely refuses to see a doctor; she will not give an explanation of her feelings, she will scarcely allow her illness to be alluded to.'[31] Four days later Charlotte wrote to Ellen again: 'I hope still – for I *must* hope – she is dear to me as life – if I let the faintness of despair reach my heart I shall become worthless ... she ... [will] take no care, use no means; she is too intractable. I *do* wish I knew her state and feelings more clearly. The fever is not so high as it was, but the pain in the side, the cough, the emaciation are still there.'[32] To

Williams, too, Charlotte described Emily's intransigence while cautioning him, once again, not to mention Emily in his letters: 'I think a certain harshness in her powerful and peculiar character only makes me cling to her more ... never allude to [Emily's illness] ... or to the name Emily when you write to me. I do not always show your letters, but I never withhold them when they are inquired after.'[33]

For Emily the light-headed dreaminess of hunger gave way to the distorted and delusional thinking of starvation. Once a certain point of emaciation has been reached, the brain too becomes starved by internal imbalances induced by fasting. As the body becomes frailer, the psychological sensation of power and transcendence over the purely physical must be protected. Hence Emily's rejection not only of food but of medical attention as well. Through her self-starvation in the early winter of 1848 she reached her apotheosis as a hunger artist.

By the end of November Charlotte badly needed someone to help share the burden of not being able to care for Emily. She wrote to Ellen, entreating her to come for a short visit, despite the bad weather, and Ellen immediately agreed. But when Emily was told of the visit, she said 'it would not do', and Ellen stayed at Brookroyd, while Charlotte continued to send her bulletins of Emily's deterioration: 'I believe if you were to see her, your impression would be that there is no hope. A more hollow, wasted, pallid aspect I have not beheld. The deep tight cough continues; the breathing after the slightest exertion is a rapid pant, and these symptoms are accompanied by pains in the chest and side.'[34]

In extremity Charlotte turned again to Williams, who suggested that she write a detailed account of Emily's condition which he offered to forward to an eminent London physician, Dr Epps, for an opinion and a prescribed course of treatment. Accordingly, Charlotte sat down to compose this document with all the care and emotional urgency she summoned to write her novels. Dating it 9 December 1848, she wrote:

> The patient respecting whose case Dr Epps is consulted, and
> for whom his opinion and advice are requested, is a female in her
> 31st year. A peculiar reserve of character renders it difficult to

draw from her all the symptoms of her malady, but as far as they can be ascertained they are as follows:

Her appetite failed; she evinced a continual thirst, with a craving for acids, and required a constant change of beverage. In appearance she grew rapidly emaciated; her pulse – the only time she allowed it to be felt – was found to be 115 per minute. The patient usually appeared worse in the forenoon, she was then frequently exhausted and drowsy; towards evening she often seemed better.

Expectoration accompanies the cough. The shortness of breath is aggravated by the slightest exertion. The patient's sleep is supposed to be tolerably good at intervals, but disturbed by paroxysms of coughing. Her resolution to contend against illness being very fixed, she has never consented to lie in bed for a single day – she sits up from 7 in the morning till 10 at night. All medical aid she has rejected, insisting that Nature should be left to take her own course. She has taken no medicine, but occasionally a mild aperient and Locock's cough wafers, of which she has used about 3 per diem, and considers their effect rather beneficial. Her diet, which she regulates herself, is very simple and light.

The patient has hitherto enjoyed pretty good health, though she has never looked strong, and the family constitution is not supposed to be robust. Her temperament is highly nervous. She has been accustomed to a sedentary and studious life.

If Dr Epps can, from what has here been stated, give an opinion on the case and prescribe a course of treatment, he will greatly oblige the patient's friends.[35]

On 10 December, the day after she wrote to Epps, Charlotte related this last desperate stratagem in a letter to Ellen which also contained the most recent news of Emily's condition and Charlotte's nearly unbearable anxiety over it: 'Hope and fear fluctuate daily. The cough, the shortness of breath, the extreme emaciation continue. Diarrhoea commenced nearly a fortnight ago, and continues still. Of course it greatly weakens her, but she thinks herself it tends to good, and I hope so. I have endured, however, such tortures of uncertainty on this subject that at length I could endure it no longer; and as her repugnance to seeing a medical man continues immutable – as she declares "no poisoning doctor" shall come near her, I have written, unknown to her, to an eminent physician in London.'[36]

Why Charlotte didn't mention Emily's diarrhoea to Dr Epps is puzzling, for this last symptom was perhaps the most dangerous. Charlotte was correct to think that it would only weaken Emily, for it prevented whatever small portions of food she ate from being absorbed and nourishing her thin, depleted body, and it also contributed to Emily's dehydration and 'continual thirst'. For Emily, however, diarrhoea may have seemed purifying; hence her belief that it was beneficial. Her physical existence was further refined by it, and she became in the process rarefied and ethereal in the most literal sense: soon she would be refined out of material existence: a chainless soul.

A week later, on Monday, 18 December, Emily was even worse, but still she would allow no one to interfere when she went to feed the dogs after tea. She prepared their meal of meat and bread scraps in the kitchen and then walked into the cold passageway with the food. She staggered on the uneven flagstones and fell back, gasping, against the wall, but she refused to let Charlotte or Anne help her. She somehow managed to muster hidden reserves of strength and fed the dogs herself. Then she joined Charlotte and Anne in the dining room. They sat near the fire with their needlework; Emily was too weak to sew and Charlotte tried to interest her by reading from a volume of Emerson's essays which Williams had sent. Charlotte read on aloud, the ticking of the clock in the hallway punctuating the gaps of silence when she looked up from the page to see if Emily was following, or even listening. Emily didn't appear to be, and after a while Charlotte laid the book aside, planning to continue the next day. They all went to bed early, shortly after their father.

It took long, dark hours and hours for the dawn to come, and when its wan, grey light filled the uncurtained parsonage windows it brought no hope with it. Charlotte had lain awake throughout the night, listening for Emily's cough, waiting for day, as if a revolution of the earth could touch or change the course of an individual life. By 7 a.m., at her usual time, Emily had managed to get up, dress, and come down to the kitchen unaided. At breakfast, Patrick Brontë and Charlotte and Anne all read in Emily's face what would befall her – befall them all – before darkness came again. Emily ate nothing, perhaps sipped some weak, milky tea, and then when the meal was over, crossed the hallway to the dining room and took up her sewing, only to drop it into her lap almost immediately out of sheer weakness.

Charlotte sat at the dining room table and did the only thing she *could* do: she wrote to Ellen of the great calamity that seemed to be battering at the parsonage door and windows no less insistently than the December winds outdoors: 'I should have written to you before, if I had had one word of hope to say; but I had not. She grows daily weaker. The physician's opinion was expressed too obscurely to be of use. He sent some medicine which she would not take. Moments so dark as these I have never known.'[37]

Later in the morning Charlotte left the house for the first time in weeks to scour the snow-covered, frozen moors for a spray of heather to bring to Emily. It took her several hours to find a withered but still scarlet-purple branch, but by the time she returned home Emily's 'dim and indifferent eyes' could no longer recognize the gift or the giver. Charlotte, in fact, was only just in time, for above all things she feared Emily dying alone. Much of the anguish of Emily's illness had been that Charlotte could not share it, that Emily had locked her out. It would be beyond endurance if Emily found her way out of the world alone.

Emily was too far away now to offer resistance, so Charlotte and Anne moved her to the sofa where she could lie down. Then there seemed nothing else to do. To watch the person you love most in the world die is both an agony and a mystery. The passage is an uncharted, unfathomable one and the watcher stands desolate on the shore. Emily was both there and not there; Charlotte and Anne could see her, touch her, but not *reach* her. Emily was somewhere else, in that dark space that is the horizon of death. Like Catherine Earnshaw, she 'was all bewildered; she sighed, and moaned and knew nobody.' Or rather, knew not Charlotte and Anne and her father. But some other, inaccessible life was going on within her even though Charlotte couldn't break the code of her utterances. Emily was speaking at last in her delirium, but in the foreign tongue of the 'world within'.

At noon, however, she came part of the way back to them. The delirium subsided for a moment the way a wave recedes from the shore only to prepare for a larger one behind it. And now, when Emily was able to recognize and respond to Charlotte again, she gave the permission she had withheld for so long. She said they might send for the doctor. Perhaps the darkness from which she had emerged and which lay ahead made her falter; more likely, the stricken faces of her sisters made Emily yield, at last and too late, to their fears and their love. At two in the afternoon, before the doctor arrived, she 'turned her dying eyes from the pleasant sun.'

On the evening of 19 December the passing bell of St Michael's tolled out over the village for the second time in less than three months, and the carpenter, William Wood, was summoned to make Emily's coffin. He took the measurements and returned with the wooden shell which was to house what was left of her. At five feet seven inches in length and only sixteen inches across, it was the narrowest he had ever constructed. Black-bordered funeral cards were ordered from Halifax and white gloves for the pall bearers. These preparations consumed time and attention, and for a short while staunched the flood of bitter grief.

On Friday, 22 December, Charlotte and her father and Anne and Emily's dog Keeper walked across the graveyard to the church for Emily's funeral. Like her mother and sisters and brother before her, she was buried under the smooth, sandstone slabs of the church floor in a vault as cold and dark as the dungeons of Gondal. In the end, she of the 'chainless soul' was confined, as we all are, by death. But it seemed wrong that she was denied 'the quiet earth' as her final resting place – the moors where, come spring, moths would flutter among the heath and harebells and soft winds breathe through the long grass.

Outside the panes of the church windows, the moors, on Emily's funeral day, were a frozen, lifeless wilderness. Within, villagers who had never exchanged a word with her, who had only infrequently glimpsed her from afar on her solitary walks on the hills, listened to Arthur Bell Nicholls preach her funeral sermon. He, too, had scarcely known Emily. They were gathered together to mourn the death of a stranger, so there could be little sense of deep loss, except for the family huddled together in their pew at the front of the church.

Charlotte and Anne and their father grieved. They felt death's sting in their hearts. Their religion – the very words Arthur Bell Nicholls preached over the narrow coffin – enjoined acceptance and resignation, but everything within them revolted against their loss. Yet perhaps comfort came from another quarter; perhaps they recalled lines from one of Emily's Gondal elegies, lines which conceded the victory of death, but also celebrated the beauty and transcendence of the life which had been:

> Wild morn ... and doubtful noon
> But yet it was a glorious sun
> Though comet-like its course was run ...
> That life so stormy and so brief.[38]

Epilogue

On Christmas Eve, 1848, Charlotte sat down alone at the dining room table and tried to summon words to express their loss. She began by speaking directly to Emily, as if Emily were not yet irrevocably beyond reach:

> My darling thou wilt never know
> The grinding agony of woe
> That we have borne for thee,
> Thus may we consolation tear
> E'en from the depth of our despair
> And wasting misery.
>
> The nightly anguish thou art spared
> When all the crushing truth is bared
> To the awakening mind,
> When the galled heart is pierced with grief,
> Till wildly it implores relief,
> But small relief can find.
>
> Nor know'st thou what it is to lie
> Looking forth with streaming eye
> On life's lone wilderness.
> 'Weary, weary, dark and drear,
> How shall I the journey bear,
> The burden and distress?'
>
> Then since thou art spared such pain
> We will not wish thee here again;
> He that lives must mourn.
> God help us through our misery

And give us rest and joy with thee
When we reach our bourne![1]

The poem was entitled 'On the Death of Emily Jane Brontë',
but Charlotte's elegy was less a lament for her dead sister than
a vivid evocation of her own anguish – her 'grinding agony of
woe'. In the weeks and months following Emily's death, even
Anne's deteriorating health scarcely distracted Charlotte from
her grief. She involuntarily and obsessively recalled the events of
the day of Emily's death, as if by ruminating on them repeatedly
she might be able in memory to halt the process of Emily's dying
before the moment of severance 'in the heat of the day'. Or
perhaps Charlotte hoped such habitual recollection would exor-
cize all remembrance of what had befallen them on 19 December
1848, the day, she felt, when, in a sense, her own life had
also come to an end. Before Emily's death, hope had somehow
survived all the blows and losses and dashed dreams that had
beset them. Now, as Charlotte wrote to Williams, she grasped
that 'life is ... blank, brief and bitter' – a description that perhaps
unconsciously echoed the last stanza of one of Emily's poems:

And Peace, the lethargy of Grief;
And Hope, a phantom of the soul;
And Life, a labour void and brief;
And Death, the despot of the whole![2]

Five months after Emily's death, Anne died of tuberculosis on
28 May 1849 in Scarborough, where Charlotte and Ellen Nussey
had taken her in the hope that the seaside climate might arrest her
illness. But, as Charlotte told Williams, Anne's 'quiet, Christian
death did not rend my heart as Emily's stern, simple, undemonstrative end did. I let Anne go to God and felt he had a right
to her. I could hardly let Emily go. I wanted to hold her back
then, and I want her back now.'[3] When Charlotte returned from
Scarborough to the empty, silent house and passed the long
summer days alone in the dining room, her father closeted with
his own grief across the hallway, she was stunned by the enormity
of her desolation. It was beyond the compass even of her own
highly developed imagination for disaster. In June she wrote to
her confidant, Williams, that, 'a year ago – had a prophet

warned me how I should stand in June 1849 – how stripped and bereaved – had he foretold the autumn, the winter, the spring of sickness and suffering to be gone through – I should have thought – this can never be endured. It is over. Branwell – Emily – Anne are gone like dreams – gone as Maria and Elizabeth went twenty years ago. One by one, I have watched them fall asleep on my arm – and closed their glazed eyes – I have seen them buried one by one.'[4]

The hardest things to bear in bereavement are its impotence and stillness; after the death and funeral and the reading of the will and sorting through of clothes and possessions, there is nothing more to be done. Yet the pain persists, and it was the passivity of her pain that Charlotte found unendurable in the summer of 1849. And so she did what she had always done in the past when in the grip of circumstances she could neither bear nor change: she picked up her pen and imaginatively refashioned a reality she found intolerable. For the next year and a half she resorted to the old Angrian tactic of 'making alive again' by rescuing Emily from the grave, first in the novel *Shirley*, which she worked on non-stop in the weeks and months following Anne's death, and then writing the Biographical Notice and Preface for the 1850 edition of *Wuthering Heights*.

Charlotte had begun *Shirley* as early as the spring of 1848, but it was only after Emily's death that the focus of the novel shifted from the industrial unrest of the Luddite troubles earlier in the century to the central figure of Shirley, who, Charlotte later told Mrs Gaskell, was 'what Emily Brontë would have been had she been placed in health and prosperity.'[5] The character Shirley, like Emily, was physically daring and strong; she knew how to shoot a pistol; her dark hair was brushed across her forehead above deep grey eyes; she whistled like a man and was called 'Captain Keeldar', just as Emily was called 'the Major'. She wrote essays in French and even had a china-topped workbox like the one Aunt Branwell bequeathed to her needlework-hating niece. Dogs figured prominently in *Shirley* too. Shirley broke up a fight between her huge, Keeper-inspired bull mastiff Tartar and some village curs, and, like Emily, Shirley was bitten by a rabid pointer and herself cauterized her wound with a red-hot iron. More important resemblances between Shirley and Emily included Shirley's refusal to go to church, her love of the moor-land countryside surrounding her house, Fieldhead, and her dreaminess and trancelike reveries.

For Charlotte, *Shirley* served a definite therapeutic purpose: as she told her publisher, 'it took me out of a dark and desolate reality into an unreal but happier region.'[6] By imagining Emily rich, conventionally happy and, in the end, married as well, Charlotte not only made her alive again in this fictionalized and highly idealized biographical tribute, she also redressed all the disappointments, pains and failures Emily had had to experience. That the novel was Charlotte's least successful book, and Shirley her least believable heroine, was perhaps inevitable given the circumstances under which it was completed in the summer of 1849. In writing *Shirley*, Charlotte gave to her sister what life had denied her. But, even more importantly, Charlotte must have hoped that by repossessing and recreating Emily in the novel, she also conferred upon her some degree of literary immor-tality.

At the same time, however, Charlotte keenly wanted Emily to win such immortality on the basis of her own work, especially *Wuthering Heights*, which Charlotte felt had been critically under-estimated and misunderstood. Hence Charlotte suggested to Smith, Elder that she prepare a new edition of it along with a selection of Emily's unpublished poems.

'An interpreter ought always to have stood between her and the world', Charlotte wrote in her Biographical Notice to the novel, and in the notice and the preface, and even in the editorial changes she made to the text itself, Charlotte became that self-appointed interpreter of her sister's life and work.[7] Her major aims in the 1850 edition of *Wuthering Heights* were to defend Emily's work against its detractors – the reviewers who had denounced its coarseness and violence – and to make the novel more accessible and readable by toning down Joseph's Yorkshire dialect, running together Emily's short, choppy paragraphs and regularizing her idiosyncratic punctuation. In the Biographical Notice Charlotte related the story of Emily's life as it had really been – harsh and troubled and solitary – the eccentricities of her character, and the pathos of her premature death. 'Stronger than a man, simpler than a child,' Charlotte wrote, 'her nature stood alone.'[8]

The new edition of *Wuthering Heights* was published by Smith, Elder in December 1850, almost exactly two years after Emily's death. And with this labour of love completed, Charlotte sank into the depression which writing *Shirley* and editing *Wuthering Heights* had kept at bay for so long. Throughout the winter of 1851, day in and day out, she sat in the parsonage dining room, listening to the ponderous ticking of the grandfather clock in the hall. She couldn't write; she could scarcely perform her household duties. She avoided walking on the moors, where every knoll of heather and stream and outcropping of rock reminded her of Emily. No one called and few letters arrived, though once again Charlotte waited with intense expectation for the post hour and was plunged into even greater misery for the rest of the day when, invariably, it brought nothing. Their common bereavement did not, as might have been expected, knit together more closely the hearts of Charlotte and her father. Both marvelled at the irony of their survival: the old man whose health had seemed so delicate and uncertain for twenty-odd years, and the 'puniest' of his brood of six who had somehow endured the deaths of all the others. The love between father and daughter remained strong, perhaps stronger than it had ever been, but it was imbued with authority and reserve on one side and timidity and obedience on the other. They did not turn to each other for comfort, but suffered silently and alone.

Somehow time passed. With the earnings from her writing, Charlotte had the parsonage walls freshly painted and the roof replaced. She even ordered curtains for the dining room but was bitterly disappointed at their garish colour when they were delivered. When the monotony of her household occupations and solitude became unbearable, and when her precarious health allowed, Charlotte was sometimes tempted and then persuaded to visit the Smiths in London. The 'great world' of London literary life was now at her feet whenever she cared to enter it. She dined at Thackeray's, was lionized by Sir James Kay Shuttleworth, met Harriet Martineau and Mrs Gaskell. She saw Macready perform in *Othello* and *Macbeth*, went to the Great Exhibition, and also visited – to her hosts' consternation – Pentonville and Newgate prisons and Bethlehem Hospital. These London excursions, as well as later visits to Mrs Gaskell's home in Manchester and Harriet Martineau's at Ambleside in the Lake District, were, to a certain extent, restorative. But they, too, could exact their own toll in the form of debilitating nervous anxiety, severe headaches and loss of appetite.

And they didn't protect Charlotte from the anguish of the past. If anything, Emily seemed to haunt Charlotte as she made her way through this London environment her sister had always shunned. After the artist, George Richmond, drew her portrait, Charlotte burst into tears because it seemed so like Emily to her. Even worse was her first meeting with the critic G. H. Lewes. She was overwhelmed by his physical resemblance to Emily, and wrote to Ellen how his face was 'so wonderfully like Emily – her eyes, her features, the very nose, the somewhat prominent mouth, the forehead – even at moments the expression.'[9]

After these infrequent trips to London, Charlotte suffered not only the after-effects of nervous excitement and exhaustion, but also an intensification of her already well-nigh unbearable solitude. The evenings and restless, sleepless nights were her worst trial. Then, when the light was too dim and her eyes too weak to read, she sat before the fire wracked with grief, longing for the past and recoiling before the prospect of a blank, hopeless future.

Finally, in November 1851, Charlotte took up her pen again and began her fourth novel, *Villette*, more than two years after completing *Shirley*. In *Villette*, too, she looked to the past, but a more distant one, for the book drew heavily on her time in Brussels and her relationship with Constantin Heger. Despite frequent interruptions because of bouts of illness – headache, toothache, side pains, 'bilious fever' and 'irritation of the liver' – she managed to complete *Villette* by November 1852 and it was published with the new year. It was to be her last book.

One night in December 1852, soon after Charlotte finished *Villette*, Arthur Bell Nicholls tapped on the dining room door on his way out from a meeting with Patrick Brontë across the hall. Towering above Charlotte, his face drained of colour and with a quavering voice, he declared his love and asked her to marry him. Charlotte was not wholly surprised by his proposal, but she was taken aback by the obvious violence of the feeling and passion which she could plainly read in his pale, anxious countenance. Nicholls, himself, expected to be rejected out of hand. But he was not; instead, Charlotte said she must speak to her father.

Patrick Brontë was enraged at Nicholls' proposal; he found the mere idea of the upstart Irish curate contemplating a union with his daughter utterly preposterous and deeply offensive. In accordance with her father's wishes, Charlotte turned down her suitor. For the third time in her life, she rejected the security and safety and companionship of marriage. Nicholls resigned his post at Haworth and threatened to go off to Australia as a missionary. Patrick Brontë offered to write a testimonial to speed his former curate's removal to the antipodes. But in the event, Nicholls went no further than another curacy at Kirk Smeaton near Pontefract. Within several months of his departure he and Charlotte were corresponding with each other, and by the following April of 1854 Patrick Brontë very grudgingly yielded way, and Charlotte and Nicholls became engaged.

Charlotte's acceptance of Arthur Bell Nicholls appears inexplicable in the light of her novels, but it was scarcely extraordinary given the circumstances of her life. She was thirty-eight years old and had been living with the most appalling loneliness for five long years, since the deaths of her brother and sisters. Her father was seventy-seven, and when he died she would be utterly alone in the world. Or if she died first, how would he manage without her in his old age? For it was one of the conditions of her acceptance of Nicholls that he should return to Haworth and serve Patrick Brontë again as curate and remain with him in the event of Charlotte's death. But above and beyond these practical considerations, Charlotte accepted Nicholls' proposal because he was so obviously and deeply in love with her. All her life she had been seeking and awaiting just this sort of passionate, unswerving, urgent love, and now at last it had come from this unlikely man who, despite his many limitations, was redeemed in Charlotte's eyes by the strength and depth of his feelings for her.

And yet Charlotte had misgivings and doubts. In May, a month after she became engaged, she took the unusual step of having a marriage settlement drawn up which stipulated that all her property and money were 'for her sole and separate use independent of ... Arthur Bell Nicholls, her intended husband, who is not to intermeddle therewith.'[10] At this date, before the passage of the Married Women's Property Act, a woman's property automatically became her husband's upon marriage. The purpose of Charlotte's settlement was to prevent Nicholls from touching a penny of her money both during her lifetime and after her death should he survive her. Yet one suspects that the settlement was more a reflection of Patrick Brontë's abiding suspicions concerning Nicholls' motives than of Charlotte's distrust of her future husband. Nicholls himself seems to have been the only one without qualms; he signed the settlement without hesitation on 24 May 1854 in the presence of Charlotte, her father, and Charlotte's appointed trustee, Mary Taylor's brother, Joseph Taylor.

A month later, on 29 June, Charlotte and Nicholls were married at 8 o'clock in the morning at St Michael and All Angels, with the vicar of nearby Hebden Bridge, Nicholls' friend the Reverend Sutcliffe Sowden, officiating. The night before the wedding Patrick Brontë made his final and most dramatic gesture of disapproval when he stunned everyone by announcing that he would not attend the ceremony. Hence Charlotte's old schoolmistress and friend, Margaret Wooler, was called upon to give the bride away while Ellen Nussey sat alone in the family pew.

Six weeks later, upon returning to Haworth from her honeymoon in Ireland, Charlotte wrote to Ellen from across the chasm of experience which separated a single from a married woman's life in the nineteenth century: 'Dear Nell – during the last 6 weeks – the colour of my thoughts is a good deal changed: I know more of the realities of life than I once did ... Indeed – indeed Nell – it is a solemn and strange and perilous thing for a woman to become a wife.'[11] The marriage was a success. Soon Charlotte positively revelled in the domestic demands of her new role; she flourished caring for her husband and aged father. Even more, she delighted in the daily and hourly intimacy of married life – the meals and walks and long evenings before the fire together. By late December she was pregnant.

But a great change approached. The happiness and contentment she had waited long years for lasted only a matter of months. The usual morning sickness that accompanies early pregnancy became increasingly severe and persisted all day and soon all night as well. Charlotte could scarcely eat, and what little she managed to swallow, she soon brought up again. She was constantly thirsty, dehydrated, restless and feverish. On 17 February 1855 Tabby died at the age of eighty-four. Charlotte was too ill to think of going to the funeral of the old servant, but on the very same day she decided to change her will. Until now Charlotte had been – however reluctantly – a survivor, but after keeping watch at the deathbeds of her brother and sisters, she knew all too well how easy it was to die. She felt the nearness of her own end now, and altered her will so that her husband became her sole heir, thereby cancelling the conditions of the marriage settlement.

Six weeks later, on 31 March 1855, Charlotte Brontë died in the bed which had been her own and her parents' wedding bed, the same bed where she had been born thirty-eight years earlier, and where her mother and aunt had both died before her. Her funeral was held on 4 April. While Patrick Brontë and Arthur Bell Nicholls sat bowed with grief in the front pew, the Reverend Sowden, who had married Charlotte and her husband less than ten months earlier, preached her funeral sermon. Then Charlotte was laid to rest with those who had gone before, under the church floor.[12]

Patrick Brontë, whose death had seemed imminent for the past quarter-century, survived his last child by six long years, cloistered in the parsonage with his uncongenial son-in-law: 'ever near but ever separate', as the sexton told Mrs Gaskell. He bade farewell to his parishioners from the pulpit of St Michael and All Angels in August 1860 and shortly after took to his bed in the room overlooking the graveyard. Here Mrs Gaskell and her daughter Meta found him in November, 'sitting propped up in bed in a clean nightgown, with a clean towel laid ... for his hands ... [with] a short white growth of beard on his chin; and ... a good deal of soft hair and spectacles on.'[13] The old man remained propped up in bed throughout the long Yorkshire winter and the following spring, 'his mental faculties unimpaired'. In June he began to fail, but he did not slip out of the world peacefully or quietly. When he finally died, on 7 June 1861, the Haworth doctor entered the cause of death on the death certificate as 'chronic bronchitis; dyspepsia, convulsions, duration nine hours'. He was eighty-four years old.

Patrick Brontë was buried five days later next to his daughters and son and wife, dead all those years, in the vault beneath the stone floor of the church. And after the funeral the crypt was finally sealed and the overcrowded graveyard closed to all future interments. Thus the end of an era was marked. It was the end, too, of the Brontë family. The Bruntys, of course, survived and flourished across the Irish Sea in County Down. But the Brontës – the creation of an ambitious, intelligent and romantic red-haired Cambridge graduate pursuing his obscure dreams in out-of-the-way Yorkshire curacies – the Brontës were no more. Or rather were no more in terms of heirs who walked the earth. But three of Patrick Brontë's children left hostages of fortune in the form of books that would endure beyond generations of descendants: especially his strangest, bravest and most gifted daughter, Emily – that 'chainless soul' who survives, 'through life and death', showing us that even the most meagre and solitary of lives may yield awe and beauty and sustenance for those who come long after.

Notes

The abbreviations used in the notes for frequently cited works are listed below. Full bibliographical information for other works which appear in the notes may be found in the Bibliography. For the most part, references are to published rather than manuscript sources, since these no doubt will be more accessible and helpful to readers. In some cases, however, such as several of Emily Brontë's diary and birthday notes and Charlotte Brontë's 'Roe Head Journal', citations are to original manuscripts because the published sources are inadequate or incomplete.

A closing caveat concerning the Brontë letters and Emily Brontë's poetry: the standard editions of both are now out of date, incomplete and sometimes unreliable. New editions of each are currently in preparation, but until they are published, it is necessary to rely on the Shakespeare Head edition of the letters and C. W. Hatfield's edition of Emily Brontë's *Poems*.

ABBREVIATIONS

Biographical Notice: Charlotte Brontë, 'Biographical Notice of Ellis and Acton Bell', in *Wuthering Heights*, ed. Hilda Marsden and Ian Jack (Oxford: Clarendon, 1976).

BPM: Brontë Parsonage Museum

BST: *Brontë Society Transactions*.

Gaskell: Elizabeth Gaskell, *The Life of Charlotte Brontë* (1857; rpt Harmondsworth: Penguin, 1975).

Juvenilia: *The Juvenilia of Jane Austen and Charlotte Brontë*, ed. Frances Beer (Harmondsworth: Penguin, 1986).

Letters: *The Brontës: Their Lives, Friendships and Correspondence*, ed. T. J. Wise and J. A. Symington, 4 vols. (Oxford: Shakespeare Head Press, 1932).

Poems: *The Complete Poems of Emily Jane Brontë*, ed. C. W. Hatfield (New York: Columbia University Press, 1941).

PREFACE

1. Winifred Gérin's *Emily Brontë* (1971) contained new factual information and, perhaps just as importantly, it dispelled some hard-dying myths. Edward Chitham's *A Life of Emily Brontë* (1987), despite its title, is an idiosyncratic bio-critical study of Emily Brontë's writing rather than a fully realized account of her life.
2. *Poems*, p. 163.

PROLOGUE

1. Gaskell, pp. 505–6.
2. Ibid., p. 55.
3. Ibid., p. 86.
4. Biographical Notice, p. 435.
5. *Letters* II, p. 52.
6. Biographical Notice, pp. 435–6.
7. *Letters* II, p. 256.
8. *Poems*, pp. 205–6.
9. Biographical Notice, p. 436.
10. *Letters* II, p. 256.
11. Biographical Notice, p. 436.
12. *Letters* II, p. 256.
13. Biographical Notice, p. 435.
14. Ibid., p. 436.
15. Ibid.
16. *Letters* II, p. 81.
17. Ibid.
18. Ibid., p. 84.
19. Ibid., p. 85.

CHAPTER ONE: SEED TIME

1. John Cannon, *The Road to Haworth: The Story of the Brontës' Irish Ancestry*, p. 99.
2. Gaskell, p. 81.
3. *Letters* I, p. 9.
4. Ibid., p. 17.
5. Ibid., pp. 18–19.
6. Ibid., pp. 21–3.
7. Ibid., p. 18.
8. Ibid., p. 22.
9. Ibid., p. 33.
10. Ibid., pp. 41–2.
11. Gaskell, p. 61.
12. Ibid., p. 84.
13. Philip Rhodes, 'A Medical Appraisal of the Brontës', BST, 16 (1972).
14. Gaskell, p. 87.
15. *Letters* I, pp. 58–9.
16. Ibid.

CHAPTER TWO: A SMALL BUT SWEET LITTLE FAMILY

1. *Letters* I, pp. 60–61.
2. Ibid., pp. 62–4.
3. Ibid., pp. 64–5.
4. Ibid., p. 68.
5. Helen H. Arnold, 'The Reminiscences of Emma Huidekoper Cortazzo: A Friend of Ellen Nussey', BST, 13 (1959), p. 227.
6. Gaskell, pp. 110–11.
7. Ibid., p. 94.
8. *Jane Eyre*, p. 63.
9. *Letters* I, p. 71.
10. Ibid., p. 72.
11. Ibid., p. 70.
12. Ibid., p. 71.
13. Gaskell, p. 102.
14. Ibid., p. 108.

CHAPTER THREE: THE WEB OF SUNNY AIR

1. *Juvenilia*, p. 182.
2. Ibid., p. 183.
3. Ibid., p. 181.
4. Gaskell, p. 115.
5. *Juvenilia*, p. 181.
6. Manuscript of 'A Day at Parry's Palace', 'The Young Men's Magazine', Oct. 1830, BPM.
7. *Juvenilia*, p. 181.
8. Ibid.
9. Quoted in Christine Alexander, *The Early Writings of Charlotte Brontë*, p. 48.
10. *Letters* I, p. 82.
11. Gaskell, pp. 121–2.
12. *Letters* I, p. 86.

CHAPTER FOUR: GONDAL

1. Joan Stevens, *Mary Taylor, Friend of Charlotte Brontë*, pp. 157–8.
2. Winifred Gérin, *Charlotte Brontë*, p. 65.
3. Stevens, *Mary Taylor*, p. 158.
4. Ibid., pp. 158–9.
5. Ibid., pp. 158–60.
6. Ellen Nussey, 'Reminiscences of Charlotte Brontë', BST, 2 (1899), p. 60.
7. Ibid.
8. Gaskell, p. 131.
9. *Letters* I, p. 88.
10. Nussey, 'Reminiscences', p. 62.
11. *Letters* I, p. 103.
12. Nussey, 'Reminiscences', p. 73.
13. Ibid., p. 75.
14. Ibid.
15. Ibid.
16. Mary Robinson, *Emily Brontë*, p. 48.
17. Nussey, 'Reminiscences', p. 76.
18. Clement Shorter, *Charlotte Brontë and Her Circle*, p. 179.

19. 'Prefatory Note to Selections from Poems by Ellis Bell', in *Wuthering Heights*, pp. 445–6.
20. *Letters* I, p. 117.
21. T. Wemyss Reid, *Charlotte Brontë*, pp. 30–33.
22. Gaskell, p. 148.
23. Winifred Gérin, *Branwell Brontë*, pp. 69–71.
24. Manuscript diary note, 24 Nov. 1834, BPM.
25. It is generally considered that Branwell Brontë painted over his own likeness before or soon after completing the 'pillar portrait'. It is possible, however, that he effaced himself some years later, in the midst of his many failures, as an act of self-destruction and despair.
26. A photograph of this destroyed painting has recently been discovered by Dr Juliet R. V. Barker, who has also identified it as the original of a crudely copied drawing of the four Brontës known as 'the gun group'. See Dr Barker's article, 'The Brontë Portraits: A Mystery Solved', BST 20 (1990).
27. *Letters* I, p. 129.
28. Ibid., pp. 130–31.

CHAPTER FIVE: HUNGER STRIKES

1. Mary Robinson, *Emily Brontë*, pp. 56–7.
2. 'Prefatory Note to Selections from Poems by Ellis Bell', in *Wuthering Heights*, p. 446.
3. Gaskell, p. 159.
4. *Poems*, p. 31.
5. Ibid., p. 146.
6. Ibid., pp. 225–6.
7. Ibid., p. 63.
8. *Letters* I, p. 134.
9. Ibid., p. 135.
10. Ibid., p. 151.
11. Manuscript of the 'Roe Head Journal', 11 Nov. 1835, BPM.
12. 11 Aug. 1836, BPM.
13. Ibid.
14. Ibid., 3 March 1837, BPM.
15. *Letters* I, pp. 147–8.
16. Joan Stevens, *Mary Taylor*, p. 164.

17. *Poems*, p. 243.
18. Gaskell, p. 180.
19. *Poems*, p. 163.
20. *Letters* I, p. 152.
21. Ibid., p. 155.
22. Ibid., p. 158.
23. *Poems*, pp. 35–6.
24. Ibid., p. 130.
25. Manuscript diary note, 26 June 1837, BPM.
26. *Letters* I, p. 161.
27. Gaskell, p. 178.
28. Mary Robinson, *Emily Brontë*, p. 107.
29. Gaskell, p. 178.
30. Ibid., p. 182.
31. *Letters* I, p. 162.

CHAPTER SIX: GOVERNESSES

1. See Edward Chitham, 'Early Brontë Chronology', in *Brontë Facts and Brontë Problems*, and Jennifer Cox, 'Emily Brontë at Law Hill', BST 18 (1984).
2. *Letters* I, p. 239.
3. Mrs Ellis Chadwick, *In the Footsteps of the Brontës*, p. 124.
4. Ray Strachey, *The Cause*, p. 97.
5. Ibid., p. 60.
6. Winifred Gérin, *Emily Brontë*, pp. 82–3.
7. *Poems*, pp. 93–5.
8. Ibid., p. 90.
9. Ibid., pp. 54–5.
10. *Agnes Grey*, p. 2.
11. *Letters* I, pp. 175–6.
12. Ibid., p. 172.
13. Ibid., pp. 172–3.
14. Ibid., p. 174.
15. Ibid., p. 184.
16. *Juvenilia*, pp. 366–7.
17. *Letters* I, p. 178.
18. Ibid., pp. 178–9.
19. Ibid., p. 181.

CHAPTER SEVEN: DIVIDING SEAS

1. *Poems*, p. 225.
2. Ibid., p. 128.
3. *Letters* I, pp. 193–4.
4. Ibid., pp. 198–9.
5. Ibid.
6. Ibid., p. 209.
7. Ibid., p. 213.
8. Ibid., p. 250.
9. Ibid., p. 216.
10. Ibid., p. 229.
11. Ibid., p. 212.
12. *Poems*, p. 163.
13. Ibid., p. 165.
14. *Letters* I, pp. 235–6.
15. Ibid., p. 238.
16. Ibid., p. 239.
17. Ibid., p. 244.
18. Ibid.
19. Ibid., pp. 246–7.
20. Ibid., pp. 242–3.
21. Ibid., p. 250.
22. Ibid., p. 253.

CHAPTER EIGHT: BRUSSELS

1. Charlotte Brontë, *Villette*, pp. 108–9.
2. Charlotte Brontë, *The Professor*, pp. 45–6.
3. *Villette*, p. 122.
4. *Letters* I, p. 262.
5. Ibid., pp. 259–60.
6. Ibid.
7. Gaskell, p. 231.
8. Ibid.
9. Charlotte Brontë used Louise's surname in *Villette*.
10. *Letters* I, p. 272.
11. Gaskell, p. 226.
12. *Letters* I, p. 267.

13. Winifred Gérin, *Charlotte Brontë*, p. 207.
14. 'Prefatory Note to Selections from Poems by Ellis Bell', in *Wuthering Heights*, p. 446.
15. Mrs Ellis Chadwick, *In the Footsteps of the Brontës*, p. 227.
16. *Poems*, p. 255.
17. John Lock and W. T. Dixon, *A Man of Sorrow: The Life, Letters and Times of the Rev. Patrick Brontë*, pp. 308–10.
18. Margot Peters in her biography of Charlotte Brontë and Joan Rees in her life of Branwell Brontë have suggested that Martha Taylor died in childbirth – her child, of course, would have been illegitimate – but there is no solid evidence to substantiate this speculation.

CHAPTER NINE: GONDAL REGAINED

1. *Letters* I, p. 284.
2. Elizabeth Branwell's will, BPM.
3. *Letters* I, pp. 280–81.
4. *Poems*, pp. 184–5.
5. Ibid., p. 193.
6. *Letters* I, p. 305.
7. Albert H. Preston, 'John Greenwood and the Brontës: The Haworth Stationer's Notebook Throws New Light on Emily', BST 12 (1951).
8. *Letters* I, pp. 305–6.
9. Ibid., pp. 293–4.
10. Ibid., p. 296.
11. Ibid., p. 297.
12. Ibid., p. 299.
13. Ibid., p. 303.
14. *Villette*, pp. 227–8.
15. *Letters* I, pp. 303–4.
16. Ibid., p. 309.
17. Ibid., pp. 304–5.
18. Ibid., p. 298.
19. Ibid., pp. 306–7.
20. Ibid., p. 307.
21. Ibid., p. 305.
22. Ibid., p. 310.

CHAPTER TEN: COMFORTABLE AND UNDESPONDING

1. Prospectus for the Misses Brontë's Establishment, BPM.
2. *Letters* II, pp. 5 and 7.
3. Ibid.
4. *Poems*, p. 208.
5. Ibid., pp. 203–4.
6. *Letters* II, p. 13.
7. *Villette*, p. 350.
8. *Letters* II, p. 23.
9. Ibid., pp. 70–71.
10. Ibid., pp. 116–17.
11. Ibid., p. 28.
12. Ibid., p. 32.
13. Ibid., p. 49–50.
14. Ibid., p. 41.
15. Ibid., p. 43.
16. Ibid., p. 52.
17. Ibid., p. 64.
18. Gaskell, p. 281, p. 273.
19. Ibid., p. 273.
20. *Letters* II, p. 43.
21. Ibid., pp. 49–51.
22. Ibid., pp. 52–3.
23. Ibid., p. 57.
24. Ibid., pp. 57–8.
25. Ibid., p. 60.
26. Ibid., pp. 65–6.

CHAPTER ELEVEN: ELLIS BELL

1. *Letters* II, p. 76.
2. Ibid., p. 61.
3. Ibid., p. 87.
4. Gaskell, p. 283.
5. *Letters* II, p. 96.
6. Contemporary reviews of the *Poems* may be found in Barbara and Gareth Lloyd Evans, *Everyman's Companion to the Brontës*, pp. 361–2.

7. *Letters* II, p. 78.
8. Ibid., p. 84.
9. Ibid., p. 107.
10. Gaskell, p. 308.
11. *Letters* II, p. 116.
12. Albert H. Preston, 'John Greenwood and the Brontës: The Haworth Stationer's Notebook Throws New Light on Emily', BST 12 (1951).
13. Gaskell, p. 284.
14. *Letters* II, p. 117.
15. Ibid., p. 127.
16. Ibid., p. 131.
17. Ibid., p. 188.
18. *Everyman's Companion to the Brontës*, p. 362.
19. *Letters* II, p. 136.
20. Ibid., p. 132.
21. Mary Robinson, *Emily Brontë*, pp. 212–13.
22. Ibid., pp. 142–3.
23. *Letters* II, p. 140.
24. Ibid., p. 149.
25. Ibid., p. 162, p. 165.
26. Ibid., p. 147.
27. Ibid., p. 144.

CHAPTER TWELVE: THE SHATTERED PRISON

1. Extracts from contemporary reviews of *Wuthering Heights* and *Jane Eyre* may be found in Miriam Allott (ed.), *The Brontës: The Critical Heritage*, and Barbara and Gareth Lloyd Evans, *Everyman's Companion to the Brontës*.
2. *Everyman's Companion to the Brontës*, p. 379.
3. *Jane Eyre*, p. 36.
4. Gaskell, p. 325.
5. *Letters* II, p. 211.
6. Ibid.
7. Ibid., p. 189.
8. Ibid., p. 251.
9. Ibid., pp. 251–2.

10. George Smith, 'Charlotte Brontë', *Cornhill Magazine*, 9 (December 1900), p. 783.
11. *Letters* II, pp. 251–4.
12. *Letters* III, p. 38.
13. *Letters* II, p. 241.
14. Ibid., p. 224.
15. Ibid., p. 124.
16. Francis Grundy, *Pictures of the Past*, pp. 91–2.
17. *Letters* II, p. 264.
18. Ibid., pp. 261–2.
19. Ibid., p. 261.
20. Ibid., p. 264.
21. Ibid., p. 266.
22. Ibid., p. 268.
23. Ibid., p. 269.
24. Biographical Notice, p. 439.
25. *Letters* II, p. 287.
26. Ibid., p. 271.
27. Ibid., p. 268.
28. Biographical Notice, p. 439.
29. *Letters* II, p. 295.
30. Ibid., pp. 286–7.
31. Ibid., p. 288.
32. Ibid., p. 289.
33. Ibid., p. 269.
34. Ibid., p. 288.
35. Ibid., p. 292.
36. Ibid., pp. 292–3.
37. Ibid., p. 293.
38. *Poems*, pp. 160–61.

EPILOGUE

1. *The Brontës: Selected Poems*, ed. Juliet R. V. Barker, p. 21.
2. *Poems*, p. 185.
3. *Letters* II, pp. 337–8.
4. Ibid., p. 340.
5. Gaskell, p. 379.
6. *Letters* III, p. 15.

7. Biographical Notice, p. 440.
8. Ibid., p. 439.
9. *Letters* III, p. 118.
10. Juliet R. V. Barker, 'Subdued Expectations: Charlotte Brontë's Marriage Settlement', BST 19 (1986).
11. *Letters* IV, pp. 145–6.
12. Charlotte Brontë's pregnancy and the cause of her death have been the subject of considerable controversy. See, for example, the arguments put forward by Philip Rhodes, Margot Peters, Helene Moglen, Robert Keefe, John Maynard, H. W. Gallagher and Rebecca Fraser.
13. John Lock and W. T. Dixon, *A Man of Sorrow: The Life, Letters and Times of the Rev. Patrick Brontë*, pp. 519–20.

Bibliography

I. PRIMARY SOURCES: WORKS BY THE BRONTËS

Brontë, Anne. *Agnes Grey.* 1847; rpt London: Dent, 1985.
    The Tenant of Wildfell Hall. 1848; rpt Harmondsworth: Penguin, 1985.
    The Poems of Anne Brontë. Ed. Edward Chitham. London: Macmillan, 1979.
Brontë, Charlotte. *Jane Eyre.* 1847; rpt Harmondsworth: Penguin, 1984.
    Shirley. 1849; rpt Harmondsworth: Penguin, 1985.
    Villette. 1853; rpt Harmondsworth: Penguin, 1984.
    The Professor and Emma. 1856; rpt London: Dent, 1983.
    The Juvenilia of Jane Austen and Charlotte Brontë. Ed. Frances Beer. Harmondsworth: Penguin, 1986.
    The Poems of Charlotte Brontë. Ed. T. J. Winnifrith. Oxford: Basil Blackwell, 1984.
Brontë, Emily. *Wuthering Heights.* Ed. Hilda Marsden and Ian Jack. 1847; rpt Oxford: Clarendon Press, 1976.
    The Complete Poems of Emily Jane Brontë. Ed. C. W. Hatfield. New York: Columbia University Press, 1941.
Brontë, Patrick. *Cottage Poems.* Halifax: P. K. Holden, 1811.
    The Rural Minstrel: A Miscellany of Descriptive Poems. Halifax: P. K. Holden, 1813.
    The Cottage in the Wood; or the Art of Becoming Rich and Happy. Bradford: T. Inkersley, 1815.
    The Maid of Killarney or Albion and Flora: A Modern Tale in which are Interwoven Some Cursory Remarks on Religion and Politics. n.p., 1818.

'The Phenomenon; or, an Account in verse of the extra-ordinary eruption of a bog which took place in the moors of Haworth on the 12th day of September 1824'. Bradford: T. Inkersley, 1824.

'A sermon preached in the Church of Haworth, on Sunday, the 12th day of September, 1824, in reference to an earth-quake, and extraordinary eruption of mud and water, that had taken place ten days before, in the moors of that chapelry'. Bradford: T. Inkersley, 1824.

Brontë, Patrick Branwell. *And the Weary are at Rest*. Privately printed, 1924.

   Poems. Ed. T. J. Winnifrith. Oxford: Basil Blackwell, 1983.

The Brontës: Selected Poems. Ed. Juliet R. V. Barker. London: Dent, 1985.

Poems by the Brontë Sisters. Ed. M. R. D. Seaward. London: A. & C. Black, 1985. (A facsimile edition of *Poems by Currer, Ellis and Acton Bell*, 1846.)

Shorter, Clement, ed. *The Brontës: Life and Letters*. 2 vols. London: Hodder & Stoughton, 1908.

Wise, T. J., and J. A. Symington, eds. *The Brontës: Their Lives, Friendships and Correspondence*. 4 vols. Oxford: Shakespeare Head Press, 1932.

   The Miscellaneous and Unpublished Writings of Charlotte and Patrick Branwell Brontë. 2 vols. Oxford: Shakespeare Head Press, 1938.

II. SECONDARY SOURCES

Alexander, Christine. *The Early Writings of Charlotte Brontë*. Oxford: Basil Blackwell, 1983.

Allott, Miriam, ed. *The Brontës: The Critical Heritage*. London: Routledge & Kegan Paul, 1974.

   ed. *Emily Brontë: Wuthering Heights: A Selection of Critical Essays*. London: Macmillan, 1970.

Arnold, Helen H. 'The Reminiscences of Emma Huidekoper Cortazzo: A Friend of Ellen Nussey'. *Brontë Society Transactions*, 13 (1959).

Barclay, Janet M. *Emily Brontë Criticism 1900–1968: An Annotated Checklist*. New York: New York Public Library, 1974.

Barker, Juliet R. V. 'Subdued Expectations: Charlotte Brontë's Marriage Settlement'. *Brontë Society Transactions*, 19 (1986). 'The Brontë Portraits: A Mystery Solved', *Brontë Society Transactions*, 20 (1990).

Beeton, Isabella. *Mrs Beeton's Book of Household Management*. London: Chancellor Press, 1982.

Bentley, Phyllis. *The Brontës*. London: Pan, 1973.

Best, Geoffrey. *Mid-Victorian Britain, 1851–75*. London: Fontana, 1979.

Black, Maggie. *Food and Cooking in 19th Century Britain*. Birmingham: English Heritage, 1985.

Blondel, Jacques. *Emily Brontë: Expérience Spirituelle et Création Poétique*. Paris: Presses Universitaires de France, 1956.

Branca, Patricia. *Silent Sisterhood: Middle-class Women in the Victorian Home*. London: Croom Helm, 1975.

Briggs, Asa. 'Private and Social Themes in *Shirley*'. *Brontë Society Transactions*, 13 (1958). *Victorian People*. London: Weidenfeld, 1974.

Bruch, Hilde. *Eating Disorders: Obesity, Anorexia Nervosa and the Person Within*. London: Routledge & Kegan Paul, 1974. *The Golden Cage: The Enigma of Anorexia Nervosa*. London: Open Books, 1978.

Brumberg, Joan Jacobs. *Fasting Girls: The Emergence of Anorexia Nervosa as a Modern Disease*. Cambridge, Mass.: Harvard University Press, 1988.

Burnett, John. *Plenty and Want: A Social History of Diet in England from 1815 to the Present Day*. London: Scolar Press, 1979.

Cannon, John. *The Road to Haworth: The Story of the Brontës' Irish Ancestry*. London: Weidenfeld, 1980.

Cecil, David. *Early Victorian Novelists*. New York: Bobbs-Merrill, 1935.

Chadwick, Mrs Ellis H. *In the Footsteps of the Brontës*. London: Sir Isaac Pitman & Sons, 1914.

Chapone, Mrs Hester. *Letters on the Improvement of the Mind*. Edinburgh: John Anderson, 1823.

Chernin, Kim. *The Hungry Self: Women, Eating and Identity*. London: Virago, 1985. *Womansize: Reflections on the Tyranny of Slenderness*. London: Woman's Press, 1983.

Chitham, Edward. *The Brontës' Irish Background*. London: Macmillan, 1986.
    A Life of Emily Brontë. Oxford: Basil Blackwell, 1987.
    and Tom Winnifrith. *Brontë Facts and Brontë Problems*. London: Macmillan, 1983.
    and Tom Winnifrith. *Charlotte and Emily Brontë*. London: Macmillan, 1989.
Christian, Mildred G. 'The Brontës'. In *Victorian Fiction: A Guide to Research*. Ed. Lionel Stevenson. Cambridge, Mass.: Harvard University Press, 1964.
Cox, Jennifer A. 'Emily Brontë at Law Hill, 1838: Corroborative Evidence'. *Brontë Society Transactions*, 18 (1984).
Craik, W. A. *The Brontë Novels*. London: Methuen, 1968.
Curtis, Myra. 'The Profile Portrait'. *Brontë Society Transactions*, 13 (1959).
Dally, Peter. *Anorexia Nervosa*. London: Heinemann, 1969.
Davies, Stevie. *Emily Brontë: The Artist as a Freewoman*. Manchester: Carcanet Press, 1983.
Delafield, E. M., ed. *The Brontës: Their Lives Recorded by Their Contemporaries*. London: Hogarth Press, 1935.
Dingle, Herbert. *The Mind of Emily Brontë*. London: Martin Brian & O'Keefe, 1974.
    'The Origin of Heathcliff'. *Brontë Society Transactions*, 16 (1972).
Dobson, Mildred. 'Was Emily Brontë a Mystic'. *Brontë Society Transactions*, 11 (1948).
Dooley, Lucile. 'Psychoanalysis of the Character and Genius of Emily Brontë'. In *The Literary Imagination: Psychoanalysis and the Genius of the Writer*. Ed. Hendrik M. Ruitenbeek. Chicago: Quadrangle Books, 1965.
Drabble, Margaret. 'The Writer as Recluse: The Theme of Solitude in the Works of the Brontës'. *Brontë Society Transactions*, 16 (1974).
Drew, David. 'Emily Brontë and Emily Dickinson as Mystic Poets'. *Brontë Society Transactions*, 15 (1968).
Dry, Florence Swinton. *The Sources of Wuthering Heights*. Folcroft, Pa.: Folcroft Library Editions, 1973.
Du Maurier, Daphne. *The Infernal World of Branwell Brontë*. New York: Avon Books, 1974.

Duthie, Enid. *The Foreign Vision of Charlotte Brontë*. London: Macmillan, 1975.

Eagleton, Terry. *Myths of Power: A Marxist Study of the Brontës*. New York: Harper & Row, 1975.

Edgerley, C. Mabel. 'Emily Brontë: A National Portrait Vindicated'. *Brontë Society Transactions*, 8 (1932).

Evans, Barbara and Gareth Lloyd. *Everyman's Companion to the Brontës*. London: Dent, 1982.

Evans, Joan. *The Victorians*. Cambridge: Cambridge University Press, 1966.

Ewbank, Inga-Stina. *Their Proper Sphere: A Study of the Brontë Sisters as Early Victorian Novelists*. Cambridge, Mass.: Harvard University Press, 1966.

Field, W. T. 'Two Brussels Schoolfellows of the Brontës'. *Brontë Society Transactions*, 5 (1913).

Fraser, Rebecca. *Charlotte Brontë*. London: Methuen, 1988.

Gallagher, H. W. 'Charlotte Brontë: A Surgeon's Assessment'. *Brontë Society Transactions*, 18 (1985).

Gaskell, Elizabeth. *The Life of Charlotte Brontë*. 1857; rpt Harmondsworth: Penguin, 1975.

The Letters of Mrs Gaskell. Ed. J. A. V. Pollard. Manchester: Manchester University Press, 1966.

Gérin, Winifred. *Anne Brontë*. London: Nelson, 1959.

Branwell Brontë. London: Nelson, 1961.

Charlotte Brontë: The Evolution of Genius. London: Oxford University Press, 1967.

Emily Brontë. London: Oxford University Press, 1971.

Elizabeth Gaskell. London: Oxford University Press, 1976.

Gilbert, Sandra, and Susan Gubar. *The Madwoman in the Attic: The Woman Writer and the Nineteenth-century Literary Imagination*. New Haven: Yale University Press, 1979.

Glynn, Jennifer. *Prince of Publishers: A Biography of the Great Victorian Publisher George Smith*. London: Allison & Busby, 1986.

Gregor, Ian, ed. *The Brontës: A Collection of Critical Essays*. Englewood Cliffs, N.J.: Prentice-Hall, 1970.

Grundy, Francis H. *Pictures of the Past*. London: Griffith & Farren, 1879.

Hanson, Lawrence and E. M. *The Four Brontës.* London: Oxford University Press, 1949.

Hardwick, Elizabeth. *Seduction and Betrayal: Women and Literature.* New York: Random House, 1974.

Harrison, Elsie. *The Clue to the Brontës.* London: Methuen, 1948.

Hayter, Alethea. *Opium and the Romantic Imagination.* London: Faber, 1968.

Heilbrun, Carolyn G. *Toward a Recognition of Androgyny.* New York: Harper Colophon Books, 1974.

Hellerstein, Erna Clafson, Leslie Parker Hume, and Karen M. Offen. *Victorian Women: A Documentary Account of Women's Lives in Nineteenth-century England, France, and the United States.* Brighton: Harvester Press, 1981.

Hewish, John. *Emily Brontë: A Critical and Biographical Study.* London: Macmillan, 1969.

Hinkley, Laura L. *The Brontës: Charlotte and Emily.* New York: Hastings House, 1945.

Kavanagh, James H. *Emily Brontë.* Oxford: Basil Blackwell, 1985.

Keefe, Robert. *Charlotte Brontë's World of Death.* Austin, Texas: University of Texas Press, 1979.

Kellett, Joyce. *Haworth Parsonage: The Home of the Brontës.* Keighley: The Brontë Society, 1977.

Kettle, Arnold. *An Introduction to the English Novel.* New York: Harper Torchbooks, 1960.

Kiely, Robert. *The Romantic Novel in England.* Cambridge, Mass.: Harvard University Press, 1972.

Lane, Margaret. *The Brontë Story.* London: Heinemann, 1953.
'The Drug-like Brontë Dream', *Brontë Society Transactions,* 12 (1952).
'Emily Brontë in a Cold Climate'. *Brontë Society Transactions,* 15 (1968).

Leavis, Q. D. 'A Fresh Approach to *Wuthering Heights*'. In *Lectures in America* by F. R. and Q. D. Leavis. New York: Pantheon Books, 1969.

Lerner, Lawrence, ed. *The Victorians: The Context of English Literature.* London: Methuen, 1978.

Lewis, C. Day. *Notable Images of Virtue.* Toronto: Ryerson Press, 1954.

Leyland, Francis A. *The Brontë Family with Special Reference to Patrick Branwell Brontë.* 2 vols. London: Hurst & Blackett, 1886.

Lister, Anne. *I Know My Own Heart: The Diaries of Anne Lister, 1791–1840.* Ed. Helena Whitbread. London: Virago, 1988.

Lock, John, and W. T. Dixon. *A Man of Sorrow: The Life, Letters and Times of the Rev. Patrick Brontë.* London: Nelson, 1965.

MacDonald, Frederika. 'The Brontës at Brussels'. *Woman at Home,* 12 (July 1894).

MacLeod, Sheila. *The Art of Starvation.* London: Virago, 1981.

Maynard, John. *Charlotte Brontë and Sexuality.* Cambridge: Cambridge University Press, 1984.

Miller, J. Hillis. *The Disappearance of God.* Cambridge, Mass.: Harvard University Press, 1963.

Millett, Kate. *Sexual Politics.* New York: Avon Books, 1971.

Moers, Ellen. *Literary Women: The Great Writers.* Garden City, N.Y.: Anchor Books, 1977.

Moglen, Helene. *Charlotte Brontë: The Self Conceived.* New York: Norton, 1976.

Moore, Virginia. *The Life and Eager Death of Emily Brontë.* New York: Haskell House, 1971.

Nixon, Ingeborg. 'The Brontë Portraits: Some Old Problems and a New Discovery'. *Brontë Society Transactions,* 13 (1958).

Nussey, Ellen. 'Reminiscences of Charlotte Brontë'. *Brontë Society Transactions,* 2 (1899).

Ohmann, Carol. 'Emily Brontë in the Hands of Male Critics'. *College English,* 32 (May 1971).

Orbach, Susie. *Hunger Strike: The Anorectic's Struggle as a Metaphor for Our Age.* London: Faber, 1986.

Paden, W. D. *An Investigation of Gondal.* New York: Bookman Associates, 1958.

Palmer, R. L. *Anorexia Nervosa.* Harmondsworth: Penguin, 1980.

Peters, Margot. *Unquiet Soul: A Biography of Charlotte Brontë.* New York: Pocket Books, 1976.

Preston, Albert H. 'John Greenwood and the Brontës: The Haworth Stationer's Notebook Throws New Light on Emily'. *Brontë Society Transactions,* 12 (1951).

Ratchford, Fannie E. *The Brontës' Web of Childhood.* New York: Columbia University Press, 1941.

ed. *Gondal's Queen: A Novel in Verse by Emily Jane Brontë*. New York: McGraw-Hill Book Company, 1964.

Raymond, Ernest. *In the Steps of the Brontës*. London: Rich & Cowan, 1948.

Rees, Joan. *Profligate Son: Branwell Brontë and His Sisters*. London: Robert Hale, 1986.

Reid, T. Wemyss. *Charlotte Brontë*. London: Macmillan, 1877.

Rhodes, Philip. 'A Medical Appraisal of the Brontës'. *Brontë Society Transactions*, 16 (1972).

Robinson, Mary. *Emily Brontë*. London: W. H. Allen, 1883.

Sanger, C. P. *The Structure of Wuthering Heights*. London: Hogarth Press, 1926.

Shelston, Alan. 'Biography and the Brontës'. *Critical Quarterly*, 18 (Autumn 1976).

Shorter, Clement. *Charlotte Brontë and Her Circle*. London: Hodder & Stoughton, 1896.

Showalter, Elaine. *A Literature of their Own: British Women Novelists from Brontë to Lessing*. Princeton: Princeton University Press, 1977.
The Female Malady: Woman, Madness and English Culture, 1830–1980. New York: Pantheon Books, 1985.

Simpson, Charles. *Emily Brontë*. Folcroft, Pa.: Folcroft Library Editions, 1977.

Sinclair, May. *The Three Brontës*. Boston: Houghton Mifflin, 1912.

Smith, Anne, ed. *The Art of Emily Brontë*. London: Vision Press, 1976.

Smith, George. 'Charlotte Brontë'. *Cornhill Magazine*, 9 (December 1900).

Spacks, Patricia Meyer. *The Female Imagination*. New York: Avon Books, 1975.

Spark, Muriel, and Derek Stanford. *Emily Brontë: Her Life and Work*. London: Peter Owen, 1960.

Spurgeon, Caroline. *Mysticism in English Literature*. New York: Putnams, 1913.

Stevens, Joan. *Mary Taylor, Friend of Charlotte Brontë: Letters from New Zealand and Elsewhere*. London: Oxford University Press, 1972.

Strachey, Ray. *The Cause: A Short History of the Women's Movement in Great Britain*. London: G. Bell & Sons, 1928.

Tillotson, Kathleen. *Novels of the Eighteen-Forties*. London: Oxford University Press, 1962.

Turner, J. Horsfall. *Haworth Past and Present*. Bingley, 1897.

Turner, Whiteley. *A Spring-time Saunter: Round and About Brontë Land*. Otley, West Yorkshire: Amethyst Press, 1984.

Van Ghent, Dorothy. *The English Novel: Form and Function*. New York: Perennial Library, 1967.

Vicinus, Martha, ed. *Suffer and Be Still: Women in the Victorian Age*. Bloomington: Indiana University Press, 1972.

Visick, Mary. *The Genesis of Wuthering Heights*. London: Oxford University Press, 1965.

Wilks, Brian. *The Brontës*. London: Hamlyn, 1975.

Willis, Irene Cooper. *The Authorship of Wuthering Heights*. London: Hogarth Press, 1936.

Wilson, Romer. *All Alone: The Life and Private History of Emily Jane Brontë*. London: Chatto & Windus, 1928.

Winnifrith, Tom. *The Brontës and Their Background: Romance and Reality*. London: Macmillan, 1973.

   A New Life of Charlotte Brontë. London: Macmillan, 1988.

Woolf, Virginia. '*Jane Eyre* and *Wuthering Heights*'. In *The Common Reader: First Series*. New York: Harcourt, Brace, 1929.

Wright, William. *The Brontës in Ireland*. London: Hodder & Stoughton, 1893.

Index

About the Author

Katherine Frank was educated at the University of Illinois and the University of Iowa from which she holds a Ph.D. in English Literature. While writing her first highly acclaimed book, A VOYAGER OUT: The Life of Mary Kingsley, she lived and taught in West Africa: first at the University of Sierra Leone and then at Bayero University in Nigeria. More recently, she was Associate Professor of English at Mutah University in Jordan. She now lives partly in England and partly in Luxor, Egypt and is writing a biography of Lucie Duff Gordon.